EDGEWALKERS

EDGEWALKERS

*Defusing Cultural Boundaries
on the New Global Frontier*

By

Dr. Nina Boyd Krebs

New Horizon Press
Far Hills, NJ

Requests for permission should be addressed to:
New Horizon Press
P.O. Box 669
Far Hills, NJ 07931

Nina Boyd Krebs
    Edgewalkers: Defusing Cultural Boundaries on the New Global Frontier

Cover Design: Norma Rahn
Cover Photograph: © 1999 Picture Perfect / IT Stock
Interior Design: Susan Sanderson

Library of Congress Catalog Card Number: 99-70153

ISBN: 0-88282-184-9

New Horizon Press

Manufactured in the U.S.A

2003   2002   2001   2000   1999 / 5   4   3   2   1

Everyone must form himself as a particular being,
seeking, however, to attain that general idea
of which all mankind are constituents.

– Goethe

AUTHOR'S NOTE

These are true experiences. The personalities, events, actions, and conversations portrayed within the book have been reconstructed from extensive interviews and research, utilizing documents, letters, personal papers, press accounts and the memories of participants. In attempting to recreate actual events and dialogue, the author has used a reasonable literary license within narrow confines of truth and credibility. Nonetheless, all scenes are recounted as closely as possible to how they were witnessed by or told to the author.

TABLE OF CONTENTS

INTRODUCTION

One morning over five years ago I awoke with a strong image that was not exactly a dream but a persistent vision hovering beyond sleep. The word **EDGEWALKERS** in bold print, all caps, sat solidly in the middle of a gently rolling cloud. Misty skeins whisping in and around the word shimmered in rainbow colors.

As I lay contemplating, I felt excited and tired, much like the time I decided to hike in and out of Arizona's Grand Canyon. Although the magical rainbow mist tantalized me, I guessed that the undefined word pointed toward rough, challenging territory. I did not address *Edgewalkers* directly for about two years, but the image stayed with me. I wondered who *edgewalkers* might be and mused about their meaning.

For most of my career, I have worked as a psychologist and organizational consultant. I grew up on the high desert of northern Arizona in a multicultural environment. I have taught in the public schools, toiled in a university, and had an independent practice in psychotherapy and organizational development. All this experience adds to my understanding of human behavior, but it hardly qualifies me to plumb the intricacies of cross-cultural relations and communication.

Nonetheless, from the first moment of my vision, I knew that dealing with cultural conflict within our world, at both practical and spiritual levels, would be the subject of *Edgewalkers*.

What does qualify me to tackle this subject is my conviction that finding the common denominator in human relations, ferreting out the nugget—that place where any one of us can connect with anyone else—is the most necessary project in today's world. We can cure AIDS, colonize Mars, desalinate enough ocean water to sustain agriculture for the growing world population and yet, if we don't use our creativity to find better ways to relate to each other, we are hindered by our own primitive aggression.

During the two years I procrastinated and obsessed about *Edgewalkers* before actually starting my study, I mulled over its meaning and relevance. In my mind, the word itself implies taking risk, existing on the edge, living between opposing forces, progressing forward and living in two worlds.

As a psychologist, I have learned over the years—both in my own personal therapy and in working with others—the importance of sustaining warring thoughts and feelings within myself. Most of us have a tendency to reduce this uncomfortable state by jumping one way or the other. Staying in the middle, looking at both sides, picking and choosing from each, challenges even the most stalwart social reformer. But that process of living through ambiguity and choosing consciously is a basic building block for conflict management. To the extent any of us can learn to expand our tolerance for internal paradox, we expand our ability to relate to people different from ourselves.

Edgewalkers began to take form.

Taking on a whole new field of study felt daunting to me, but I began to study the literature on cross-cultural relations to see if anybody else had done a project like this. I could not find much that had to do with people walking the edge, staying true to themselves *and* dealing with the dominant culture effectively. The multicultural material I found has more to do with the dominant culture making room for diversity on one hand, and with people knowing about and respecting their cultural roots on the other. Both are important steps in an ongoing process, but the connotation of separatism that comes through this kind of multicultural view troubles me.

In the beginning, from my naïve perspective, I felt I simply needed to find people who lived in two cultures, discuss how they do it, collect data and recount some of their stories so they could be role models for others who want to better understand cross-cultural relations, drawing inferences as I went along. To my surprise, this idea did not pop out as clear, comprehensible and perfectly logical to just about everyone.

Something about my approach, the subject matter, or where we are in history, made academic people and researchers defensive. Not the *edgewalkers* themselves. Most of the people I approached to interview were excited about the project, and generous with their analogies and ideas. People who did not know me well and who I *told* about the project seemed put off.

What is so special about them? Are you an edgewalker?

Suddenly, I realized, though not in terms of bicultural birth, but in terms of viewpoints, I was in the same situation *edgewalkers* are in. I had alienated myself from my birth culture, and now I had to translate my motivation to outsiders whose support and understanding I had taken for granted.

Finding *edgewalkers*, interviewing them and understanding their perspective proved to be more difficult than I'd first imagined, both in terms of the work involved and the discomfort of intruding on people's lives. But interesting. Exciting. Deeply rewarding to me, and I hope to them.

I began to seek out people who see themselves as part of mainstream life, but who also have a strong connection with some cultural, spiritual or "counterculture" group. I asked them questions about how they put up with this precariousness and why, what it feels like, and if and how they teach others to tolerate ambiguity.

The *edgewalkers* I interviewed educated me. I thank them for their trust, their candor, their patience, their generosity and their wisdom. They spoke with me openly, often sharing painful, personal material, with only my word that I would guard their trust. I hope I do them justice. I have not quoted from every interview, but every interview guided my path.

Though many strangers were dubious, to my friends who arranged contacts and interviews for me, and who encouraged me even when the path was vague or lost, I owe a great debt. Thank you especially to Melissa and Jim Leehan in Indianapolis who made it possible for me to talk with *edgewalkers* in the middle of our country.

People who read my early manuscript, especially Jacqueline Horn, Karen Brown and Rosalee VanStelten offered direct and useful feedback, and I appreciate their efforts and honesty—true gifts of friendship.

My writing group, particularly Mary Bolton, Andy Ennis, Howard Figler, Steve Figler, Marj Stuart, Elizabeth Varadan, heard a lot about *edgewalkers* as the ideas crystallized in my mind and became an epiphany. They know what it is to take an idea from fluffy rainbow-colored fog to black and white print. They supported and challenged me, always with love and patience, and anchored me as I grappled with the challenge of saying hard things so the reader would want to know more. My women's creativity group—Beulah Amsterdam, Mary Bolton, Ruth Ghio, Connie Gutowsky, Jacqueline Horn, Regina Miesch, Phyllis Watts—is the oasis in the often trackless desert of writing, offering cool water and honey cakes.

Literary agent Patricia Smith Snell honed my first proposal, lending both insight and technical skill to help me build a solid structure.

Her interest in my fledgling project came at a crucial time. I am deeply grateful for her undaunting support, which, over the long haul, brought the book to the market place.

My heartfelt thanks to Dr. Joan Dunphy and the team at New Horizon Press for choosing to publish *Edgewalkers*. I am grateful for their artful and sensitive editing, smoothing my words but leaving my intent intact and for their timeliness in bringing this book to press.

Karen and Erica, as always, said, "Do it, Mom," and offered unguarded optimism. Seeing them take for granted social progress that has unrolled in my lifetime reminds me change does happen.

David Krebs, my husband and soul-mate, has sat at the mail-box with me, listened to my exhilaration and frustration, cooked meals, cleaned house, clipped articles, challenged my circuitous thinking at times and loved me throughout this process. He, more than anyone, knows what this book is about and how much work went into it. Thank you, Dave, for your sacrifices, support and enduring love.

And so, this book is dedicated to those around the globe who do believe in the positive elements of both diversity and mainstream culture, with the hope that the *edgewalker* concept can point the way to shrinking the racial/cultural/spiritual divide which prevents all of us from finding a common meeting ground.

part one

DEFINING *EDGEWALKING*
The Real Meaning of Treading Through the Morass

"*The larger vision of life and Earth is something that you see in ceremony. These lessons are given to us in many guises. You must make special arrangements to access the truth,*" says Frank LaPena, a university professor who stays connected with his Wintu-Maidu tribal community. "*I'm a singer and a dancer at my people's ceremonies. I make a very conscious effort to participate.*" Frank, a university department head and an artist, who among other credits worked with the group who planned the format and installed the first exhibit for the Smithsonian's National Museum of the American Indian in New York, also engages the mainstream.

My criteria for selection were people of assorted ethnic, spiritual or cultural backgrounds who had 1) comfort, if not identification, with a particular ethnic, spiritual or cultural group, 2) competence thriving in mainstream culture, 3) the capacity to move between cultures in a way the individual can discuss with some clarity, 4) the ability to generalize from personal experience to that of people from other groups without being trapped in the uniqueness of a particular culture.

I have talked with many educators and conducted in-depth interviews with forty *edgewalkers,* people who use their intelligence, creativity and stamina to solve problems, promote harmony and find a better way. Their efforts contrast with the daily news that overflows with what doesn't work between people from different cultural groups—gang conflicts, political gridlock, ethnic warfare.

Unlike most people, they have chosen to embrace cultural complexity, to see differences as enriching rather than debilitating, to walk the edge. Because *edgewalkers* embrace cultural complexity with unusual creativity, they provide insight into ways groups and individuals can deal effectively and openly with difference.

It's encouraging to encounter people who acknowledge conflict in their own multicultural experience and yet manage to walk a steady path through it. These chapters define *edgewalkers* and explain their importance. These frame-setting chapters raise questions about whether or not cultures *should* blend and what it means for an individual to spin in the space between competing, often-conflicting, demands of family, community and spiritual tradition.

one

WALKING THE EDGE
A Two-way Street

The way Meme and Mother explained each other to me did not add up. As a little girl I had no way to understand that when one said something mean about the other, or made her sound better than life, they were doing what they had to do to feel okay about themselves. So I learned to get along one way with Meme and another with Mother, shifting back and forth between two cultures that operate on different tracks.

Meme, a Papago Indian woman, took care of me from birth, and I loved her as if she were part of me, or I a part of her. I called her Meme, short for Amelia, and she centered my young universe, although my mother was alive and well and definitely in charge. I spent my child-hood in two cultures, walking an edge between Meme's way and Mother's, but it has taken a lifetime to understand what the meaning is of those times past and how it extends beyond my small-town roots.

My first lesson in race relations grew out of my experiences with Meme.

"Come here. Let me fix your dress," Meme looked me in the eye and wiggled her index finger toward her broad body. Then she tugged and pulled and smoothed my perfectly ironed, starched dress, hugged me and sent me on my way. She never seemed to hurry and, unlike my mother, appeared incapable of getting upset.

Long brown fingers on my straight, but often tangled hair, combed gentler than Mother's. Meme took each strand and sorted the tangles, rather than just combing through. She didn't smile much but hummed under her breath as she did mounds of laundry, mopped the floor or ironed the starched and sprinkled clothes she had rolled and tucked into a tub-size wicker basket. I never quite knew how Mother felt, but the tone of Meme's hum broadcast her mood.

I got in her way sometimes, but she included me in whatever project occupied her so I "knew" all about chores she let me pretend I was good at. She had nearly as much authority as my mother and didn't hesitate to use it. She talked with looks rather than words, with nods, points or a twitch of her shoulder. Sometimes just with her eyes; so dark they were mirrors.

In the earliest days, Meme lived with us. She slept in a tiny room facing the alley in a small building at the back of our property. It was crammed with lumber and other construction odds and ends. This was hard for me to understand, since I knew she had been around even before my birth and seemed to me a member of the family. I puzzled over why Meme would want to live in a place that didn't seem very comfortable.

"Honey, I have something to tell you," Mother said to me one day when I was in the second grade. "Meme is moving to her own house."

I couldn't imagine life without Meme at our house all the time. She would be there three days a week, but that seemed very different to me.

She and her husband, George Addington, moved to Laguna Village out where the Winslow, Arizona, city limits met the tumbleweeds. When I went to visit her there, I found that the adobe apartments were stuck together and faced a clay and gravel square through torn screens and cracked or broken windows.

"It's a fire trap," I overheard Mother say to her friend Wamble. Horrified, I visualized a huge flaming mousetrap with Meme in it. "But she likes it out there," Mother went on, "Her place is so clean you could eat off the floor." I knew Meme would never let me do that.

I loved visiting when my sister Judy and I stayed all night with Meme and George. We slept on a narrow iron bed in the living room, which served as a sofa by day, and I tried not to think about the firetrap. Meme and George slept in their room, which was separated from the living room by a flowered print curtain hanging in the door.

Meme originally came from south of Tucson. The story I heard was that she was an orphan and had grown up at the San Xavier Mission. How or why she came to Winslow, I don't know, but she was not among her own tribe. People of several tribes, and some Mexicans too, lived at Laguna Village. My classmate, Leonard Begay, a Laguna, lived out there. Judy Chamema and her family, Hopis, lived in a separate house across the alley from Meme. They had a round Hopi bread oven in their yard, which impressed me mightily. When I asked about different people I saw out there, Meme would say, "Oh, he's a Navajo," or "She's a Laguna," as if that should tell me something.

Going to the ceremonial dances down the street from our family's home opened questions I had not considered before. On summer evenings we could hear chanting from our front porch on Elm Street. Meme took Judy and me by the hand and we walked a few blocks west to the "Government Units," familiar territory, because I played out there with friends.

These night journeys felt different than playing kick ball in bright sun. The tawny, magical quality of Arizona darkness embraced bell jingles, rattle shimmers, and the drum's rapid heartbeat, whirling sound around and through the dancers who circled on a cracked cement platform.

"Hey ya, hey ya, hey ya ya ya," they chanted.

"Hey ya, heeeeyy!" and a harder than usual accent on the biggest drum.

The wildness of the drums, the singing I couldn't understand and costumed dancers scared but fascinated me. Sometimes chills crawled up my spine and goosebumps came out on my arms. But Meme was there. She talked to her friends about regular things that didn't have anything to do with what we were watching. She pointed out people I knew in the lines of dancers.

"See. There's Joe. An' there's Henry Lomatewa," she directed my eyes around the circling line.

Sure enough, familiar shapes supported masks or head-dresses. When I could recognize real people I relaxed and sleep pushed my eyelids shut. The drum, the chanting, the air wove their magic into my sleep.

A few times Meme took us out to the Hopi mesa villages too, not to the snake dances, but to some other ones.

"Hurry!" Meme cried out, suddenly, one bright feast day at Mishongovi. "We have to run inside," she whispered loudly. "The whip boys are coming." I felt real fear. My heart pounded hard as she pushed us in the door of the nearest house. The gamy smell of mutton stew, garlic and human sweat saturated the tight space so I could hardly breathe, but we were safe. We had to stay away from the windows for a while, then, carefully, we tiptoed outside and perched on a high wall where we could see the excitement from a safe distance.

Red-bodied mudhead clowns with round eyes, round heads, and ball-like topknots chased each other, climbed walls and ladders and took prat falls. Bare-bodied, muscled adolescents acted as comic foils. Whip boys chased and pretended to sting them. Rows of dancers swayed, circled, came and went, endlessly stepping to pulsating drums and chants. Crazily dressed men played jokes on people who watched. The technicolor action felt scary, exciting. A crowded, hot and strange afternoon in the high desert air compounded dense, dreamlike feelings and images. Attracted and overwhelmed, I loved being there.

Exhausted, I fell asleep before the trip home and have no memory of slipping into my own bed on that magical night. The transported quality of mesa afternoons never evaporated completely for me. But modern technology, in the form of movies, began to intrude as I grew into adolescence.

At that point, Saturday afternoon movie matinees became special treats for Judy and me. Occasionally, Mother dropped us off downtown at the Rialto, and we timidly bought our fourteen-cent tickets and settled in for an afternoon of cowboys and screaming hostile savages. I liked the music, swooned over the beautiful horses, and hated the killing. The Indians were heartless, but, no matter, the good guys—the cowboys—always won.

Seeing those movie Indians who were sneaky, conniving and bloodthirsty, a slick worm of doubt about my earlier experiences with Indians began swelling into a serpent. In every movie, they would pretend to be docile or friendly and then concoct some vicious trick. They whistled like birds to tell each other the cowboys were coming, and then they'd ambush.

On the streets of my hometown, schooled by Meme, I could tell Hopis from Navajos both by dress and physical appearance, and sometimes I was right about Zunis and Lagunas. Of course, I knew

Papagos by heart. The Indians in movies, bare-bodied and screaming, just slightly resembled some of the dancers I had seen. To me they looked more like fair-skinned people wearing brown shoe polish. Their bloodthirsty wildness didn't fit at all with the people I knew. I decided they must be Eastern tribes, yet somehow the resemblance was one that rankled.

On the day that my undermining question snaked in, I agonized through chilly feelings of embarrassment and fear. Meme was not around on Saturday afternoons anymore, and I was relieved that I wasn't going to have to face her immediately. A gnawing sense of disloyalty made me even more miserable as the weekend dragged on. I was embarrassed for her that her people were so bad, and for the first time, I was afraid I couldn't rely on her anymore. Could she be so different from the rest? Yet, I knew she was the person I trusted most in the world.

However, after I saw these films, I began noticing other things which suddenly embarrassed me about Meme. She said "ain't" and used other bad grammar. I craved my friends' approval and wanted to be like them. I grew self-conscious about bringing my classmates home when she was there. Her color was different from mine, and I knew she wasn't *really* my family.

Years later, after Meme's death, I wouldn't have to put up with her old-fashioned ways or explain her to my friends any more. Quietly guilty about betraying her, nevertheless, I would feel relieved and push my sadness away, trying not to feel anything.

I thought about those times at the mesas and wondered if I had just barely escaped being scalped or some worse fate. I had always felt the safest with Meme, or with Meme and George and the other people I knew, possibly because Meme stayed close physically, while Mother moved around more, and was not usually in the same room with me. Maybe I had made a terrible mistake trusting Meme so much. I had to find out.

Monday morning my hands shook as I pulled on my clothes. Meme came in the back door, as usual, and humming under her breath, started filling a tub with cold water and lots of Clorox to bleach the sheets and other white clothes. She stuffed the white clothes in the tub and then moved to fill the latest model wringer-washer with scalding hot water. I knew the routine well, and I knew that soon she would be so involved there would be no time for questions.

I tapped her solid brown arm and she looked down at me. For the first time in my life, she didn't seem like the most comforting person in the world. She seemed huge, and maybe mean.

"Meme," my voice squeaked a little.

She knelt down beside me.

"Are you a *wild* Indian?"

She kept the same expression, but her face seemed to smooth out and become even more round. A little tear came out of one eye.

"No, Neenums." She put her arm around me in the usual comforting way. "I'm a *real* Indian."

And a real person, with a real heart and real feelings.

The conversation about who she was for me, as compared to movie images, or even the way I heard my family or some of my classmates talk about Indians, changed me. From that time on, I knew the importance of seeing people for who they are, not through the eyes of others.

In a small way, and at a very young age, I experienced what many people in different countries, but especially in America, live with as wrenching conflict in their daily lives. The people in my family's world made fun of the people in Meme's world, although they pretended otherwise. Sometimes when I had been with Meme and met her friends, they had said *Pahaanas,* the Hopi word for white people, using a tone that made my skin crawl. I had loved both my family and Meme, and it tore me up when they said mean things about each other.

I was clear that Meme and Mother saw each other as very different for reasons I could not comprehend, but they occupied equal space in my heart. So I learned to behave one way with Meme and another with Mother, shifting back and forth, in a small way, between two cultures that operated by sometimes incompatible rules.

Estranged from my family for a few months for reasons I never knew, Meme died when I was ten. I didn't attend her funeral or talk with anyone about my sad feelings, but I went on with my life and did the regular things. But I didn't forget her or our relationship. It was as much a part of me as combing my hair, breathing and deep and undying attachment to the Southwest.

One time, I overheard my mother talking to her friend about Meme and the influence she had on Judy and me. She laughed and said, "The girls thought they were little Indians until they started school." As a child, I had no words for the loyalty conflict I felt.

That comment jarred me. Her tone implied not only that Judy and I were silly or stupid, because of course we should know we were "white," but also that being a "little Indian" was undesirable, that if in fact it were true, it would be bad. I did not tell Mother how her statement hurt my feelings and made me want to stay away from her. But I also knew I couldn't live with Meme. She was gone forever.

If you think about it, culture shifting of this sort is not unusual. We operate in one culture at work and another at home. We have different expectations for ourselves in these different environments without giving much thought to the transition. We dress differently, move differently, speak differently, perhaps even think differently at work than at home. We tend to shed our home selves when we go to work, and shed our work selves when we come home. Since the differences are not too great or too demanding, we manage them with little notice.

If you amplify that difference though, so it involves more than work style and home style, the problem becomes bigger. Role-shifting does not work as a way of life when the differences are great between one environment and another. Over time this way of getting by will mean loss of connection with who you really are. For instance, if a woman of Puerto Rican decent who was taught to be outspoken and self-expressive is expected, at work, to keep her convictions to herself rather than saying what she thinks, the stress of censoring herself will become unbearable. Such a woman, Miriam Acevedo Davis, one of the *edgewalkers* whose story comes later, finds ways to speak her mind *and* deal effectively with her work environment, creating new possibilities. She takes care of herself, doesn't "become socially constipated," as she says, and others in her workplace gain a new perspective.

The difference between role-shifting and *edgewalking* is that *edgewalkers* do not shed one skin when they move from their cultures of origin to the mainstream and back. An *edgewalker* maintains continuity wherever he or she goes, walking the edge between two cultures in the same persona. They handle the implied or direct criticism that their difference stirs up and explain what they are trying to accomplish.

This process is painful, and as a psychologist I have heard from many how hard it is to stay true to oneself rather than just taking what looks like the easy way out. It causes less controversy to be "white" among white people, "yellow" among yellow people, "black" among black people, live on the reservation or abandon traditional ways entirely and become an Apple—a "white Indian"—than it is to manage clashing loyalties.

This *splitting*—amputating part of myself to lessen conflict or pain—caused me great damage over time, yet it is what we do when we do not have the skill, support or maturity to embrace paradoxical feelings. My work as a psychotherapist over the past twenty-five years has taught me that integrating the painful or conflicting parts of one-self, rather than *splitting,* is crucial for mental health. Accomplishing this personality integration is not easy, but, with hard work, it is pos-sible.

Partly because of my love for Meme, a "real Indian," and partly because I think it is a crucial moral, political and economical issue for our world, I propose the possibility that if we, as individual people, can acknowledge and harmonize our conflicting parts in the interest of becoming mentally healthy, the same process can work on a cultural level.

Our nation and many others tend to deal with conflict and heartbreak the same way I did as a child. We reject the parts we do not like or understand or that do not glide smoothly into the mainstream. I believe that with the knowledge in individual and organizational psy-chology that has grown in the past few years, and with good old inge-nuity, we can do better.

People with mixed backgrounds—a description which fits much of the world—who do not abandon one cultural strain or another, accomplish on an individual basis what countries need to do on a socio-political one. Society's vitality depends on dealing effec-tively with the differences among our people.

Similar to the theory as it applies to individuals, is it possible to integrate rejected, painful or conflicting parts as nations and be truly healthy?

In America, our mythology proclaims egalitarian inclusion of all our peoples, yet we do not embrace cultural diversity as well as we pretend. Progress over the years has certainly occurred, but racism, sexism and other forms of discrimination, continue as givens in American life, more subtly than in the past, perhaps, but insidious nonetheless. And yet, I am convinced that a healing trend is at work, which remains largely unnoticed because it happens on a person to person basis.

If we can talk about our own personal process, how we manage living in two or more cultures, what that feels like, what works, what the payoff is, we create possibilities for cross-cultural understanding. We figure out how to love and work with people different from ourselves without abandoning parts of who we are. We explain to others about our backgrounds or what we do in our lives so they can understand us. And we ask the same of them.

It is important to keep in mind that *edgewalking* isn't limited to people of color, and it occurs on a two-way street. It is not the sole obligation of those within minority groups to teach those in more powerful places how to relate. People who move *from* the mainstream culture to explore and support other possibilities are significant contributors.

Morris Dees, founder and Executive Director of the Southern Poverty Law Conference is an example of a mainstream-to-alternative *edgewalker*. His background is solid establishment, but he decided to dedicate himself to work in an area that identifies him much more with the underprivileged. He risks his life for his values and commits himself to making a difference.

Rachel Guerrero, Frank LaPena, and Satsuki Tomine, *edgewalking* individuals I know, and others I have tracked down, are making a difference. They dedicate their lives to understanding and promoting social change, especially in the area of racial or cultural relations. They don't become *Oreos*, *Bananas*, or *Tia Tomasas*, whatever color on the outside and white on the inside, although they are sometimes accused of this. They stay true to who they are, to their cultures of origin, *and* become part of mainstream culture. These people are *edgewalkers*.

They are strong, know who they are, say what they think. In my travels, as I listened to them in person and later on tape, their humility and their directness often touched me. I was intrigued by how they use their experiences to understand their complex worlds and interpret them for others. I am learning from these *edgewalkers* how to find the places in myself that connect with people from different backgrounds and cultures and to speak from those places.

In November 1993, traveling in New Mexico on business, I had a few unscheduled hours before I needed to be in Santa Fe. As Garth Brooks sang to me from the car radio, *Sometimes you're the windshield, sometimes you're the bu-u-ug...* I responded to a whim and pulled off the freeway onto the side road to the Santo Domingo Pueblo. A half-hour later, having enjoyed the traffic-free country road and the wide-open spaces, I pulled into the outskirts of that high desert village. It seemed deserted. Where was everybody? I parked the car and stepped out. I heard the faint sound of a distant drum. As the smell of dust and flinty, cool air engulfed me, so did an overwhelming memory of Meme, so powerful I could feel her presence. A hot tear hit my cheek and I brushed it away.

I glanced around the village outskirts, deciding whether or not to explore further. Across the way a quilted silver lunch wagon shone against the red earth buildings. I bought some nachos with slick yellow-orange cheese, pickled jalapenos, and a diet soda.

"Where is everyone?" I asked the man behind the counter.

He turned to glance in the direction my car pointed. "They're all at the dances."

Dances? I *had* heard drumming.

I drove deeper into the village and parked. Leaving the car, I imagined my hand slipping into Meme's. Although I had not been at Santo Domingo before, it had the feel of the Hopi villages I had visited as a child.

Moving toward the plaza, I inched sideways through a narrow passage between two adobe houses, touching the rough skin of brown bricks flecked with gold straw, glittering faintly, even in the shadow. The eerie tenderness of returning home raised prickles on the back of my neck. I squinted into the chill white sun and snugged my denim jacket around my shoulders.

A line of men, carrying drums and rattles filed out of the community house facing the spot where I entered the street. Then dancers, some men in black-face, others in traditional dress, most wearing black ruffs around their ankles and carrying spruce branches, followed. A column of women stepped out. Each carried rattles and wore bells as well as black ankle ruffs above their moccasined feet, turquoise satin mantas on their shoulders and the big flat painted wooden headdresses of the Butterfly Dance on their shiny black hair. Another group of women, similarly adorned but wearing red mantas, came forward.

Be quiet. Don't call attention to yourself, I could hear Meme's voice. I felt just as excited as I had as a little girl when we went to the ceremonial dances, now without the fear. I wanted to jump up and down with pure joy, but I stood still, waiting.

The lines of dancers snaked down the street, accompanied by the flank of drummers, lightly beating a steady rhythm. Singers chanted just louder than the breeze. They turned right off the street, between earthen walls and disappeared.

I followed them into the plaza where they disappeared for a while, and then returned.

The drums and chanting resumed.

Fifty or so dancers, painted and costumed, lined and swayed to ancient chants. Colors flashed, rattles and bells decorated the drum sounds. Magic unfolded before me. The steady beat, moving feet, singers offering prayers in song, would continue long into the night, moving them deeper into a trance far beyond weeping blisters and aching knees. Soaking in the scene before me, opening to the rhythm, I drifted into another time and place.

Shadow darkened the plaza, stealing even the illusion of warmth the winter sun had lent the afternoon. The dancers would continue, but it was time for me to leave for Santa Fe and the conference I would be attending. My steps lagged as I turned away from the afternoon's intensity and enchantment of the Butterfly Dance.

Relinquishing the nostalgic comfort of Meme's presence, I climbed into the rented Ford and turned the key. I felt grateful for the remaining drive into Santa Fe that would allow time for me to shift from my reverie into a more social mood.

As I dwelled on my experience, it convinced me how important it is to honor the complexity and delicacy of our personal, cultural connections and to share them. The dramatically shifting cultural and ethnic mix in our world is bringing people with real differences together on the job, traveling and at home. It no longer works to assume most countries are made up of one stereotypical kind of citizen.

The next frontier in our global perspective is personal and emotional, not geographic. It will take all of us stepping beyond current boundaries to affirm the enlightened values by which our world must go forward.

The *edgewalkers'* stories I have chronicled in this book show how people I have talked with take those important steps. They claim all of who they are and work as translators between cultures. They move through the difficulties of cultural subtleties, teach others, and create opportunities for communication in daily encounters. Informed by deep knowledge of more than one way to be complete people, transforming what it means to be citizens of their countries and the universe, the *edgewalkers* dance between their worlds with grace and tenacity.

This dance is for all people.

The beat of the drum has begun.

two

BLENDING CULTURES
The Melting Pot Assumption

> I am visible—see this Indian face—yet I am
> invisible. I both blind them with my beak
> nose and am their blind spot. But I exist, we
> exist. They'd like to think I have melted in
> the pot. But I haven't, we haven't.
>
> Gloria Anzaldua
> *Borderlands - La Frontera: The New Mestiza*

The traditional melting pot idea with its emphasis on conformity and the minimizing of diversity has great limitations. We lose opportunities when immigrants or other identifiable groups surrender their cultural identity by "melting" completely into the homogenous culture of the new countries, but what is the balance? What will happen if in America, and the rest of the world as well, populations on the move blend into one assimilated mass? What are the alternatives, and how can *edgewalking* contribute?

Since the early 1970s, *multiculturalism*, group loyalty and organization around identity, and political and funding issues, assert that cultural groups should maintain distinct boundaries and create their own power bases. As this movement rolls on, regardless of which "side" they may be on, people in schools, governments and businesses who struggle with multicultural issues find themselves deeply mired in controversy and nit-picking. Fairness is in the eye of the beholder, as demonstrated by the difficulties surrounding affirmative action in America, which is just one example of the effort to manage multicultural issues. Resulting bitterness and backlash feed cynicism about cultural change, even among people of good will.

The new global frontier is not physical but cultural, a borderland between the total assimilation of a melting pot ideal and clearly defined multiculturalism. It fosters neither blending nor isolation. This edge, a meeting place, is easier to think about as a theory than it is to locate or maintain in real life. However, it is one thing to believe that diverse people have a right to coexist with equal opportunity, but quite another to work out the terms of that coexistence.

Many countries have, at one time or another, welcomed immigrants, some groups more graciously than others. In the United States, this is consistent with the idea that America is a melting pot into which everyone will blend. That blending also applies to the people who were here before any of the immigrants. The assumption until quite recently was that this amalgamation would be a rough and ready variation on British, or at least Western European, style. In *The Spirit of Community*, Amitai Etzioni wrote: "The view of the American culture as a melting pot does imply that new Americans and their children are to abandon their heritages and become homogenized Americans, without distinct traits or culture."

There was a bumper sticker that read VISUALIZE WORLD PEACE, then someone modified the phrase to read VISUALIZE WHIRLED PEAS. The whirled peas idea is consistent with the melting pot philosophy. No particular pea, whether it's a green pea, a lentil or a black-eye pea, stands out. And to some extent, in our country, this blended ideal has come true. Despite cultural and geographical diversity, urban environments grow hauntingly similar. A shopping mall in London could be replaced with one in America, Japan or Australia, and few would notice.

The melting pot philosophy would be convenient if it would just work. It does, to a point, and then it falls apart because people treasure their uniqueness, which, for many, evolves from ethnic, cultural or spiritual history. To make life more complicated, recognizable groups, such as Hispanics, Native Americans and Asians, often have their own subdivisions. As my friend Rachel Guerrero says, "Who do they mean when they say 'the Hispanic community?' Mexicans, Chicanos or Bolivians?" Each of those clusters again divides into distinctive sub-groups, which then divide again and again.

Until relatively recently, many immigrants, not only to America, but to other countries around the world, embraced the melting pot idea and worked diligently to lose accents and Old World ways, wherever Old World happened to be. People persecuted for their religious or ethnic ties clutched the anonymity of blending as a protective shield. Using this strategy, some avoided sharing family history with younger generations and refused to teach them Old World language or traditions.

At the opposite extreme, other newcomers made little attempt to blend and surrounded themselves with other like souls. They settled near their cultural neighbors, learned little of the spoken language, and reconstructed a microcosm of their Old World, transplanted.

Neither approach is quite right for the cultural complexity that's brewing in the world. In America by the year 2000, people of color will compose more than half the population of California. Here, as well as in other countries, collections of Asian, Latin American, Eastern European and African progeny make it clear that previous assumptions about the identity of inhabitants of a particular nation can't be taken for granted. Descendants of families who have worked hard to dissolve their roots in order to assimilate are now digging through layers of family history, dusting off old photos and artifacts, asking uncomfortable questions in their efforts to uncover and reclaim those very roots.

Whether or not cultures *should* blend is the subject of Daniel Gordis's book, *Does the World Need The Jews?* Gordis asks, "What would happen if the world woke up one day and there were simply no Jews left? No genocide, no persecution. Just a gradual fading away. Would the world be worse off?" The same question could be asked of any group. The special qualities each group adds bring out the flavor and vitality in our country. The challenge is to find the key that turns conflict among these groups into synthesis and its resulting creativity.

Daniel Gordis fears that the Jewish people may lose their distinctive identity by melting into mainstream culture of the country in which they settle. At times this process of assimilation has been very intentional. In the early 1900s in Atlanta, Georgia, for instance, a Jewish man, Leo Frank, was accused of raping and killing a "white girl," Mary Phagan. The Atlanta Temple urged members to move from Jewish neighborhoods to other parts of the city in case of reprisal. The reprisals did not occur, so either the strategy worked, or it was not necessary. However, blending has unanticipated costs. Gordis said, "The evidence is in: Being just like everyone else will make it difficult to survive." And, according to Jewish tradition, if the Jews make no special contribution to their own religion, and through it, society, survival is essentially irrelevant.

It seems easier to define oneself, or one's group identity, when it's necessary to mobilize against opposition. Defining self in an open system is a harder task.

So Gordis suggests a search "for the voice that made us different, the voice that set us apart...Today, it is up to us," he declared, "to remind ourselves that we're Jewish. Unless we recapture a sense of why we matter and what made us different, we'll have difficulty explaining why we should go on."

The melting pot philosophy has served its purpose by creating the idea of an open system from which something more complex can emerge. It may be useful to consider this philosophy as a step in our society's, as well as America's development, rather than as an end goal. Now the problem is to determine how much uniqueness and how much blending provide the optimal cultural mix.

This idea that everyone will maintain a certain degree of similarity, or at least work hard at it, isn't going well. For instance, across America, the Women's Movement made a dent in the assumption that men are in charge. Now, a real shift in the ethno-racial composition of the population unravels the basic supposition that to be a real American is to be white, Anglo-Saxon and Protestant. A shift to the other pole, multiculturalism, or what historian Arthur Schlesinger terms "Balkanization," results in an attempt to deal with diversity that isn't any more successful than the melting pot.

In America, as in other countries today, complexity grows apparent. The decision to change the system for Census 2000 in the United States so that people of mixed race can register their multiple identities rather than forcing themselves into one of the five formerly used ethnic/racial groups has profound political implications. The double bind about ethnic identity squeezes tight in this situation.

Listing oneself as African-American, Native American and Caucasian, if that's the case—has a different statistical impact than simply saying African-American, which would have been expected before. If the census truly reflects the population, what will the impact be?

In addition to overwhelming institutional decision making, multiculturalism threatens to unhinge the consensual connections in the America of the past. For the system to work, based on democratic ideals, people have to agree on some operating principles which recognize the needs of *all* the people, not just whoever can marshal political clout at the moment. Highly organized and politicized ethnic groups fighting for money, power and influence—on the basis of their ethnicity—don't contribute to the general welfare.

Most western nations are highly technical societies, united through major legal, philosophical and physical infrastructures. Each one's unique history proclaims certain rights of the individual and particular opportunities. But we have yet to see whether, at the very heart of society, we can move beyond the melting pot philosophy, through multiculturalism, and create a sanctuary for diversity that really works. It is the heart of many parts of our world, strangely empty and out of sync, that is at stake.

Trying to solidify votes during the 1984 U.S. presidential election, Jesse Jackson appealed to a number of minorities, labor unions, farmers and environmentalists to follow him to a new America, a "rainbow coalition," in which people of all backgrounds would be culturally and socially equal. Unfortunately, he didn't clarify quite how this would work. The *idea* of creating a society in which people of different ethnic or racial identities participate fully isn't new. *Implementing* and *sustaining* such a society is a formidable undertaking, as George Orwell pointed out long ago in *Animal Farm*. Even after all the animals were equal, some became "more equal" than others!

Historian David Hollinger, a professor at University of California, Berkeley, is more specific about what might work. In his book *Postethnic America: Beyond Multiculturalism*, he outlines "a democratic-cosmopolitan society, respectful of its ethno-racial heritages, but not imprisoned by them." It's then up to the individual to *decide* whether he or she wishes to emphasize or diminish the significance of ethno-racial identity.

When I spoke with David Hollinger he stressed the significant part that economics plays in whether people emphasize or diminish their ethnic ties. He wondered whether some of the people I described as *edgewalkers* rely on their ethnicity as a commodity of sorts. His concern was that if you make a business of selling art or artifacts from your culture, you are not necessarily *in* the mainstream, but rather allowing yourself to be exploited *by* (or exploiting) the mainstream.

New immigrants, or others who have been largely sequestered from the mainstream of a nation, are not likely to be *edgewalkers* while they are making the major transition into the culture. To move into the mainstream, or close, people have to blend in enough to avoid bouncing out or going under. Basic ability to get around in the culture and some semblance of economic security come first. Then, questions of personal expression, style and loyalty grow more pressing.

A National Book Award winner for his young people's novel, *Parrot in the Oven*, Victor Martinez described his approach that bypasses both the melting pot philosophy and multiculturalism. When he speaks at schools and talks with children of any marginalized national group, not just Hispanics, he tries to help them redefine their perspective. "It has to do with how we view the world we are inhabiting. Whose world is it?" he asks. Rather than feeling like they are on the outside looking in, he urges, "Put yourself in the middle of this world. It is *your* country, *your* culture. You are not going back anywhere, you are here to stay. Make it yours!"

Martinez's advice is solid for anyone moving to a new environment.

In a country like Germany, where the assumption is that the main cultural group will be German, not an immigrant society like the United States, *edgewalking* becomes a social survival skill. Now, foreigners comprise roughly 9 percent of Germany's population, the highest proportion in Europe. "Foreigners seeking German citizenship must, through their behavior, show a credible integration into our social and state order," said Erwin Marcschewski, a spokesman on internal affairs. Unlike the United States but like most other European countries, Germany does not automatically grant citizenship to children born in that country of foreign parents.

Almost one-quarter of all foreigners in Germany are under eighteen, and more than 60 percent of those were born in that country, a phenomenon which German officials call "immigration by birth." Increasingly, the definition of who is German is being challenged by people like Ozlem Inci, whose parents emigrated from Turkey to Germany. Born in Germany, educated in German schools, she speaks the language with confidence and is open to mixing with Germans, even dating them. Quoted in the *New York Times*, Inci said, "I'm not thinking of going to live in Turkey; I grew up here... People like me are foreigners in Turkey. They call us the Deutschlanders. There you are not a real Turk, and here you are not a complete German. We are somewhere in-between."

The *opportunity* to move beyond the expected, lives in people who make it into the mainstream and who have the *emotional fire* and the *means* to embrace and articulate their culture of origin. A double message about fitting in is a basic part of modern culture, and a direct message in countries with more traditionally homogeneous culture like Germany. This overt message is that everybody should jump in the melting pot, but some people, because of their skin color or other differences can never really melt.

At some point where assimilation has occurred over time and been fairly complete, a reflective or assertive individual is likely to grow interested in affirming or reclaiming the traditional ways of his or her people. The strong incentive to embrace one's cultural heritage, or to engage the struggle of aligning with two or more cultures, surfaces as an individual becomes disenchanted with the elusive promises of the melting pot. Of course this process is different for different people. For these *edgewalkers*, inspiration seems to flow through having a catalytic experience, awakening spiritually, seeing one's children with no idea of their history, moving through different perspectives over time and seeing others like oneself claim their heritage.

Jahi McCurtis, a man who has engaged the assimilation process from one end to the other and back again, teaches and works as a clinical supervisor at Christian Theological Seminary in Indianapolis, Indiana. He is one of a handful of people of color on the staff there and was willing to talk about some turning points in his life.

Jahi grew up in East Saint Louis, Missouri, living with his grandparents from the time he was eight days old. "I consider myself having a very, very good life. My grandparents were what you would call black bourgeoisie in attitude—from the old school. Residentially, we lived on the fringe—that is, the white neighborhood was just around the corner from our house. Since there were no kids my age in the black neighborhood, my main playmate was a white kid, Bobby Hanks."

From childhood, Jahi was in touch with two cultures, although his family certainly did not promote that fact.

"I remember the first time I had a negative confrontation with a white—a little white boy in the store. He called me a nigger. I was with my great grandmother, who didn't make any big deal out of it, as I recollect. I didn't have any feelings about it because I had not been taught by my parents what a nigger was supposed to be."

Describing this incident, Jahi seemed completely neutral, as if he were discussing the weather. It illustrated his innocence and how children take for granted that their world is just fine, if that is the way adults interpret it for them.

"I went to an all black high school where we weren't socialized to be anti-anything, but focused more toward the realities of life at that time. I was a basketball player and track athlete. We had exceptionally good teams all the time, and we would be cheated out of the regional title or the local title. That's how racism came upon me. My family never taught me that I had a place."

As a student leader and athlete, Jahi was at the center of the action in his high school. Although he had a sense that something was off, in regard to the school not winning the championships, he still did not communicate much concern when he talked about the incident. Here, though, he picked up the tempo, and moved forward in his chair.

"It was after leaving my first year of college that I began to get mad. At college I had learned to play tennis, so in the summer after my freshman year I got together with a black friend from college at the park back home—a white park, where all the tennis courts were. We finished a game, and two white girls came over and asked if we were leaving. We said we had two more games to play so they waited. While we were playing, all of a sudden, these white guys came over and started yelling at us to get away from those girls. A crowd started to form, and I turned around. I was alone. My friend had run away and left me.

"It got pretty scary, a big crowd screaming racial stuff at me. The police were circling, but they were laughing at the situation. As a teen, I had been in a gang in East St. Louis because it was necessary for survival, so I knew how to act tough. I walked through the crowd looking mad and went to the trunk of my car, got out my jack, and screamed at them, 'Okay, you may take me, but somebody's going with me.' They backed away; I got in my car, and nervously drove off.

"That was the beginning of my anger, rage, hate. I did it two ways. I began really thinking about these things. Was there something wrong with me? Processing was part of it, but the other part was hating whites. Going back to Southern Illinois University in the fall, I was extremely active on campus. Some of my anger was directed toward my friend who took off. I wanted to beat him up."

Jahi's face telegraphs pain still in him after all these years, as if even now he can't believe this betrayal. Shreds of shock and wrenching disappointment cling to his images of that day. His friend's desertion was a powerful catalyst which initiated him—changed his view of the world.

"At Southern Illinois University in the early sixties we blacks had to go through town to the black section to party. We were allowed to go upstairs at the movies, but weren't admitted to certain places downtown. My fraternity became very active in turning the city around. Even though my friends and I were active on campus, that was different. It wasn't sufficient for me to be cool on campus and then walk ten miles to the black section to have a hamburger. I tell people I paid my dues in that process. My fraternity actually was instrumental in opening up Carbondale."

Jahi directed at least part of his energy into social action. Similar to his high school experience, on his college campus as an athlete and student leader, he was at the center of things. He couldn't tolerate the contrast between being accepted on campus, but treated as undesirable in town.

"When I left there I went to the University of Southern California. Again my uncle said, 'Why is it you're the only black guy to get in all these places?'"

Then, as now, Jahi made choices to go against what most people expected of him. Whether those choices came from a sense that the opportunities were available to him and why not take them, or intentions to make a difference socially, he put himself in situations that required dealing with difference.

"I was active on that campus as well. I created a stir around the fact that there were no blacks in the Helen of Troy homecoming pageant and none of us were allowed to be counselors at Troy Camp, a summer program for underprivileged youth, ninety-nine percent of whom were black. At USC many of the black students were unhappy with me for rocking the boat.

"I moved from there, angry, to Manhattan Beach in southern California with two Jewish friends and was the first African-American to live there in ages. The landlord said to me, 'Well, you're the first black to come here in twenty years. If you've got enough nerve to ask me to rent my house, I'll rent it to you.' I had a very pleasant experience there."

With his superb communication skills and sensitivity to others, Jahi got along well with the people he met. Although his dark skin made it impossible to "melt" completely, his white friends and associates welcomed him in situations where most people of color couldn't go. He had made it into the white world by adopting the ways of the people around him.

"In looking at myself then, I say I was an Oreo. Something about my attitude. I didn't hang out in Watts. I hung out in Hollywood. I hung out in Manhattan Beach. Most of my associates were white. The women I dated were white. I didn't feel a need to go to Watts to see an African-American woman."

And then, another shift began, which seems to be the kind of awakening many people who have assimilated at the expense of their cultural heritage recount. Seeing other people like himself claim their heritage opened Jahi's eyes to new ways of seeing himself.

"When I graduated from college and went to my first job at Cal State University, Dominguez Hills, the older students demanded a certain degree of blackness that made me very nervous. That was a starting point of beginning to re-attach. The difference between me then and me now is that up to then, I felt like I was in prep school for learning how to be white. I grew from learning how to be white— believing that was the only way to positive selfhood—to realizing that attitude had me all out of sync. When I started to study metaphysics, I began to come back home. Now, I know how to 'be white' and do all those things that make for success in white society, but I no longer claim that whiteness as part of who I am.

"I went from being, let's say, whitewashed, to exaggerated blackness, wearing African clothes, taking an African name and avoiding white people in social situations as much as possible. When

I graduated from SUNY, Buffalo, I was a medical epidemiologist. I studied cancer—social, psychological causes of cancer. I was, again, one of the first black epidemiologists in the country, flying all over, doing workshops and speeches. Then I turned against what I called my 'slavemaster' by not being a good old boy, stopped playing the game. The funds, the access and the workshops disappeared.

"I started challenging their theories, their research findings, because I got tired of hearing that all the cancers that black folks had was because we were more sexually active and more promiscuous than whites. That was a theory. At national and international conferences, I had had it. At one point, I just went over to the microphone and lambasted them for their theory and their conclusion. That was the end of my funding. I wasn't politically savvy."

Jahi had reached a point where he was no longer willing to submit to his internal slavemaster to gain the approval of others. Although it caused uproar in his life, he dropped the white professional facade and stepped forward.

"I say the same kinds of things now, but I have a way of saying them that doesn't annihilate me or intimidate others. Like here at the school, I call them to task about their lack of awareness and sensitivity, but I do it in a way that isn't hostile. It's aggressive, but framed in a way that they can see me as walking on water."

Jahi leaned back in his chair and laughed. His laugh communicated to me that he was fully aware of the paradox of his position. He is *in* the culture of his work environment, but he is also an observer of its inconsistencies. From that position he can make judgments about when and how to emphasize difference, when and how to support social change. And he has the confidence of his colleagues as one who understands the flow of the mainstream.

"My experience has been that they do listen to me, and I don't have to resort to my ghetto side to be heard. The white community is a little more accepting than my own. I have a professional article coming out entitled, 'Can't We All Get Along?' I take us both to task because I don't believe we resolve anything by blaming. It's time to come together as a community and work with some of the stuff we can change."

Jahi confronts the melting pot myth and proposes a process that acknowledges differences rather than trying to blend them. He no longer pretends that everyone is the same.

"The Europeans [referring to white people] have to work in-house with their own stuff. We can have a coalition where we all come together, but I think the work we need to do needs to be done separately. The one-upsmanship and fragmentation in the black community needs to be eradicated.

"At this point in my life, my choice is to affirm and assert who I am—how much of that I want to give up, how much I want to put on hold. I'm not very good at putting much of my blackness on hold. I have learned a better way."

Jahi's path through innocence, betrayal and awakening, identifying with the white majority, time out in "exaggerated blackness," and attempts to make sense of it all tells his story as an individual.

America, like many other countries, exhibits developmental steps which may be somewhat similar, beginning with birth in relative naiveté, a struggle through crises of revolution, civil war and international conflict. Then, as the country grew, idealistic efforts to create a melting pot made room for immigrants from around the world.

This melting pot stage in the development of America and many other countries is like the early stages of life or of a relationship. Symbiosis with the mother, or merging, is where the baby begins life. Falling in love and merging, total togetherness, is also often the first part of a romantic relationship. But, at some point, the individual is no longer content to sacrifice individuality to be part of another. Multiculturalism, a need for separate, distinct identity and recognition, may be the cultural rebellion against the pressure for conformity that is inherent in the melting pot philosophy. It makes sense that in countries where individuality is highly valued, pressure for conformity creates a reaction—a swing to what we now call multiculturalism.

Jahi knows deep inside that neither extreme reflects who he is. As an African-American familiar with white institutions and manners, he appreciates the importance of separateness with cooperation. His comment, "It's time to come together as a community and work with some of the stuff we *can* change," captures the essence of *recognizing and working with differences* rather than *melting* them.

Edgewalking isn't just about minority people moving into mainstream culture or back and forth between different groups. It's just as important for mainstream people to gain comfort with people outside that mythical center. If the melting pot ideal is not the model for dealing effectively with diversity, experimenting with edges and finding new models is the challenge.

As with any social or spiritual shift, artists often have a sixth sense for being on the forefront of emerging trends and, through their work, clarifying and interpreting them for the culture at large. Several years ago, some friends and I attended a creativity workshop at Judy Tuwalestiwa's studio near Healdsburg, California, in the rolling hills along the Russian River.

On the day of the workshop, after we left the freeway, we traveled down a road that meandered through acres of vineyards until we entered a misty green space, enjoying the symmetry of sinuous grapevines entwined on trellises. We shared a feeling of shrugging off the demands of our everyday lives.

Judy's studio, nestled near her home among the vineyards and a grove of redwoods, offered materials and spacious tables for experimenting with clay, paint and words on big sheets of paper.

The day's activities included viewing photographs and a videotape from her three "Continuing Paintings," large monochromatic canvases of red, black, and white. Under each of these final colors is a series of approximately eighty buried images, one painted on another, some with a few embellishments, some new work. Before painting over any particular image, Judy photographed it, creating an evolving series that holds the memory of paintings that existed for a brief time.

Watching the video of the varied images, each appearing only to be replaced, I became agitated and anxious. I wanted to know more about some of the paintings, savor them longer. My sense of loss and regeneration burgeoned as light and color rolled on. I harbored the unsettling knowledge that each finished painting—that huge one-color canvas—contained much more than appeared on the surface.

"The Continuing Paintings are an example of process and end combined. I knew each painting was ephemeral," Judy told me.

These paintings offered a powerful melting pot metaphor. From the viewer's perspective, the large one-color paintings, like the melting pot, submerge the original components of each individual work, obscuring its uniqueness. The painter is different for having painted them. Each image is inscribed in prints and on the video. But the individual images melt away, becoming memories, leaving marks as traces on the canvas under the final color.

Five years later, Judy Tuwalestiwa's paintings and poetry were featured at the Linda Durham Contemporary Art Gallery in Galisteo, south of Santa Fe. I attended the gallery and arranged to interview the artist.

Arriving at Linda Durham's compound on one of the gravel streets in the tiny New Mexico town, I found Judy sitting cross-legged, planted on a spacious plot of red earth inside adobe walls. She poked at the ground in front of her with a knobby twig, moving aspirin-size clods from one side to the other of an oblong water-darkened plot. At her left were three triangular sandstone slabs, stacked.

Sheet lightning blinked in the distance. The smell of rain saturated the air.

"I buried a dead bird here. I buried it to begin the piece," Judy said, pointing to the sandstone stack. She had sprinkled ochre pigment on one part of the gritty patch, gray on another.

Four years earlier, Judy made a significant cultural transition, moving from the luxuriant wine country of northern California to what she calls the "harsh and beautiful" landscape of the Hopi reservation in northern Arizona where she lives with her husband, who is Hopi. How has she made that shift? Does she see herself melting into the way of life at Hopi? What are her feelings about separation and inclusion as someone who has moved from mainstream to immersion in another culture?

"Talking about edges helps us define our own," she began. "In my art, I always work at the edge of what I know. When I complete a painting, when it resolves itself, I am happy. Then I become curious again, wondering what would happen on another canvas 'if I...' The 'If I' comes from questions that have been raised by the canvas on which I have been painting. I learn visually, emotionally, intellectually from my paintings."

The sky darkened. Thunder rumbled. We decided to stay until the first drops arrived. I was curious about what Judy was making.

"I wanted to stay in Galisteo during the show, but I also wanted to do some work that might serve as ground for the next series. I'm working with the earth each day, exploring with no finished piece resulting. Playing in the mud seems like a good idea. I loved doing that as a child growing up in the desert sunshine of Los Angeles."

Judy stared at the earth piece for a long time and then spoke, her head still slightly bowed. "My experience at Hopi is very different than living in northern California in what we call mainstream culture. I lived in a forest, a creek flowing by my house, grapevines covering the Dry Creek Valley, a great city, San Francisco, seventy miles away. I raised my children there and was deeply immersed in the life of my community through creating art programs in the schools. Living on the reservation, in a demanding landscape, in a different culture, at a different phase of my life, I am very aware of survival and human strength and fragility. The membrane between worlds is thin at Hopi."

Judy stretched her legs, looked up at me and smiled. Her reference to a "thin membrane between worlds" suggests awareness of a different edge, more spiritual than geographic. Her next statement unveils a paradox about the blending process. Although she does not blend into Hopi culture, the connection the Hopi people have with their ancestors and their sense of place tune her in to the importance of her own ancestors. *This recognition of part of oneself as reflected in an entirely different culture is an important aspect of edgewalking.*

"At Hopi I am also much more conscious of my ancestors because of my awareness, through the ceremonies, of the ancestors that exist here. The Hopi have lived on the mesas for over a thousand years. Before that they spent millennia leaving their 'footprints' throughout the Southwest. Their relationship to the land is different from most of ours, not in the romanticized way, but in a profoundly rooted way. Their ceremonies grow directly out of this landscape, out of their dependence on it as farmers of corn in a land of both little rain and great visionary distances.

"My people have been wanderers for many generations. I express my relationship to my ancestors in a stanza from my *Canyon Poem*, which grew out of a three week rafting trip on the Colorado through the Grand Canyon:

> "My ancestors, a people scattered
> Over the earth, abide in my heart,
> In my bones, in my marrow.
> Together, we float on this thick
> Red river, spinning a chrysalis
> From strands of water, rock,
> Sand and sky. We coil into
> Silence, listening for the
> Heartbeat of a star."

It is lonely living between cultures. *Edgewalkers* repeatedly speak about not fitting in, feeling more participant-observer than integrated into a group. The promise of "belonging" is one the melting pot has not been able to fulfill. Learning how people handle this question of the "not quite right fit" is key in expanding our *edgewalking* capacities.

"As an artist, I spend a lot of time alone in my studio," Judy continued. "I have friends at Hopi, as I have friends in the other parts of my life. I also have a role at Hopi as a maoui, an in-law, but I have no shared history over a thousand years. And, since Phillip and I do not have children together, I have no future history in terms of Hopi. I am a guest.

"I have always, since I was a child, been aware of death. I became even more aware of my mortality at Hopi. I'm in a slice of time in terms of that culture. I have no relatives eight hundred years back who reacted to someone else's relative. It is not my cultural continuum. But I believe the unconscious also holds a universal human continuum. An artist has the responsibility to heal herself and then to form the personal into a universal expression. As an artist, I live in many worlds: I live my work.

"I have learned about being an outsider. I didn't go to Hopi either to become Hopi, as a 'wannabe,' or to take things from the Hopi. I went there because my husband is Hopi. I didn't go there looking for something, but I have found much."

Judy is no stranger to diversity. Practice at relating to people different from herself makes her a skilled observer.

"Growing up in the 1950's in racially mixed East Los Angeles, I attended synagogue with my Grandma Rosie on the High Holy Days. The murmuring of praying men mesmerized me, the trumpeting of the ram's horn transformed me. In the Buddhist temples of my Japanese friends, I experienced visual silence. At Catholic mass, with my Mexican friends, I experienced the cadences of Latin-chanted golden ritual that has been handed down for centuries. In the small, wooden Baptist churches of my black friends, heart-felt songs moved me to experience joy and sorrow inextricably mingled.

"Sight and sound united so that those images, colors, the rhythms of various languages, prayers, chants and songs of my childhood helped to form the ground in which my art takes root. In this sense, the 'melting pot' has influenced me and my work.

"I learn from each person I meet. I am always surprised by people's lives, what they have done, where they have been, how they perceive. You can look at the outside of a person, but you have no idea how they perceive the world."

Judy immigrated, in a sense, placing herself in a culture very different from her own. She participates in the Hopi community, contributing where it is appropriate, while maintaining her own center. In some ways, living at Hopi has helped her to know her own center better. Since she neither desires to become Hopi, nor could if she wanted to, melting into the pot is not an issue. She neither melts nor holds herself apart. She has created a balance that works for her.

It's a tall order to negotiate the ill-defined and often treacherous edge between the melting pot blend (*merging*) and multicultural clustering (*splitting*). Both Jahi and Judy have personal qualities that support them through the cultural transitions they choose. They stand astride two cultures, staying connected with their culture of origin, engaging equally in a second one that is meaningful to them.

Each of us possesses personal qualities we can develop to promote sure-footed edgewalking for the journey into the borderlands between cultures. Following are comments from Jahi and Judy that illustrate some of these qualities.

Self-knowledge.

Jahi: I grew from learning how to be white—I thought that was the only way to positive selfhood—to realizing that attitude had me all out of sync. When I started to study metaphysics, I began to come back home.

Judy: I've always been aware of death, but at Hopi I became aware even more of my mortality because of experiencing it in a cultural context of which I am not a part.

Flexibility.

Jahi: I know how to be white. I know how to do all the things that make for success in white society. But I no longer claim that whiteness as part of who I am.

Judy: I painted a canvas knowing that none of the images on it would exist except as memories expressed as small images in photographs. I was working to free myself of self-censorship.

Curiosity.

Judy: When I complete a painting, when it resolves itself, I am happy. Then I become curious again, wondering what would happen on another canvas 'if I...' The 'If I' comes from questions that have been raised by the canvas on which I have been painting.

Personal strength and self-confidence.

Jahi: My experience has been that they do listen to me, and I don't have to resort to my ghetto side to be heard.

Judy: I have learned that one of my resources is my sense of being an outsider as well as a participant. I suspect that comes in part from my upbringing and from my being an artist, being both a participant and observer.

Willingness to dissent.

Jahi: I started challenging their theories, their research findings. I got tired of hearing that all the cancers that black folks had were because we were more sexually active and more promiscuous than whites.

Ability to see oneself in a "different" culture.

Jahi: When I graduated from college and went to my first job at Cal State University, Dominguez Hills, the older students demanded a certain degree of blackness that made me very nervous. That was a starting point of beginning to re-attach.

Judy: At Hopi I am more conscious of my ancestors because of my awareness, through the Hopi ceremonies, of the ancestors that exist here.

Either diving into the melting pot or embracing multicultural separatism is easier than taking on the complexity of doing both. Independently, though, neither honors a certain intractable drive many people have to expand into all the complexities and potential of human beings. Seeing how individuals get around in the borderland between melting pot and multiculturalism offers some clues to what could happen in our world on a broader scale.

The *edgewalkers* in this chapter have peered into the melting pot and backed away, choosing not to jump in but to stay true both to their heritage and to their unique experience. They offer hope that it may yet be possible to *visualize world peace* without blending into *whirled peas.*

part two

STROLLING ON THE EDGE
Barriers to Overcome

*R*obert Lew, a financial planner in San Francisco, returned from a national conference in Chicago where he was a speaker. "Of the fifteen hundred people there, only three were African-American and four, Asian. That alone put me in the spotlight. In Sacramento and in San Francisco, I don't think much about it. But there, being a speaker and Asian, I really stood out. I couldn't get over feeling conspicuous."

The contrast between myth and reality in the United States and other lands which have varied populaces is deep. The following chapters explore the ideas of diversity and open-mindedness and, in the words of people who run hard into economic, political and social walls, challenge a sort of habitual self-satisfaction many people have on this subject.

Watching the fireworks extravaganza in the night sky from Marine Park in San Francisco on the Fourth of July, I had no doubt that being an American is a thrill and a privilege. I couldn't stop my tears and my pounding heart as the "Star-Spangled Banner" sailed heavenward during the finale. On that occasion, counterpointing my emotion, my mind monitored the music that poured through the throbbing speakers, listening to see if the selections would be exclusively American folk tunes and military marches. Sure enough, very few ethnic traces were woven into the medley, and only because of *West Side Story*, a quick rash of mariachis, hot jazz licks, and Mahalia Jackson. I scanned the crowd and saw that there, white faces were not a majority.

three

MULTIRACIAL HERITAGE
A Refreshing, Confrontive Approach

In 1990, one in 33 children born in America
was of mixed race; in 1995, the number had
risen to one in 20. In California, the numbers
are much higher, where, in 1995, one in every
six births was a child of mixed race. Mixed-
race births now constitute the third largest
category of births, after Latinos and
Caucasians.

Stephen Magagnini
Sacramento Bee, October 12, 1997

"I am the product of two great cultures. On my father's side I am
African-American, on my mother's I am Thai...I feel very fortunate,
and equally proud, to be both African-American and Asian...The bot-
tom line is that I am an American and proud of it." Golf phenomenon
Tiger Woods prepared and delivered this statement to the press at the
US Open he won in 1995. By rejecting the media's facile label for him
as an African-American and embracing a wider concept of his humanity, Tiger Woods stepped onto a new frontier, an edge of complexity
where people own and live their mixed heritage.

Not only in real life, but in our commercial images as well, the stereotypes are being replaced. The image of a white housewife as Betty Crocker, who reigned over syrup bottles and cereal boxes for decades, has been modified. The woman who now represents General Mills' products in Betty's place is a computer-generated composite of seventy-five women of various racial and ethnic backgrounds. Commercially driven as it may be, this new portrait reflects a real change in modern life.

Similar shifts are visible in other arenas as well.

The reflections of change in the sports world and at the breakfast table, two of America's most lucrative commercial venues, echo the optimism of Basho Fujimoto, a recent college graduate, and some of his contemporaries as they discuss mixed race.

Basho opened his conversation with me directly. Typical of many people in his age group, he liberally sprinkles his conversation with a ubiquitous "like," which I have edited. "My friends and I realize we are part of the first generation of racially mixed people in this country. The last anti-miscegenation law was repealed in 1967, in Arizona. We call ourselves 'fitties,' fifty percent this, fifty percent that. Our interest is not about taking traditional elements from our old cultures and mixing them altogether, making a nice, evenly distributed multiculturalism. It is more like taking just the consciousness of all of our heritage and bringing in one point and working with that to create something new."

Basho Fujimoto spoke from a new center built on *edgewalking*. That center includes conscious choice from many cultures. Mixed race is as legitimate a classification as white, African-American, Asian, or any other designation. And why not?

In *The Disuniting of America: Reflections on a Multicultural Society*, Arthur Schlesinger, Jr. argued that it is essential for America to have some kind of cohesive center. The noted historian puts it well: "Our task is to combine due appreciation of the splendid diversity of the nation with due emphasis on the great unifying Western ideas of individual freedom, political democracy and human rights. These are the ideas that define the American nationality—and that today empower people of all continents, races and creeds."

In line with General Mills' marketing department's decision to acknowledge that the "typical" homemaker is no longer a white housewife, a look at the new center reveals a major change. The center is not dissolving, it is sliding from where it has been to someplace new. Since Schlesinger writes from the perspective of the white male establishment, the shift must feel *to him* like the nation is coming apart at the seams. He clearly recognizes and abhors his own prejudice, "...how sadly our interpretations are dominated and distorted by unconscious preconceptions, how obsession of race and nation blind us to our own bias," but he doesn't experience the impact of that elitism on his point of view.

As Schlesinger stated, "American history was long written in the interests of white Anglo-Saxon Protestant males...The Anglocentric domination of schoolbooks was based in part on unassailable facts. For better or for worse, American history has been shaped more than anything else has by British traditions and culture. Like it or not, as political scientist Andrew Hacker puts it, 'For almost all this nation's history, the major decisions have been made by white Christian men.'"

These white Christian men are the people who have defined and shaped the cohesive center of American life, and up to this point, the way to join the American establishment was to pare off vestiges of difference in order to melt into that center. Basically, what that means is that women and people of color who can't or won't change their stripes, cannot really be part of the center. With the population shift and women's liberation, the Anglo-centric values and standards that have defined the center to this point are no longer cohesive for the majority of the population.

So is the world ready for a new look?

In an article on the Census 2000 procedures and related struggles of people of mixed race, Stephen Magagnini writes in the *Sacramento Bee*, "For a long time, mixed race meant mixed up. Throughout their lives, many multiracial Americans have felt like outcasts, forced to identify with one race over another, or check 'Other' on forms. Constantly they are asked, 'What are you?'"

The dehumanizing word "*what*," rather than "*who*," is significant. "*What* are you?" is not a pretty question. Race mixing, understood by some to contribute to the threat of mongrelization, is still seen as negative. *Half-breeds, mixed-bloods, métis*, historically have found themselves objects of scorn—as if having two parents who match each other ethnically is some kind of requirement for being whole. These genetic *edgewalkers* often identify with one side of their heritage or another rather than claiming both. When he broke the mold publicly by asserting the legitimacy of his racially mixed background, Tiger Woods came out with a refreshingly confrontive approach.

When a symbol as common as Betty Crocker becomes multiracial, we can see change is happening. Even if the new woman only reflects General Mills' attempts to tap a broader market, the shift is important. Basho and his friends know that the old role models don't fit them and trust themselves to create something new.

Basho spoke of his own image. "When I was in high school, I was kind of preppy. I would go to Macy's and get clothes. I started to notice the more I tried to fit in, the more I realized I stuck out. When I was cutting my hair short, in a crew cut, I realized that there was something funny about doing that."

For young people to grow up with a healthy sense of who they are, they need to see their reflections in the world around them. Black History Month, Women's Studies, H'mong New Year's celebration, even controversial bilingual education, give people mirrors that affirm their images as Americans. People of mixed race are growing more vocal about the importance of cultural mirrors. Hapa Issues Forum, a five-year-old mixed-race organization with 500 members nationwide, and other groups like it, are determined to break down racial barriers and promote a new, race-free consciousness. "People here don't have hang ups about race," so founder Greg Mayeda told the *Sacramento Bee*. "By connecting all these diverse people, it builds a chain with links in each community and tears down the walls that divide people."

This idea of linking is more powerful than any legislation because it is personal. In recreating our country's center it is essential to "crisscross commonalities," as Martha Minow suggested in her book *Not Just for Myself: Identity, Politics & the Law*. Through overlapping communities, families that extend over marriages and divorces, and groups that make music, play sports, or stage benefits together, cultural change becomes real. Race and politics crisscross more than ever. This re-working of cultural associations weaves new relationships between old-fashioned American individualism and group pressures for identity and recognition.

Edgewalkers don't typically feel they are part of the unifying center. They see themselves as outsiders, different, not a part of the main culture. Yet they care deeply about making our country better for everyone and see the potential for doing so. Many of them want to be a part of a new center, a new sense of what it means to be American.

"I would love it if there were more unity between all of us *edgewalkers*. Through that we will really be the ones to help everyone else along," Malik Johnson, one of Basho's friends said to me.

Joey Garcia, a Sacramento poet, spiritual adviser, and advice columnist who was born in Belize but grew up in the United States, descends from Mayan, Welsh, Honduran and African forebears. "My ethnicities are tools for me to understand myself," she said.

Joey remembered watching President Bush on television talking about the *New World Order*. "My aunt said, 'I don't think he realizes *you're* the New World Order.' Everywhere in the world, people think I'm from there," she said. "That's what the New World Order is—we begin to accept each other as kin."

Redefining the center is a work in progress.

High school students have started a quiet revolution. According to a USA *Today* Gallop Poll (1997) 57 percent of teens who go out on dates say they've been out with someone of another race or ethnic group. Their views on race seemed inconceivable just two decades ago. But that depends on who's talking.

When he first heard about *Edgewalkers*, Basho Fujimoto was interested.

"I relate to being mixed," Basho explained. "I am biracial in heritage, my mom is Irish Welsh, my dad is Japanese American. I try to come to terms with that and not choose one or the other."

A bandanna crowned picturesque clumps—not quite braids—of the young man's brown hair. His open smile, warm handshake and energetic "Come in!" proclaimed enthusiasm. We talked at the kitchen table while the answering machine picked up repeated phone calls. A bulletin board nearby, crammed with colored snapshots, suggests a full life. Basho had just finished college and was feverishly preparing to leave in a few days for a nine-month stay in Japan. The first American ever selected, he would be an intern with an internationally known Taiko drumming group, Kodo.

"The whole thing will be in Japanese. I'll have to eat every meal with my opposite writing hand, run ten kilometers each morning, work in the rice fields with the people who live there. They're set up for having apprentices from Japan, not America. I'm going to take it day by day."

Basho and his friends view life with optimism, along with some stringent suffering. They obviously think about their racial heritage and their place in the world.

"We have other friends who are mixed, too. People are always asking, 'What are you? Where are you from?' We would never fit certain stereotypes or certain generalizations about people. I am what is known as *Hapa*, a Hawaiian Japanese term. I think it was originally not a good term—like *Hapa/Haoulie*, which meant half-white or half-foreigner. But now it's more of an affectionate term, a good way to describe people who are part Japanese.

"Other than on the university campus, there aren't that many Asians in a place like Davis, California, where I've lived off and on. There's not a Japanese community, not an Asian-American community where Old World culture is passed on. My friend Mark, who is Hawaiian Japanese, and I grew up American. And so in this place, it's not just by chance we were friends. It's because we're Japanese American. We were also friends from a long time ago—along with Wendell Fishman and some other people. Wendell is half-African-American and half-Jewish. We started to realize that we don't have anything racially that connects us except the fact that we're completely different from everyone else. When we first started college, Wendell and I would yell, 'My Fittis!' It would always arise in people's throats, talking about our ethnicity. That's one of the first things that becomes an issue—race—one of the first things out on the table. People say, 'You kind of look like you're Puerto Rican?' or, 'Maybe you're from the Middle East?' I've been mistaken for Persian, Mexican, you name it."

Basho's confident presence is a far cry from someone who feels diminished by a mixed ethnic heritage. He has embraced his differentness and regards it as a strength. It is clear that his confidence is the result of learning to get along in a variety of environments, with plenty of bumps along the way.

"It is okay for me now. I grew up in a variety of locations, so I had this perspective that was always kind of different. I was born in Davis. Then I moved to Oakland for elementary school and lived there for six years—went to a totally mixed school—predominantly black, but I consider it mixed. I came back to Davis for junior high and high school. I lived in England for a semester, then went to

Denmark. When I was there people thought I was a Middle Eastern refugee. Oftentimes, Middle Easterners would say, 'Ah, Salaam!' I had some Iranian friends and Palestinian friends.

"Situations like that can reinforce how being mixed can be positive.

"A lot of times people will say things like, 'I'm just a white girl,' or 'I'm just a white boy. I have no culture.' My friends and I try to be inclusive. We're not just about us being in the mix and excluding others. Especially with our music [he and his friends have a band]. It's all connected for us. We play African, Latin American, jazz, Asian. We are trying to come up with a new definition of American. The thing is, right now, 'American' still conjures an image of baseball-playing, apple-pie-eating, Chevrolet-driving people. It doesn't necessarily incorporate all the mixed bloods."

Basho and his friends are direct about being "fitties," as they say. They create a forum for confronting the ugliness of what the Ku Klux Klan termed "mud babies," and other insulting attitudes toward miscegenation.

"It definitely is about trying to find a place where voices can be heard. For us, it's in the music. Our group survived several phases, but our latest incarnation is 'The Free Association.' We can talk about racial things in the music, and we do. We sing about being 'fittie', and being mixed blood, and make jokes about it. We say, 'We're The Free Association and we officially sponsor race mixing!'

"People look uncomfortable and make sounds like, 'Hehhh.' It all depends on the delivery. People are shocked. They like it. It gives them a chuckle. But they're uncomfortable. In what other situation would you hear someone say, 'We officially endorse race mixing?' It's kind of an inside joke for us. We try to do it in a positive light."

Despite Basho's up-beat attitude and creativity, his pain came through as well.

"The whole thing can be frustrating—finding your identity and having to deal with figuring out what it means to be black, Japanese, Native American in a society where you don't have your traditional culture. People look at you and assume you must be culturally astute. That can be a detriment, leaving me blank, or feeling left out, or feeling like a sellout, or feeling at a loss. It is almost like there is a responsibility to reiterate the old and be traditional, without being able to explore a new self."

Being caught between demands for conformity to an old model or stereotype and a personal yearning for self-exploration is a common theme in *edgewalker* conversation.

"The mixed identity is something that is being created as we talk. We're starting to see more mixed blood faces come up in the media—fashion models in advertising. I don't know if that's positive or not.

"Most of my friends are part Caucasian, have some kind of European ancestry. We don't identify as white. We actually question the notion of white. What is white? You look it up in the dictionary and it just says 'absence of color.' It's not a color. It doesn't say a race of people. If you look up black, it says African-Americans. Both are social constructions."

Basho revealed that he equates "white" with "mainstream."

"I don't identify with being white. I think a lot of it has to do with my own personal life story with a lesbian mother. She can't lump herself in the mainstream category. She's part of a whole alternative culture, against the mainstream of everything I think white stands for. I think a lot of confusion comes up in the definitions of white, especially in our discussions when we talk about race with our friends or other colleagues or contemporaries. It always reaches this point where it gets really confusing.

"A lot of European Americans don't have an identity to have a basis of discussion of what they want to do with the whole notion of a collective identity or personal identity—one that works together. Right now there are no venues for that kind of discussion other than private, personal ones, so that's what we do. We acknowledge people as mixed bloods or 'fitties'.

"My friends and I are mixed bloods but we're not a new race. People have been mixing for a long time. It's just that in our country right now we're part of the first generation where it's okay. We don't suffer the racism that people did thirty years ago. We don't have that direct stuff much—Nigger, Jap, Chink, Kike.

"You look around and there are mixed bloods that are tremendous inspiration for us—real people, fictional people. Bob Marley on one hand, Spock in Star Trek on the other."

As the phone rang one more time and Basho looked at the kitchen clock, he summarized, matter-of-factly, describing his personal solution to biracial life in a world struggling with the same question on a much larger scale.

"When I speak of being a mixed blood, I speak of it as being a person of color, but someone who does have access to white America. I don't feel like I'm compromising or selling out in any way. I've been raised in both. If anything, I'll try to explore my cultural heritage. Next week, when I go to Japan, I'm returning to the source, for which I feel very fortunate. Most people don't have the opportunity. The thing I'm going to do now will put me in touch with the culture, more so than most Japanese people in America."

Wendell Fishman is as quiet as Basho is outgoing.

"I've traveled my whole life—ever since I was seven months old—all around Europe and the United States with my family—been in a lot of countries, in Africa and Jamaica, Brazil, Hawaii. That experience helps me. Sometimes I'll be in a situation and be able to draw from one of those other cultures and just say, 'Whatever is happening, it's not a big deal.'

"The older I get, the less I think about being mixed. I'm in the process of becoming more myself. There have been times in my life where I've been in situations where I've definitely not fit in. But these days I just have a pretty good sense of where I am and where I want to go with my life. I am myself. I accept myself. When I have that viewpoint, most people accept me.

"I've taken a lot of trips, lived in Denmark for half a year, went to Africa. I can't remember which trip it was, but one time I left the country and my attitude was, 'This place is fucked up! The United States, California. I don't have any intentions of coming back in the near future.'

"But after a while, I missed being in a place where people got my jokes or understood my sarcasm. I came back with a different perspective. Yes, this place is fucked up, but it's my home. This is my tribe, my community. I'm going to spend my life trying to make things better. That's why I believe in working within the system rather than standing outside and criticizing it. That's what I do. I educate the young people in this culture and try as an example and a teacher to help things—to help us unlearn some things we've learned. In a sense, by leaving the United States, you can look at it. If you leave the planet Earth, you can look at the planet Earth.

"We're in the process of growing or overcoming. We have a lot of different cultures and groups represented here. But historically, the white male power structure has imposed their way of seeing the world. If you look at the media, that's the way it still looks. We do have a lot of amazing technical ways of connecting the species. The problem is, the people who are running this technology represent just one group, and they impose their way of looking at it. The Internet, for example, is an amazing thing, but it is not balanced.

"My father, being a white male, gives me a close-up look. Something I get after him about—and I think a lot of white males could work on—is not giving his opinion as if it is the truth. That's a fundamental thing people do a lot—impose their beliefs upon other people and don't even realize they're doing it. That's been a big problem at many levels.

"From the black culture, I've learned the whole idea of asking, checking in every once in a while. You stop and say, 'Right?' or just raise your voice in a question. You're aware of your audience. You're saying, 'This is what I believe, but I'm open to other views.' It's just respect. I even see this style overflowing into the classroom where traditionally, lectures were once the main method of teaching. I like the process I'm seeing where the teacher is the 'guide on the side' instead of the 'sage on the stage.' When I run a class, I look at it as though everybody has something to offer. I think about it like in *The Celestine Prophecy*. Energy goes from one person to another. I get that in music, in sports, in the classroom. It's like a ball. The ball goes from person to person. That's been a problem in the white culture, where they don't allow the ball to go to another person.

"I want to teach and play music. I'm going to graduate school next year at San Francisco State to study educational technology.

"I learned to claim my difference from a Jordanian friend of mine who's very involved in Arab women's issues. It can be a blessing or a curse. Her motto is 'claim it!' You can claim anything that's in your environment. If you want to talk in a British accent, if you want to be a dancer, you don't have to just sit and watch people do it. You can do it. You can claim you're *edgewalking* with two worlds—you don't have to move into this one or that one.

"If you don't know that, life can be very painful. You can be excluded from both worlds. I've definitely experienced that before when I've been very excluded, from either the white world or the black world.

"Both Basho and I play in a number of groups. We play together in The Free Association, which is a fascinating group with several mixed race members. At so many levels we're different. At the same time, the fact that we've agreed to do this project together makes it really strong. It's like chemistry. If you have two things that are being bonded that are different, then the bond is strong. We've gotten to a point where I think we do a nice job of dealing with each other as human beings. We create this energy that just liberates people. We have discussions all the time. Stylistically, we often segue in one song from rhythm and blues, to punk rock to reggae, to Latin, and then, maybe, to free jazz. We're performing, setting the tone for the whole room. It opens things up, creates a platform on which people can do whatever they want. The more creative the better."

Malik Johnson, a friend of Basho and Wendell, had just completed his master's in Fine Arts at the University of California, Davis, and will soon be leaving the area. He had contacted his long misplaced biological father in Wichita, Kansas shortly before our interview.

"When Basho first told me about that name you're using, *Edgewalkers*, I thought, 'Wow, that's a great name!' I look around when I'm out, and it's my biggest hobby to recognize someone who's mixed. I think Basho told you about the 'fittie' thing. It's not really about blood quantum at all. It's about awareness. My mom and my dad to some extent could be considered 'fitties' if they choose because without them there would be no me. They are essentially the sparks that create the 'fitties,' so they're 'fitties' also. It's not a strictly defined category. It's a fluid thing, and it's about an understanding. From time to time I get upset about people who consider themselves white—although I'll use 'I'm black and white,' and I can understand how it's useful. There are times I'll say to myself 'I don't like that because there is no white.' There is no white person. We're all 'fitties'. I love looking around and feeling that connection.

"I was born in Wichita, and I have this Wichita mentality. Growing up in New York makes me feel really cosmopolitan. I have a lot of experience interacting with different cultures. When I was an undergrad in Pittsburgh, I worked in an Indian restaurant for two years waiting tables, and I got along really well with the people in the kitchen. When I first started working there, people asked, 'How do you understand what he's saying?' I said, 'It's really easy. You just have to open up to it—listen and understand what he is trying to communicate. All of us essentially say the same things, just different words,

different sounds.' It was easy for me to understand what he was trying to communicate, even if I didn't understand every word.

"One of the painful aspects of all this is doubt. For example, my
name is Malik, and it's a Muslim name. It was ironic to discover my
father changed to a Muslim name after he lost touch with my mother.
My brother and I both got our names because my mother was Muslim
when we were born. I feel like my name is a really big part of who I am.
People always want to know about it, and I'm willing to answer questions, or speculate myself. At one point when I was about ten and
moved to Queens, Mom was Muslim, but we weren't going to temple or
anything. She decided to get back into religion, so we started attending
the Methodist Church, which is what she was raised—United Methodist.

"I spent a lot of my formative years at the youth group and
Sunday School, and I actually worked at the church for three years
when I was in high school. I learned about Christianity and about that
kind of spirituality. And yet, I can clearly remember a time when I
rejected it—not fully—but just in the form it has taken. And so those two
major things are within me. I go back and forth between them. That
process creates doubt. It's painful sometimes to feel that if I were just
born this certain way with these certain paths, with this certain religion, I wouldn't have to question so many things. Seems like taking
your identity for granted would allow you free time to do whatever
interests you. I'm in pain sometimes because what really interests me is
this figuring out—this flip flopping. It makes me feel like I have more
room to choose certain things for myself, but yet it's scary to have that
much choice.

"I was in the honors classes growing up. Honors classes in
whatever school I've ever been in are predominantly white and Asian—
even when the rest of the school is predominantly Hispanic and black.
I had a lot of interaction with kids like that. And then I would go to
camp every summer—for eight years—and the camp I went to was predominantly inner city kids—poor, black and Hispanic—from all the
boroughs in New York City. I had this back and forth thing. I'd be in
my neighborhood in Queens and I'd have people who were my friends
who would jokingly say 'nigger,' and I'd be at camp where I'd have
friends who would jokingly say 'whitey,' or 'honky,' or 'white boy.' That
built a kind of distrust, but I also needed to understand why I was in
this position—because this was coming from my friends. Sometimes it
was just horrible. Depending on who it was coming from, I could just
laugh it off. I would have to. Or else I would have to go home.

"Emotionally, I would always react, but on the surface I might be very strategic about it. It's the kind of thing that's happened to me all my life. I can remember several incidents, like one not long ago. I was crossing a bridge here in Davis and some guys drove by in a big pick up, yelling 'Nigger! Nigger!' shaking their fists out the window at me. Those experiences are so valuable in helping me learn not to get hooked. I wouldn't trade them for anything.

"Although I will always appear and feel like an outsider, I think more than many other people, I am able to slip in and out of many different communities. I can be in a middle class academic arena and feel like I'm supposed to be here. I'm doing well. I'm useful and necessary. And yet, I'm also right now working in a restaurant—in the kitchen. Here, I have a master's degree—I feel like, 'Oh, I shouldn't be working in the kitchen.' But it's fine. When I look out of the kitchen, people assume certain things. I've been called paranoid before. I wouldn't say that's untrue. I'd say it's all part of my intuition.

"Since I was young I've been told I'm a relatively good-looking person. That quality helps me slip in and out of these different situations. I'm inclined to believe that mixed people are among the most beautiful people in the world. I'm sure that's because that's what I was taught. I've overheard people say that to my mom in front of me.

"I do feel special. That's why I was saying before, even with all the negative, I just wouldn't trade it. It's not like I feel that I'm on top of anything or I'm some kind of chosen one, but I just feel special enough."

The people in this chapter claim their mixed race with pride, think about it, talk about it and see themselves as the wave of the future. They experience their heritage as an asset, not without its pain at times, that promotes understanding of others different from themselves. They value building relationships with others and supporting people who are open to learning about crossing cultures. Some of the themes they brought out in their conversation include the following.

Elucidate *all* their cultural influences.

Basho Fujimoto: I relate to being mixed. I'm biracial in heritage, my mom is Irish Welsh, and my dad is Japanese American. I try to come to terms with that and not choose one or the other.

Wendell Fishman: I learned to *claim my difference* from a Jordanian friend of mine who's very involved in Arab women's issues. It can be a blessing or a curse. You can claim your *edgewalking* with two worlds—you don't have to move into this one or that one.

Malik Johnson: From time to time I get upset about people who consider themselves white—although I'll use 'I'm black and white,' and I can understand how it's useful.

Acknowledge their pain.

Wendell Fishman: If you don't know that you can claim both your worlds, life can be very painful. You can be excluded from both worlds. I've definitely experienced that before when I've been very excluded, from either the white world or the black world.

Malik Johnson: It's painful sometimes to feel that if I were just born this certain way with these certain paths, with this certain religion, I wouldn't have to question so many things. I might just take all of that for granted. It seems like taking your identity for granted would allow you free time to do whatever interests you. I'm in pain sometimes because what really interests me is figuring out this flip-flopping. It makes me feel like I have more room to choose certain things for myself, but yet it's scary to have that much choice.

Use what they have learned about themselves to reach out.

Malik Johnson: I would love it if there were more unity between all of us *edgewalkers*. Through that we will really be the ones to help everyone else along.

Wendell Fishman: That's why I believe in working within the system rather than standing outside and criticizing it. That's what I do. I educate the young people in this culture and try as an example and a teacher to help things—to help us unlearn some things we've learned.

Joey Garcia: Everywhere in the world, people think I'm from there. That's what the New World Order is—we began to accept each other as kin.

Basho Fujimoto: We started to realize that we don't have anything racially that connects us except the fact that we're completely different from everyone else.

Wendell Fishman: I think about it like in *The Celestine Prophecy.* Energy goes from one person to another. I get that in music, in sports, in the classroom. It's like a ball. The ball goes from person to person. That's been a problem in the white culture, where they don't allow the ball to go to another person.

Create something new.

Basho Fujimoto: It's not about taking traditional elements from our old cultures and mixing them all together and making a nice, evenly distributed multiculturalism. It's more like taking just the consciousness of all of our heritage and bringing in one point and working with that to create something new.

Basho Fujimoto: The mixed identity is something that is being created as we talk. We're starting to see more mixed blood faces come up in the media—fashion models in advertising. I don't know if that's positive or not.

Wendell Fishman: I've traveled my whole life—ever since I was seven months old—all around Europe and the U.S. with my family—I've been in a lot of countries, in Africa and Jamaica, Brazil, Hawaii. That experience helps me. Sometimes I'll be in a situation and be able draw from one of those other cultures and just say, 'Whatever is happening, it's not a big deal.'

Wendell Fishman: We create this energy that just liberates people. We have discussions all the time. Musically, we will segue in one song from rhythm and blues, to punk rock to reggae, to African groove, and then, maybe, to free jazz. We're performing, setting the tone for the whole room. It opens things up, creates a platform on which people can do whatever they want. The more creative the better.

Tiger, Basho, Joey, Wendell and Malik live at the world's new center. Each, in his or her way, embraces mixed heritage and feels richer for it. The perspective they share offers integrity to a New World Order, and optimism, as well. From childhood they've walked the maze of tangled identity, and answered with pride the question, "Who and *what* are you?"

four

DIVERSIFYING CULTURALLY
Unconscious Structures of Belief

"**W**HITE PEOPLE JUST DON'T GET IT!**" screamed the headline of the free paper I picked up at San Francisco's temporary City Hall. The article was an interview with filmmaker Peter Bratt about his work, *Follow Me Home*, which the audience at the 1996 San Francisco International Film Festival had declared the best in the festival. The film is about a journey by a group of Latino, African-American and Native American artists and activists into memory. Along the way, they encounter the remnants of some lost faux United States cavalry troops. Film critics' perception of what the troops are doing differs.

Bratt pointed out that people of color, intellectuals, writers and others had hailed the film, the audience responding to it strongly. At the same time, Bratt said, "...film critics...say it's the most puerile, banal, trite, piece of shit we've seen in a long time... We saw something similar in America with the Rodney King verdict, the O.J. Simpson verdict, and in California's Propositions 209 [curtailing affirmative action] and 187 [tightening controls on illegal aliens]. There are such polar opposite reactions to those issues, oftentimes along racial lines, because we have such different perceptions. We don't really understand each other culturally and historically."

It is not the fact that we *are* different that is so important. It's what we tell ourselves and try to tell the world about how we handle those differences.

In his film, and in discussing critical reaction to it, Bratt confronts one of the most powerful myths that blocks social change in the United States. Despite the fervently held belief—social construct, even—that comfort with diversity is a way of life in the United States, cultural, ethnic and religious differences aren't easily accepted on a practical basis.

In America, national identity is built on the idea of openness. Innovations, improvisation and acceptance of change all contribute to a people in process. Granted, all kinds of people in the U.S. have more mobility and more access to privilege than any place in the world. But the intention to honor diversity operates better at a theoretical level than at a daily, personal one.

"Can white people be *edgewalkers?*" my friends have asked me with a recognizable look in their eye.

In fact, American culture is quite British, despite the anti-British sentiment of the Boston Tea Party, and people must either buy into the Anglo style or remain outsiders. In an *Atlantic Monthly* article, Benjamin Schwarz named this double message the *diversity myth*, the belief that in America, diverse groups co-exist peacefully and productively and are good at resolving conflict. He challenges American naïveté and grandiose attitudes—the view that we deal with diversity so well at home we can help other nations with their internal ethnic conflicts. Even though Schwarz's focus is on international relations and the absurdity of American hubris in playing diversity leader, his naming of the problem is helpful here for understanding its subtlety.

When a gay resident of the Castro District in San Francisco, California, and a dairy farmer from nearby Marin County, California, happen to find themselves briefly thrown together for one reason or another, they probably will not see each other as having much in common. No matter that they are of the same cultural heritage, approximately same economic group, and are both native Californians.

When Peter Bratt called attention to the difference between audience and critic reaction to his film, a barrier rose. These barriers also occur at personal levels when individuals stand up for difference rather than hiding in the cloak of conformity. Their actions happen in the business of everyday life, rarely making it into the newspaper.

I met with one *edgewalker*, Miriam Acevedo Davis in Indianapolis, Indiana and found her friendly, maybe a shade formal, though she laughed easily. Of Puerto Rican descent, she grew up in Brooklyn, New York. She had thought deeply about this business of living in more than one culture, knew her feelings and was willing to express them.

"When you said *edgewalker*," she began, dark eyes looking at me directly, "I got an image of someone who is standing along the side—on the perimeter—and has the alternative perspective that stance would offer, as opposed to being more in the center. In my mind I was trying to picture how that would be. That would give a more rounded view. Too often we become bifurcated, but an *edgewalker* sounded more rounded, rather than split."

Miriam has lived in the Midwest part of the United States for eleven years. Her navy and white dress, stylish shoes and bag, and leather briefcase, communicated an ease with the business world. She contrasted her years growing up in Brooklyn with the ways she's learned to behave in the business world and her personal life as an adult.

"We spoke Spanish at home, ate Puerto Rican food, even though we were right in the middle of the dominant culture. I can remember in high school we went out to Stratford, Connecticut, to see a Shakespeare play and stopped at the Howard Johnson. Our family never went out to dinner, so that was big time. It was my first exposure to a setting like that other than by watching TV.

"The flip side of the trip to Stratford is being marginalized. In school, we were told by the teachers not to speak Spanish, to behave in a certain manner. If we laughed too loud or spoke emotionally, it was a negative thing. If you were stoic—I called it socially constipated—that was more valued. Too many of my Hispanic friends were tracked into vocational or general education. The sense of not being valued could be spoken or unspoken.

"On the East Coast, people like to banter and tend to be straightforward with their differences. Here, if you challenge, no one says a word to you. No one says, 'Well, wait a minute!' They just stare at you. You come to the meeting next month, and it's almost like a shunning in some religious traditions. They don't say, 'Girlfriend, you stepped out of line. We don't do that here,' and let you know. I call it the Arctic Blast that comes in with you when you enter the room. You're not included in the little parties or coffee klatches afterward.

"So if you say, 'I notice there isn't a whole lot of diversity in my daughter's grade school curriculum, has anybody thought about this?' Or, if you challenge some of the milquetoasty ways things are done, oh my!

"I find a constant guarding against change of any kind. That can really mess with your mind if you don't have a strong sense of who you are, or if you don't have friends on the outside that you go and talk to. Being in the mental health profession I understand the effects of being ostracized—having everybody turn their back on you. You start gathering a sense of what that is. I can be more sensitive with clients in helping them get support so they can hold on to their experience.

"It makes me think about when we were kids playing Double Dutch. We'd yell 'Yeah, Girl! Yeah, Girl!' and be a cheering section for each other. That's what's missing here if you don't fit in. When you don't have that, you can't value what you're doing. You can't know how to gauge it.

"It's funny. It would be easier if it were arrogance. I can fight arrogance. The problem is really the valuing of sameness. Diversity is wonderful, as long as you are just like us. People here want compliance and fear anything beyond that."

Miriam persevered in spite of the pressure for conformity. She talked about helping her daughter of multicultural heritage choose an African-American inventor for a school project. Nobody had ever heard of the individual her daughter, Kamile, reported on, but they were interested in learning about someone new.

The core of Miriam's strength highlights her straightforward communication. Her strong sense of who she is made itself known when she walked into the room—a little intimidating, maybe, but effective in establishing her presence. From that place, she is willing to connect, willing to be open with her feelings and opinions, and receptive as well.

The *diversity myth* is no mystery to Miriam. However, she is substantially prepared to use her experience as being different from her colleagues to help others who are in situations where they are in the minority.

Edgewalkers pay a price either way—if they push for change, they have to deal with the resistance, and if they don't, they violate themselves and their beliefs. There's pressure to maintain what many perceive as the natural state of things, the white male establishment in charge with everyone else seen as a minority. The message is something like: *The United States does a better job than anyone dealing with diversity, so don't make me uncomfortable about my insensitivity.*

A good example of how this point of view is taken for granted is illustrated in Schlesinger's *The Disuniting of America: Reflections on a Multicultural Society*. The author laments the loss of what he considers America's core. He observes that the cult of ethnicity has its price, and pressed too far, poses the danger of "the fragmentation, resegregation and tribalization of American life." He cannot see that his view is from inside the establishment, and it is *his* point of view, which is at stake.

Schlesinger is a great scholar, and he acknowledges that his view is influenced by his place in the culture. But, he still does not get it. Viewing life from the perspective of the majority culture carries with it many assumptions that don't hold true for everyone—the *invisibility of privilege* that only shows up when seen from outside.

An expanding proportion of America's population comes from the Far East, Africa, Latin America or indigenous North American peoples, but remains invisible or underrepresented in the media, government and business. Years of exclusion make it difficult to repair the damage. Often, inviting other-than-white, middle-class people into new places opens controversies of race, class, economics, discrimination, favoritism, victimization and affirmative action. Look around at the next official or ceremonial occasion you attend to see if the food, the service, the dinnerware and the guests reflect who your nation really is. Does patriotic music include everybody's tunes?

An *edgewalker* who has grappled with these complexities, Dr. Rufus Burrow, arrived for an interview at a friend's office in the Indianapolis seminary building where they are colleagues, and we tiptoed onto the shaky ground of getting acquainted. Rufus, a man of athletic build with a modified Afro hairstyle, wearing a scarlet safari shirt, made a colorful statement in the subdued surroundings.

Rufus, a Boston University graduate, a teacher of ethics and writer of the Liberation Theological Movement, has built a career in a mainly white world. He has done so on his own terms and at great personal cost.

We sat in an office on the second floor of the seminary where he teaches—a beautiful facility with marble lining the floors and the walls of the corridor. The interior of the building, enclosing a square, offered a view of the tailored green courtyard through its enormous glass walls.

"One of the things I did early on was establish an outside support group—pastor-types, but also Sam Jones of the Urban League," Rufus said. "From time to time, when I felt like I just couldn't take it anymore in this building..."

This is where he stopped, sighed, and extended his arm—circling as if to encompass the entire square. "I had this problem with the building. Still do. The place is too white for me! If you've been through the building, you've seen that everything's white. The walls, the floor. Most of the people are white. From time to time, I just feel a need to be away from this white place!"

As Satsuki Ina, who will be introduced later, had said to me early on, "Minority people don't find ourselves reflected in the research."

Rufus' sentiments were similar, "We don't find ourselves reflected in the architecture, in the physical environment."

Rufus continued, "In the early days, it seemed to me there were people around who didn't quite understand when I got a little bit cocky. The message was that I needed to fit in, be more like them. I felt like 'I don't have to explain it to you,' since a good number of them, particularly on the faculty, were involved in the civil rights movement. They should know better. I shouldn't have to spend my time educating them."

But now, Dr. Burrow has been on the faculty for more than thirteen years, has seen people of color come and go, both as faculty and students.

"I've stayed in touch with African-Americans in other schools. One of the things that was said to me by James Cone, major leader in the Black Theology Movement, '...since you're there by yourself, you're in the unique position of having to be there for the black students. Of course, you're there for all the students. But you are all the black students have, and there will be times when you will think that they are all that you have.'"

Rufus Burrow explained to me that he had given up dropping by his white colleagues' offices to chat and didn't reach out much anymore: "If someone stops by to chat with me, I invite them in, and then later, I return the call. It just doesn't happen much."

Rufus does his *edgewalking* mostly by staying in the situation and asserting his presence. And by not capitulating to unspoken, as well as more direct, pressure for conformity. He challenges the *diversity myth* by being the diverse one. Rufus frowned as he explained the lack of understanding about his situation by people who were ostensibly committed to civil rights but missed the personal connection. He helped me understand the importance of white, establishment *edgewalkers* who are willing to risk rebuff to shake the fence from the safer side.

Rufus could do the things that would gain him easier acceptance among his colleagues, but he wants them to respect his culture, his artifacts, his style, rather than assume he will, or should, blend into theirs. His story, like those of other *edgewalkers*, has history, complexity and politics. He shares in some aspects of his work environment, but doesn't perceive himself as sharing at a core level.

It's easy enough to walk into a seminary and think, *Oh, no! Christians should do a more faithful, hopeful, charitable job of managing diversity!* In reality, it is not easy. From inside any system, it is difficult to be in tune with one's fallibility.

Caught in a blind spot recently while driving, I was reminded how hard it is to be aware of my own assumptions and be in tune with someone having a different point of view. In my psychotherapy practice, a woman from Alabama whose contract had not been renewed after a year in a high-level corporate position came to consult with me. She had accepted the job, knowing that one other woman had worked there for a year and then departed voluntarily. No other women or minorities had held high-level positions in this firm. When she went after a top-level job and captured it, she felt pleased that the firm had recognized her competence, and she put her career on the line. Her previous success as an entrepreneur gave her every reason to believe she would do well. It didn't occur to her that anything but her competence would be evaluated, and she knew she could do a good job.

I was amazed that a woman with her skill and sophistication had not seen the potential problems, or at least asked some questions about where the other women and minorities were in that organization. In consulting with a colleague later, I queried, "Hasn't she flipped through a copy of *Ms.* in the last twenty years?"

My colleague, who grew up in Mississippi, laughed at me.

"You need to understand southern culture. They don't think that way."

It made sense. A woman who lives in a culture where women tend to be ostensibly valued, would not be as likely to look askance at a business that did not have women in positions of power. She might not see that distinction as a warning sign. She would assume that her competence would carry her.

Of course, my friend's statement doesn't apply to all southerners, but I had to accept that my feminist bias made it very difficult to comprehend this particular individual's naïveté. One of my first questions in looking at an organization is always, *Where are the women? Are they on the board? In top management positions?* I am not saying that she shouldn't have tried for the position, or even accepted it. But that she would be surprised when she bumped into barriers tougher than she had ever encountered was difficult for me to understand.

America is comprised of people from most of the nations in the world. It is home to people with every possible belief and background. Metropolitan areas play a symphony of language from all over the globe, backing up people in saris or sombreros, dashikis or turbans, pursuing daily life. Many neighborhoods retain the ethnic flavor and color of the dominant cultures that inhabit them. More Jewish people live in America than in Israel, more Cubans in Miami than in many Cuban cities.

Coco Fusco's book, *English is Broken Here, Notes on Cultural Fusion in the Americas*, deals with the *diversity myth* from the inside out. The author agreed to meet and talk with me when she was in San Francisco. Coco, the daughter of an Italian father and Afro-Cuban mother—both physicians—grew up in New York City and attended the Ethical Culture School, and later, an Ivy League college. "The school that I attended was mostly Jewish kids who were children, or at most grandchildren, of immigrants. The idea that people came from other places or spoke other languages at home was very much a part of my life. A lot of the teachers—blacklisted during the nineteen fifties and forced out of universities—were politically progressive. I think that was one of the reasons I wasn't crushed.

"The sixties leftist position—to be anti-racist—was to eliminate any reference whatever. Assimilation was the accepted method. To assimilate meant to excel, and I didn't question that for a long time."

Here Coco described the *diversity myth* in full bloom. According to the myth, we should deal with diversity by being alike. In other words, don't acknowledge diversity. Difference is only skin deep. Coco's experience painfully demonstrates that no amount of wishful thinking, well-intentioned or otherwise, could make it so.

"Once I left the protected environment of home and the

school, I encountered a very different world where people perceived me in terms of my difference, not in terms of my similarity. It had a big impact on my social life at college, my experiences in jobs and interactions with professors. I kept marginalizing myself more and more, thinking that if I could find where all the weirdos were, then all of these problems would go away. I was still trying to find myself solely in terms of what I was interested in and what I wanted to do. When I finished college, something in me felt like I had completed all the requirements for assimilation. Now, maybe I could get more interested, or do more about the kinds of things that relate to my culture."

Coco Fusco now teaches what she calls the "race requirement," a course that fulfills a multicultural curriculum spot at an art school in the East, and spoke about her experience this way:

"My Utopian view is that my students are racist because it's comfortable for them to be racist. They think the demands of people of color are unreasonable because they believe America is a democracy and everybody is equal. What enables them to believe that is that they don't have access to information about inequality. They live in a society that supports the view that everything is fine and anyone who doesn't succeed doesn't succeed because there is something wrong with them. Some of them didn't even know about the Japanese internment camps until I told them."

In *English is Broken Here*, this scholar, artist and social critic describes a performance piece she and Guillermo Gomez-Pena presented internationally. For this slice of living street theater, they put themselves in a golden cage, dressed like "noble savages," and played that role. They situated their performance at museums, parks and other public places.

When I asked Coco about her goals or intentions for this ambitious project, she said, "...basically to challenge how Westerners see exotic or primitive people." This project was a theatrical challenge to the *diversity myth*. What do people do when they encounter someone really different from themselves in an unusual situation?

Two things happened that the performers hadn't counted on: 1) a large portion of the public believed they really were natives from some far-off place called Gatinau, and 2) the decision makers at museums or other public institutions tried to deflect attention from the performance itself and focus more on their view that Fusco and Gomez-Pena had duped the public.

"When Guillermo and I started the project, we didn't know

what reaction we would get. I didn't think people would believe it, and so that was a big surprise. What it presented for me was the possibility of tapping unconscious structures of belief."

Here Coco is looking at something central to dealing with difference. It's not what people say about it, it's how they reveal the feelings and beliefs they don't even know they have—how they react.

For instance, my *unconscious structure of belief* in dealing with my client from Alabama was that since she was a very bright woman, she would anticipate that discrimination would be an issue in a corporation where no other women were in positions of power. I would certainly make that assumption. Why wouldn't she? I formed opinions about her based on my own *unconscious structures of belief*, not her background and experience.

Unlike my earlier misconception, Coco's observations got to the heart of the *diversity myth*. Very few on-lookers approached the performers, wanting to know more. Nor did they question whether they were really natives from Gatinau.

She stated the issues clearly: "I feel there's a way we can talk about racism to death. But we can't really deal with the deeper level of how it touches people and forms their sense of the world unless we can actually get to what they don't want to talk about. Everybody wants to be perfect. Most of the people in the world know that it's bad to be racist. But most of the people in the world don't want to admit that they are."

From their positions, labeled "noble savages," caged in a public place, Fusco and Gomez-Pena were literally able to observe the results of the *diversity myth*. They could see that people didn't question, but accepted the performance as real—that the two people in the cage were, indeed, the *other*, and as such, not the concern of the everyday citizen. They were seen as objects, oddities, not people who might have feelings and concerns. They evoked indifference, ridicule and rejection more than curiosity, concern or compassion.

This project was not without its design and presentation problems. However, Coco's experience, putting herself in a situation from which she could observe the uninhibited response of onlookers confronted with others who are different, leaves small room for doubting the difficulties that differentness evokes.

The *diversity myth* includes not just the idea that we have and tolerate diversity, but that we thrive on it, benefit from it. The reality is that most of us want to think we do well with diversity, but it's not that easy.

By looking for the *unconscious structures of belief*, as Fusco put it—*those things we believe that we don't know we believe*—we begin to have a handle on our own biases. And we can work with them and change them if we are willing to invest the energy. Since these belief structures exist outside our conscious awareness, we are most likely to become aware of them when someone else points them out.

Miriam Acevedo Davis, Rufus Burrow and Coco Fusco have felt the sting of racism and talk about the *diversity myth* from personal experience. Here are some points they raise that demonstrate that although many people believe diversity is an important aspect of modern culture, our behavior does not consistently support that belief.

Use experiences with racism to understand the pain of others.

Miriam Acevedo Davis: Being in the mental health profession I understand the effects of being ostracized—having everybody turn their back on you. You start gathering a sense of what that is. I can be more sensitive with clients, in helping them get support so they can hold on to their experience.

Coco Fusco: Once I left the protected environment of home and the school, I encountered a very different world where people perceived me in terms of my difference, not in terms of my similarity.

Garner outside support to deal with the double message of the *diversity myth*.

Rufus Burrow: One of the things I did early on was establish an outside support group—pastor-types, but also Sam Jones of the Urban League.

Be clear that the underlying cultural assumption is white.

Miriam Acevedo Davis: In school we were told by the teachers not to speak Spanish, to behave in a certain manner. If we laughed too loud or spoke emotionally, it was a negative thing. If you were stoic—I called it socially constipated—that was more valued. Too many of my colleagues were tracked into vocational, or general education. That sense of not being valued could be spoken or unspoken.

Rufus Burrow: I had this problem with the building. Still do. The place is too white for me! If you've been through the building, you've seen that everything's white. The walls, the floor. Most of the people are white. From time to time, I just feel a need to be away from this white place!

Satsuki Ina: Minority people don't find ourselves reflected in the research.

Coco Fusco: My Utopian view is that my students are racist because it is comfortable for them to be racist. They think the demands of people of color are unreasonable because they believe America's a democracy and everybody's equal.

Acknowledge the *diversity myth*.

Miriam Acevedo Davis: 'Diversity is wonderful, as long as you are just like us.' People here want compliance and fear anything beyond that. I find a constant guarding against change of any kind. That can really mess with your mind if you don't have a strong sense of who you are, or if you don't have friends on the outside that you go and talk to.

Coco Fusco: I feel there is a way we can talk racism to death. But, we can't really deal with the deeper level of how it touches people and forms their sense of the world unless we can actually get to what they don't want to talk about. Everybody wants to be perfect. Most of the people in the world know that it is bad to be racist. But most of the people in the world don't want to admit that they are.

Edgewalkers operate from at least two *structures of belief* and tend to know when they move from one to another. They have working knowledge that no one system has all the answers. They are in a perfect position to challenge the *diversity myth* and offer the tools to dissemble and reassemble it so that, together, we can build a new reality.

five

SEARCHING FOR A CULTURAL MIDDLE
Beyond Color and Race

"My parents shipped me off to a Japanese orphanage for the summer, eight hundred miles from where they were living in that country. That is where I learned to speak Japanese. I didn't learn their reasons until much later. I was at the orphanage two summers and some winter breaks. After the end of the first summer, I almost refused to come home. This was the genesis of my *edgewalking*. Over a period of thirty-five years, I lived in Japan for eleven or twelve years."

Barbara Arnn has a Ph.D. in Japanese language, but that is not the main basis of her employment now as an editor in Connecticut. Crossing cultural barriers has both enriched her and caused such pain that she rarely works in her hard-earned area of expertise.

"I see *edgewalkers* as people who are willing to blur or cross lines. I'm thinking culture. I don't perceive ethnic groupings as having boundaries on them. My family didn't identify themselves with any particular group, except my father was part Commanche. He knew very little about that, but it influenced his life philosophy. His view was that you lived your life, didn't organize it around money, didn't listen to other people's opinions, did not subscribe to such organized evil things as politics and Christianity. Where were you in the landscape? Where's the water?

"In thinking about *edgewalking*, I decided the trick is you have to make choices across patterns. First of all, you have to recognize the patterns. That happens to be something I'm good at. Then you have to start making choices across them.

"I can't even imagine a situation where you can be in both cultures at the same time. When I take my culture into the orphanage it's always within me, but the orphanage completely surrounds me. You have to decide either to meet the expectations of the other people in whose culture you are—to disappoint them or to defy them. Or ignore them. You can choose to intrude or set yourself apart. Or you can try to make as many choices as possible to fade in. If you're a foreigner in Japan, you'd better try to do that if you can. That's the pressure.

"You know the term *comprador*? It's used to describe people in China who served as go-betweens with the Chinese and the other cultures. They became kind of a class of people in specific places who knew enough about both cultures to translate, to run errands. On those people, the West depended entirely for entry. Yet, they were universally reviled because they didn't belong.

"When I start thinking about *edgewalkers*, those people come to mind. As an *edgewalker*, you have to know who you are. If you let go of that, you can't make choices. They're just kind of thrust on you. There has to be a core, absolute assurance of at least some values."

In bringing up the *comprador*, and the idea that they were seen as odious, Barbara raised an important issue that every *edgewalker* knows about. If you are not clearly in one place or another, some people are going to see you as disloyal, a traitor, a bad person.

People who don't fit in, who don't operate in a predictable way, are threatening to others. One way to reduce the internal confusion this may cause is to reject them out of hand. *You're either with us or against us.* If you are not like me, you are the enemy. This psychological defense pattern which operates at an unconscious level is called *splitting.*

Splitting, within an individual, is an unconscious mechanism that slips into place in response to fear. The urge is to oversimplify and distance rather than open up and explore. If you think about the positive and negative aspects of living in the city or living in the country, and then decide to stay in the city, that is not a split. If you decide with very little information that country living is inferior to city living, that everyone that lives in the country is uneducated and you don't want anything to do with them, that is more like splitting.

As an outsider, it is definitely easier to divide things into black and white, see them as all bad or all good—to fight off, or at least avoid, differences. Psychologists are familiar with this self-protective process at the individual level. If someone offends me or hurts my feelings, it is easier to see him as a jerk, or as unimportant, than it is to look at my responsibility in the situation, or understand his point of view. If I reject that person, I don't have to deal with him at all. He has no credibility in my eyes. On the other hand, it is easy to believe that others will see me as a jerk and then I can decide not to approach them.

It takes very little to activate this splitting mechanism.

Splitting is making the other person all bad or all good. Or, even making yourself all bad or all good. Everybody *splits* from time to time at a personal level. *We split as a culture, as well.* Cowboys and Indians, blacks and whites, good guys and bad guys. If it's not this, it must be that. Our cultural tradition disenfranchises complexity.

This dualistic way of dealing with the world appears early in life, helping a baby get along. People or situations seem all bad or all good, from the toddler's knee-high view. Through supportive parenting and education, people learn that most things have more than two sides.

Rather than acknowledge fear and work with it, some people experience fear or vulnerability as hatred of someone else and develop a righteous attitude about it. Propagandists expand on this human tendency by portraying the enemy as subhuman, for example. Beer commercials operate on the same principle in the opposite direction. *Drink this beer, and you'll be surrounded by beautiful people in paradise (and all your troubles will disappear).*

In his book, *Fear of Strangers and Its Consequences, The New Thinking About Ethnic Strife*, David Allen goes even further. It is his opinion that "the true cause of discrimination and prejudice is not moral failure alone...but innate fear of strangers...which surfaces in human infants in the eighth and ninth months after birth in diverse cultures. It is this natural withdrawal from outsiders that is responsible for ethnic conflict in multiethnic societies." It is human destiny to fear or reject strangers.

That babies develop stranger anxiety in the eighth and ninth months after birth is well-supported in psychological literature. How people learn to tolerate that anxiety as adults, however, seems more important than the reality that we are prone to have it. It is the capacity to get a handle on this anxiety at an individual level, and the motivation to work with it at a group level, that can make a difference.

In America, I believe people *split* in major ways when winning is more important than anything. Dehumanizing the other team or one's business competitors makes it easier to go after them. You cannot care about their fate. *America, Love It Or Leave It*, summarizes *cultural splitting*.

It could be easy to think that the making of any choice is a split, but of course that is not the case. Barbara Arnn explained a little about what it was like for her to live in Japan. "There are patterns of physical behavior to which women in Japan adhere. If you are on a train, holding a train ticket, you hold it one way. If you are a man, you do it another. Women generally pitch their voices higher. When I was living there doing research, speaking a lot of Japanese, I had a raw, sore throat because I made a choice to pitch my voice high. It was very physically painful and a very conscious choice, so that the people from whom I needed to get information would not spend minutes sitting there thinking 'this is a stupid, big, loud, masculine sounding, aggressive gaijin female.' You can understand how Americans have an incredibly difficult time. In a way it seems like a counter example of *edgewalking*."

It is. What she is describing here is more like assimilation, the melting pot idea. It is not *splitting* because she's making a conscious choice. It is not something that is happening outside her conscious awareness. In fact, Barbara was diligent about learning Japanese behavior patterns.

The good news is that not everybody splits all the time. Even though splitting is an unconscious defense mechanism, we can learn to deal with it, with some effort.

I asked anthropologist Ruth-Inge Heinze how she thought the deep conflict between the fundamentalist right and those interested in a multicultural point of view would be resolved, or whether it could. She pointed out to me that world history is full of parallel cultures. Conflicting cultures, religions, political movements co-exist—with some views surfacing for a while and then becoming less prominent.

Collectively our society has the capacity to tolerate plurality. The point of view from any one group, or any one individual, is likely to be less tolerant because it is hard to perceive the whole picture and understand how there is room for all the parts.

The *edgewalker* undoubtedly embodies this process on an individual basis. When the *edgewalking* professor/artist is in the classroom, one part of his personality is prominent on the stage; his studio, another. But the less subdued part never retreats entirely. It is present for him to draw from—when it is desirable. He does not have to make a choice and abandon either part of who he is.

In a country like Canada that is officially bilingual and has two equally prominent cultures, opportunities for *splitting* are rampant. In fact, in recent years, the country voted by a narrow margin to refrain from splitting in two. Thus, for some people, animosity continues. Rosalee VanStelten, a former Navy petty officer, instructor and poet from Calgary sees the positive aspects of the situation. "As a nation, Canadians are *edgewalkers*. We are the link between our American cousins and our British motherland. In Britain, I am often thought to be an American. In America, until Canadians learned to say 'aye,' where Americans say 'huh,' we were often thought to be Brits."

Rosalee descends from both French and Anglo-Saxon roots like many people in Canada, and although she blends with the dominant cultures in her own country or in the United States, she is tuned in to and values her mixed cultural background: "I'm Heinz 57 on my mother's side; Scottish-with lots of Scots phraseology in family stories—English, Dutch and Protestant Orange. I'm French Canadian on my Dad's side, where the older members of his family [raised in the Ottawa Valley] were fluently bilingual and raised their kids to be the same. My father and his younger siblings, raised in an English community, were unilingual. So are their children. They were Roman Catholic. I started off in the Catholic Church 'til my Dad went off to the war and my Mom shunted me over to the Protestant side. But, nonetheless, she made French pea soup and johnny cake for us!

"I consider myself a *Canadian* and have lived from coast to coast. But when I am in Holland or Britain, they think I'm 'one of them.' And, because I lived in London and married a Dutchman, I have a great affinity for those places."

Rather than *splitting*, Rosalee works to embrace the conflicting facets of her personal history. She feels equally at home in many different settings, and finds that she is readily accepted in many different cultures.

Just as the psychologist works with the individual who splits, the first step in changing group behavior is awareness of the process. People can only change their response if they can begin to understand they are splitting—that they are ignoring one whole side of a situation, when they are immersed in the other. When they can remember, "Yes, I hate him now, but sometimes I love him," psychological integration becomes possible.

When I visited the Hopi Reservation, I spoke with a man who I thought might tell me some things about Hopi tradition and shamanistic practices. He talked with me, guardedly, about those traditions, but was clear that there is plenty of anthropological information about his people in the library. He chose not to share personal knowledge or experience in that realm. His observation on cultural splitting turned out to be quite useful, however.

During our conversation, I learned that white people were not allowed on the mesas for dances at that time, and had not been for about four years. There is a cultural split from the Native American side—us and them.

Evidently, some of the Hopi people were deeply incensed because *Marvel Comics* had published an issue about the Hopi involving two sisters. In the story, one of the sisters left the reservation and abandoned her heritage. As the epic progressed, one of the ceremonial dancers, a *kachina*, was unmasked. I am not sure which was the greater affront, the bad behavior, the unmasking, or both. Later, *Marvel Comics* apologized, but the damage had been done.

"It was just like Los Angeles," the Hopi man said, referring to the Rodney King verdict, which had come down the week before our conversation. L.A. still burned.

"The idea to close the mesa started with one person, and it spread through all the clans. Not everybody agrees. I don't really agree. But that's the way it is for now."

The decision was to close the villages. To *split*. To shut out those who are different. He did not agree with it. He would have preferred a different solution, but he understood why the decision was made.

Hearing this analysis from a man whose people inhabit the oldest continuous settlement in our country, gave me chills. He is connected with something bigger than himself. It scares him and gives meaning to his life simultaneously. He carries the deep tradition of his people along with his ability to drive heavy equipment and supervise a work crew. He moves between life on the reservation and life in the mainstream, each of which contains everything about what it means to be human. Each of which is in conflict with the other.

"My village is the only one that doesn't have electricity. That will change too. We have to deal with that. The young ones want conveniences."

Comparing closure of the Hopi mesas on the Arizona high desert to race riots in Los Angeles dramatically telescopes life styles in the United States. It is difficult to find designs that can weave a cultural middle ground in such places.

Despite David Allen's implication that stranger anxiety is permanent and we might as well split and have everyone go along with the majority, there are some things that help. Here are seven steps for effective *edgewalking*, ways to build a cultural middle ground.

Know thyself.

Gail Christopher: I'm always mindful of the need to value myself, not to seek that value from others. It's a daily issue. But that struggle makes me more respectful of differences in others, so I can facilitate the group dynamic. For me, it harks back to a basic principle of human behavior. We extend to others the compassion we have for ourselves. *Edgewalkers* have had to work through self-hate and can extend what they've learned to others. It all boils down to love.

My tendency to make wrong choices about my life interfered with my ability to give to the world. I became determined to do something about it. One of the things I've learned is the importance of not getting enmeshed by other people's needs. I can be a force in their lives without becoming part of them. I learned in my late teens a sense of spiritual sustenance, independent of other people or institutions.

Stay flexible.

Carol Parrish-Harra: At times I feel different. In real traditional settings, I now feel like a stranger in a strange land. A shift happens, and I feel myself slow down, become more of a listener. I listen for a point of identification, stay quiet for a time and gather information. It seems like I go right down a little line, wanting to know where I can identify—where they're going to identify with me. When it is my turn to contribute, I start out utilizing those points of identification. I know that the other part of me is so foreign, that if I don't build a bridge I'll never get to say what's important to me.

Risk being alone.

Barbara Arnn: You have to be willing to be different and alone. I felt lonely when I was doing my research in Japan. When you are moving from one culture to another, it's got to be true that you are alone. You have to be willing to be lost. Even though you disagree with someone, you learn to listen, look at what's happening before you have something to say. I'm perfectly content to sit, not to talk, but eavesdrop and pick up on conversations.

Be willing to risk accepting help.

Barbara Arnn: During that time, my hair fell out. I didn't have a dream for a year, and I didn't have a period for a year. There were a handful of people, teachers and mentors, elderly men, who had nothing to lose by helping me. They were secure in their positions. They were respected. One of them was a great scholar. They were passionate about their work, as I was passionate about mine. There is a spot in Japanese culture for sensei-deshi, teacher/pupil, disciple relationship. These scholars erased barriers for me. That was their choice and they made it. They tolerated my difference; and I, theirs.

Seek your sacred path.

Patricia Nell Warren: On my vision quest that became my book *One is the Sun*, I learned these things the hard way, going back to my prayer of really wanting to find a teacher. We think of teachers as people who know more than we do, who are going to give us the key that's going to unlock the door. All during this time I was journeying, I still had this belief, because it's part of the Judeo-Christian thing of giving up your authority. There's always a bigger authority—the Church in Catholicism, or The Bible in Protestantism.

This ten years was a time of really beginning to look at these ideas. Are these my ideas or someone else's? I realized that this whole thing was predicated on giving up your own authority to other people. And all of the grief, the pain and the sad confusion that came in my life—especially my struggle to meet my husband's image of what women were supposed to be—and the whole cultural idea of sexuality and what that is, I had accepted.

And even through the years on the path of teaching and holding ceremonies and being with people who were outside of this frame of reference, I was still looking for that authority outside myself. Until the moment came when I realized that the teacher is my own life. The teacher is life. The teacher is the earth. It was then that I finally got other people out from between me and my own life—from between me and the earth.

Recognize commonalities.

Miriam Acevedo Davis: As the world becomes smaller through communication and travel, in terms of business and diplomacy, that shrinking process will help us value a sense of the mother, which is the way I think of our planet. My hope is that as the world becomes smaller, we, its members, will be challenged to value it differently.

Having been a history major in college, I know that means challenging some of the myths we live by—the myth that you do it on your own—that the highest need is self-actualization. In no other culture except the American one do you have people saying 'My greatest need is to be self-actualized.' In my culture, we say we live together. We live in community so you help each other. I think it's going to take a real challenge to the myth of that individualism that you do it alone. No one does it on their own. I have clients who reject affirmative action and say, 'I did it on my own,' and I say, 'You've had affirmative action for three hundred years.'

We're going to have to get away from talking about rights for people and talk about behaviors. What gets missed is what happens when we discriminate against someone. It could be because of sex, race, ethnicity or religion. We look at it as rights, but we don't ask what could be behind that. I think it's going to have to shift from that legalese language into looking at the effect of these laws in a particular situation.

Honor your own complexities.

Joey Garcia: Part of the gift of being an *edgewalker*, being from many cultures, is always learning to bridge. It's very easy to come out angry, or at least, that's the reactive thing to do. What I would rather do is try to reach back, no matter how faulty the hand is. I feel that people like me are here specifically to be the bridge to the future, to the present and to the past. If we don't reach back, the pain of non-connection is always present. It will always be like this—sore scabs all over, and then someone bumps it again.

For a long time in my life, it was my challenge and my pain to carry so much—to understand so many cultures. Now I see it's my greatest gift, like a wounded healer metaphor. I can move anywhere with this now. I've traveled in different places in the world, and where I go they claim me. It's not just because of the way I look. It's because I can understand the culture. It's like all of this exists within each of us. It's like little doors that we can open inside of us—like a door to understanding a particular pattern of speech, or way of seeing the world, or a way of sitting down and relating to a person. When we're from many cultures we have no choice but to open those doors."

Pay attention when you step back and forth.

Satsuki Ina: When I'm back home taking care of my mother, or in the Japanese community, I know exactly how to click in to being the Japanese daughter. I don't offend anybody. There are things I don't like about Japanese value systems that go against what my direct experience has been, but I want my mother to feel proud of me in the Japanese community as well as outside, and it's familiar.

When my father died and I was in Oregon working on my doctorate, I was right in the middle of this Gestalt group process where I was confronting somebody. Someone from the school knocked on the door and said, 'Your family needs you; you need to go home.' So I left, just in the middle of this process in which I was saying, 'Well, what do you experience right now?' The student I was talking with said, 'I'm having a hard time because you look like a nice Japanese lady, but I feel like you're being really bossy.' And then, the knock came on the door.

I thought about her words while I was flying home—how incongruent it was for her. Although I was enroute somewhere else, I still felt like I was in Oregon where I'm a doctoral student. Working with the master's students there, I had been doing a very traditional process of controlling and manipulating, creating the atmosphere for intense emotional interaction. Then, I got on the plane and arrived at the airport where my two brothers were waiting for me. I knew they were going to make all the decisions. They had already made the plans. My job would be to just sit beside my mother and serve tea. When the question came up about whether we should have an autopsy for my father, I was never consulted. And so, accepting the stereotype they had created for me, I just went into automatic pilot—all the ritual ceremonies, the Buddhist rituals—but a little part of me was observing, saying, 'This is not the real you sitting so quietly, not making your opinions known.'

Edgewalkers in this chapter demonstrate the key difference between *edgewalking* and other ways of dealing with conflict. Satsuki, for instance, having split first to the white side, then the Japanese side as she grew through early adulthood, now has the ability to weave both through her life. She can walk on one side without losing sight of the other. Her choice to work with both sides of her heritage came from discovering that she couldn't really reject one or the other. Both are important to her, and through strengthening her core self, she experiences her Japanese-American complexity as special. She doesn't need to reject either.

Edgewalkers integrate complexity rather than *splitting* differences into conflicting components. They manage paradox as a way of life. Whether or not *any* nation can accomplish this complex task on a broad socio-political scale, the seeds are planted on the new global frontier. Can they thrive?

six

MIXING OIL AND WATER
The Multicultural/Feminist Paradox

In its demand for equality for women,
feminism sets itself in opposition to virtually
every culture on earth.

Katha Pollitt, *Boston Review*

"Whistling girls and crowing hens always come to some bad end," my grandmother would say to me when I whistled, which I loved to do, especially around her. Then she would explain why boys and men can whistle, but it is not proper for girls. My introduction to sexism shocked me. I could see no reason that girls should not do something just because they were girls.

I still can't. It only makes sense that women or men do things they enjoy and have the skill to do regardless of whether they are women or men. That is my basic definition of feminism, by the way. Women and men are equal. Neither is superior nor inferior, privileged nor underprivileged.

As it turns out, though, the gender edge is a tough one to walk. The women's movement has not quite leveled the playing field in the work world, as many had hoped, but it has made a difference. If the competition for jobs has not exactly doubled because women have more access than in the past, there are female contenders these days who would not have been applicants even twenty years ago. An understandable outcome is that some men have become more adamant about guarding what they perceive as masculine territory in the work world, and that flows over to domestic life, sharpening the edge between women and men.

Then, if you think about Katha Pollitt's statement quoted at the opening of this chapter, life becomes even more complicated. Many cultures in the world assume that men are superior and women are there to serve them, especially in the personal realm dealing with family and sexual issues.

But most women worldwide want to be full citizens of their nations. Here we are in cultural quicksand. What if women choose to adhere to old ways? Do they have all the information they need to make that choice? Where does that leave their children?

Susan Okin wrote in a 1997 *Boston Review* article, "...it is clear that many instances of private sphere discrimination against women on cultural grounds are never likely to emerge in public, where courts can enforce their rights and political theorists can label such practices as illiberal and therefore unjustified violations of women's physical or mental integrity. Establishing group rights to enable some minority cultures to preserve themselves may not be in the best interest of the girls and women of the culture, even if it benefits the men."

The assumption that an informed woman's opinion is as important as that of an informed man's is revolutionary. The concept that a woman has as much say-so over her reproductive system as a man has over his may be even more revolutionary. A recent article caught my attention.

According to a February 11, 1999 Associated Press article in the *San Francisco Chronicle*, "In a lightning-quick six months, the impotence-treatment drug Viagra got the go-ahead from Japan's notoriously slow Health Ministry. The birth control pill, meanwhile, has been languishing in the approval line for nine years."

Japanese women have made strides in the business world, in education, in their own mobility and in their capacity to impact public policy. This article, however, points out a discrepancy in the power structure when it comes to control of reproduction. Access to birth control is essential if women are to manage their own lives.

In the United States, where birth control has been widely available for more than two decades, the right to choose to terminate a pregnancy continues to polarize public opinion. Where religion, tradition or government defines reproductive practices in such a way that women have no choice, where are women's rights?

Separation of church and state, a concept accepted in many cultures and considered fundamental in America, should not mean that religious hierarchies can negate women's civil rights. For those who accept a doctrine of individual feminine choice, a true dilemma emerges. The foundations of any culture, and religion as well, are based on the status of men and women. A basic tenet of modern thought in the Western World is that women and men are moral and legal equals. At the risk of greatly oversimplifying, I believe this is an area where the value of the core culture takes precedence. "Group rights" to cultural integrity must not outweigh an individual woman's rights. Even though such an adjustment does great damage to the integrity of the alternative culture, individual freedom, for women as well as for men, is a core value that cannot be compromised.

Another example from Susan Okin's article makes the point that such issues can become complex. In the 1980's, controversy arose in Paris about whether Magrébin girls who had immigrated to France should be allowed to wear the head scarves required by their Islamic religion. Defenders of secular education, some feminists and far-Right nationalists spoke out against the practice. The old Left and those favoring dominance of group rights asserted the view that the choice belonged to the girls' cultural identity group. At the very same time, however, the public was virtually silent about a problem of vastly greater importance to many French, Arab and African immigrant women: polygamy. The women affected by the acceptance of polygamy regarded this practice as an inescapable and barely tolerable institution in their African countries of origin, and an unbearable imposition in the French context. As Okin pointed out, "The French accommodation of polygamy illustrates a deep and growing tension between feminism and multiculturalist concerns to protect cultural diversity."

In Arabic nations, where religious fundamentalists believe women should not freely move around or show their faces in public, the values are contradictory to those in the Western World. When people emigrate to other cultures, they take their values with them. Even though no Western culture, including the United States, has perfectly attained gender equality, the concept is a guiding one, and cannot be sacrificed to a group identity that denies it.

Multiculturalism and *feminism* are strange concomitants with a rough-and-tumble history of *splitting* and merging. Many people of color see the women's movement as catering exclusively to the white, middle class. Yet, the feminine principle is about inclusion, not exclusion.

One day I agreed to accompany a friend to a hospital near San Francisco where she was going for skin cancer surgery, which requires waits between different serial procedures. During the hiatus, we sat in close quarters with strangers who were similarly stressed and in pain. As people often do in coping with tense situations like this, one woman talked unguardedly. In this case, discussing with her sister a problem she was having with an employee in her role as supervisor at work.

"He acted like he didn't even hear me!" the woman exclaimed. "I told him that unlike the country he had emigrated from, women have authority here. Whether I am a woman or not, I am his supervisor. When it comes time to do his evaluation, I will determine whether he stays or goes. He started taking my instructions seriously after that, but I know he never liked it."

This chance eavesdropping hit me full force. The assumption that men give directions to women rather than taking them is deeply embedded in some cultures. It begs the question to ignore the patriarchal structure of many *edgewalkers'* cultures, not to mention the patriarchal push central to the Western World. In the United States, women achieved the right to vote as proclaimed by the 19th Amendment to the Constitution, August 26, 1920—not that long ago. Until World War II, when women, symbolized by Rosie the Riveter and her colleagues moved into the civilian work force, the right to vote, *per se*, may have caused domestic tension in individual households but it did not cause a major social shift. It wasn't until women's experiences during the war, picking up the responsibilities of working to support themselves and their families while men were away, and subsequently the women's movement in the seventies, that American culture became more closely aligned with the humanistic ideals of individual freedom and equality for women as well as men.

When the practices of minority cultures or religions clash with the norm of gender equality, ill-defined as that norm may be, those groups tend to isolate. People with little power in those groups, often women and children, find it difficult or impossible to seek the benefits and protection of mainstream culture. It is tough enough to balance the cultural uniqueness of any group with the general welfare of the people. When feminism enters the equation, achieving that balance becomes even more difficult. If women have had a sub-servient role to men in their culture, the assumption that men and women are of equal standing is difficult to implement. But it is possible.

Even in war-torn Algeria where women have been subjected to unthinkable atrocities and continue to deal with oppression, *edgewalkers* emerge. Aicha Barki, a former high-school principal who heads the Ingra Foundation, which fights illiteracy among women, said in the *New York Times*, December 26, 1997 issue, "We have crossed the cape of fear. Remember how much more difficult it was in 1993. We were afraid to dress like modern women. Some of us wore the veil for protection. This is over. Just look around you in the big cities. Hundreds of thousands of girls are going to school unveiled. The schools are open, they are still mixed. The terrorists have failed....Now, it is up to us...to make it clear that being a Muslim, as I am, does not mean denying your womanhood, our right to education and work and our place in society."

A huge paradox arises when support for women's civil rights in a culture seriously undermines the historical integrity of that culture which has been organized on the assumption of masculine dominance. In this situation, *edgewalking* becomes even more challenging. When men who are relinquishing power can see the benefits of sharing not only privilege but also responsibility with women, they become leaders in social change. It is more likely, however, that women will be the *edgewalkers* in such a situation. The need for someone to translate between the old ways and the new becomes crucial in determining which parts of the old culture can survive and contribute to the new environment.

Several women of color and white women from traditional religious backgrounds whom I interviewed chose to talk more about their feminist liberation than about their ethnic or spiritual ties. They could do very little to explore their cultural roots or spirituality until they confronted and dealt with the masculine domination inherent in their particular backgrounds. Just as it is important for all people to feel relatively secure about the basics of life before moving into the exploration of identity, it is essential for women to feel secure in their ability to guide their own lives.

In March 1995, a time of awakening according to the Mayan calendar, I went to the Yucatan to celebrate the Equinox. At that time of the year, the sun is positioned so that the shadow on the great pyramid at Chichén Itzá imitates the ascent to heaven of the mythical plumed serpent, Kukulkan. Forty thousand visitors, mostly from Mexico, but from far away as well, arrived to partake in the ceremonial celebration.

One of the seminar presenters at the event I attended was Reverend Carol Parrish-Harra, Executive Director at Sparrow Hawk Village, a spiritual community in Oklahoma. She is a Christian, receiver of the 1997-98 Earl Award for Religious Futurist of the Year, among many others, and also a protégé of Hunbatz-Men, the Mayan shaman who led the conference. Her eloquent talk, accompanied by music and dance, focused on global enlightenment and disclosed no particular religious bias, but rather integrated spirituality from varied epochs and religious systems.

Carol Parrish-Harra finds value in varied, often conflicting spiritual systems, creating an environment at Sparrow Hawk where people from assorted Christian, Eastern, Mayan, Celtic and New Age persuasions, among others, teach, work and play in harmony. In addition to leading and participating in her own community, Carol travels internationally, working with people in management training, as well as more spiritual realms.

When we spoke, rather than delving into the esoterics of spirituality, foreign or domestic, Carol took a personal tack. Her story echoes many I have heard before, and I offer it here, because it illustrates such an important link. Women claiming their own lives in patriarchal systems are *edgewalkers*, especially when they do not break completely from the old system. As they establish themselves in their own choice making, they can move forward with the confidence needed to relate to challenging cultural differences.

"You find persistence, stubbornness, survival instinct, bedrock in yourself," Carol said. "If everybody in the world is different, you have to face it. You have to be willing to be the bad guy, which is the hardest part of all in the spiritual field. Women aren't prepared for that, especially a nice southern lady like me."

From a traditional Catholic background, Carol found herself in a situation she could not resolve within that religious framework. She could not continue to comply with her religion *and* acknowledge the truth of her life experience.

"I had ten children. My husband had left me time and again, but I wasn't going to violate the relationship. After the last child, he left. Two years later, he called, wanting to come back. I was caught between knowing the children had had the best period of their lives in a harmonious, though single-parented home, a better life without constant struggle. However, since I believed divorces were detrimental, I called an attorney friend to see about a legal separation. He said, 'It is not worth it. Get a divorce or don't get a divorce.' I took out my checkbook, paid the retainer and knew at that point I had to rethink my life."

The first step in a woman's liberation is her willingness to act on her own based on her experience and judgment rather than what others expect of her. This decision is central, whether it is about challenging religious tradition or cultural practices that keep women subservient to men. Since political and financial power is mostly in the hands of men, it is dangerous for women to defy the system and assert independence.

Carol left the religion she had grown up in, but she continued her spiritual life, bringing what was meaningful to her in the faith she had known into one that became more expansive and inclusive.

"The experience of life is different than theory," Carol said. "*Edgewalkers* challenge theories rather than letting them define life without question."

It is important to note that despite Carol's ecumenical feminist message at the Mayan Solar Conference, Hunbatz-Men, the conference organizer, spoke at length on what he called "Sexual Education." He pointed out the disproportionate number of women at the conference, suggesting that women are currently more spiritually attuned than men, and then argued for rigidly stereotyped sex roles based on masculine dominance as the Mayan way to harmony.

More and more women in Latin America own and operate their own businesses, are elected and appointed to government positions and assume major responsibilities outside the home. But to say that women have achieved complete political, financial and moral equality in Latin culture is far from true. The attitude of masculine dominance permeates, even though many women argue that the cultures are truly matriarchal, that women just operate behind the scenes. Latina women, even when they live in other countries, speak about the necessity for personal strength and the ability to overcome stereotypes.

Representative Loretta Sanchez, who defeated nine-term conservative Republican Bob Dornan for her seat in the United States Congress, stays connected with her Hispanic roots and identity, embodying the ideal life for many Latinos in her southern California district. Becoming known as the "dragon slayer," she does not stay behind the scenes. The daughter of Mexican immigrants and the first Head Start child to become a member of Congress, Loretta remained undaunted by the male-dominated establishment as she carried on, despite Dornan's prolonged challenge to her election. She became an *edgewalker* at an early age, crediting her family with teaching her to rely on hard work as a response to life's challenges. In a September 26, 1997 *USA Weekend* article, she quoted her father. "Never let them call you a dumb Mexican," her father told her. "Study and become something, because that's what this country is all about."

Using the support her family provided, a traditional Mexican value, Loretta Sanchez stepped out to assume a public leadership role, not a traditional move for a Latin woman. One political consultant commented that Loretta had "...a great rainbow coalition. She had moderate Republicans...Hispanic voters, her base and she was the beneficiary of the gender gap, as well." Loretta's active political career provides visibility and at least one public voice for the fastest growing minority in the United States.

Gail Christopher, another woman who deals with feminism and multiculturalism every day, lives in Washington, D.C., but she travels broadly, speaking and teaching. She has been designing and administering holistic educational programs since 1974 and has received national recognition for her work. Co-director of *Americans All*, the national non-profit education program that "reinforces and promotes the concepts of both diversity and democracy" in the class room, she also wrote *The Peopling of America: A Teacher's Manual for the Americans All Program*, which provides the conceptual framework and overview for the program. Her other book, *Anchors for the Innocent, Inner Power for Today's Single Mothers & Fathers*, is a no-nonsense parenting guide.

Gail is adamant about her concerns for gender balance. She traces her lineage through her Native American ancestry, primarily Seminole, and through her African-American ancestry as well. Until she entered the healing profession herself as a naprapath, she had not paid much attention to stories that women on both her mother's side of the family and her father's, were healers. The work she does now relates to empowering women and dealing with family violence as well as diversity issues.

"I have survived a tremendous internal struggle, and the gender piece, in particular, has been difficult. The men in my life have had a high level of immaturity. When you couple that with a woman who has accomplished as much as I have in the public policy and human service arenas, I come off as intimidating. That sometimes appeals to men, especially white men, but whether they can live with it is another story."

Gail's matter-of-fact assertion of her competence as a teacher and leader does not fit old-fashion feminine stereotypes. It is no coincidence that she dedicates herself to empowering women and children as well as to promoting diversity education. Breaking through both race and gender barriers, she knows how easy it is to get pulled off balance and lose touch with her own inner core.

Direct and compassionate at the same time, quick enough to laugh, but absolutely centered about saying what she has to say, Gail's view outlines the *edgewalking* process:

"I've worked hard to stay true to myself in the face of these conflicts, always mindful of the need to value myself, not to rely on others for a sense of well-being. It is a daily issue and makes me more respectful of differences in others. *Edgewalkers* have to work through self-hate and, when they have reached a certain point, can extend to others a sense of the self-respect they have gained. It boils down to love. My work is about helping other people get in touch with their wholeness, and then they can extend that confidence to those around them. We have to have gender balance as well as balance among people of color."

Bridging the gap between a feminist perspective and a more patriarchal culture requires just such strength if there is going to be effective communication rather than a standoff. Mary Lee Daugherty is a white, Christian woman who knows about walking this edge. If you met her in the elevator, you would probably assume she is more or less a mainstream person. However, her work with the people in Appalachia is anything but.

Mary Lee is Executive Director of a program she created called Appalachian Ministries Educational Resource Center (AMERC). She is as comfortable in a Manhattan boardroom, where she finds herself with some frequency, as in some of the most isolated parts of the United States. She grew up in the coal mining region of West Virginia, spent three years in Brazil as a missionary, did her dissertation on the snake handling Pentecostals of Appalachia and now directs an immersion program out of Berea, Kentucky, for people, mostly pastors, who are headed for jobs in Appalachia and beyond. She is an ordained Presbyterian minister.

"Did I mention to you that I published a major book for the women of my state—and was fired for doing it? It's a self-help book," she said to me as we headed upstairs to her apartment over the library in one of the two main buildings on the AMERC farm.

"You know the *Boston Yellow Pages*, a directory of services for women? I had been teaching in the Department of Religion in an Appalachian college in West Virginia for nine years as one of the few women on the faculty—the only ordained woman on any faculty in my entire state. I had tried over and over again to help women resolve the problems associated with going through divorce, trying to gain custody of their children, going back to school, getting a job, managing money and even working in the major industry of this region, which is coal mining.

"All during the seventies I worked on that book, and it was finally published in nineteen seventy-seven—sold thirteen thousand volumes. It was written very simply because so many of the women in my state are lucky if they can read at the sixth grade level. It was presented to Rosalyn Carter at the White House as the first book of its kind for women in a rural state. At about the same time, I was fired from the West Virginia college at which I was employed.

"I didn't have tenure. One of the very wealthy donors to the college said to the president, 'If you keep this woman on the faculty, I'm not going to give you my money.' You can imagine who won."

Mary Lee provided this background with straightforward punch. She is not easily intimidated and trusts the instincts that lead her across unpredictable edges.

"I had included pro-life information and pro-choice, and this patron was strictly pro-life. He was extremely upset that I had included the pro-choice information for women who wanted abortions. We had been trying to help women deal with that issue before there was any safe way to terminate their pregnancies. In five or six years, I had seen so many horrible things that women in rural areas do to their bodies. But that book opened the door for me to go to Harvard Divinity School and teach for two years as a research associate in feminist studies.

"Teaching at Harvard was like going to the moon. It put me in a different ethos. There, I was the typical, traditional southern woman who was still married to the enemy and was not in with the main crowd. I was teaching a course on Appalachian women. They ordered six copies of the materials for my course in the bookstore. Seventy people showed up the first night—women and men. I think thirty-six actually took the course."

Mary Lee had ample opportunity to demonstrate her flexibility while she also stood up for her beliefs. As she walked the edge between Harvard and Appalachia, she could not rely on the opinions of colleagues close to her in each of those very different places to guide her.

"It was the weirdest two or three years of my life. When I would go home to West Virginia, I was the radical, militant feminist. And, when I'd go up to Boston, I was the traditional southern woman wearing lipstick and married with older children. I remembered asking some of the women there, 'What do you want us to do? Throw away our kids?'

"Gloria Steinem had helped me get some money for the West Virginia Edition *Yellow Pages*, and then I raised the rest of the one hundred and twenty-five thousand dollars, and got forty other women and men to help me write and work on the different parts of it. When Gloria Steinem saw it, she said, 'My goodness, Mary Lee, is this feminism?' I said, 'Gloria, it's all the feminism that rural women can stand.'"

One of Mary Lee's many skills is knowing just how far to push. Tactful, but direct, she managed to bring a powerful feminine presence to bear. She circulates in a religious context that may be more progressive than some, but is still unmistakably patriarchal. She lives in a region of the country where women are expected to serve, not lead. Her ability to see and relate to both sides of the issue and keep on plugging right through the middle, getting things done, is apparent not only in the program she directs, but in the facilities she has brought into existence.

Intrepid edgewalking women like Carol Parrish-Harra, Gail Christopher and Mary Lee Daugherty, who risk being rejected, fired and ridiculed to give their ideas birth, continue to change the world. They do so through trusting their experience, honoring their beliefs and doing what needs to be done despite any obstacles. In the face of barriers, including the patriarchal ones, they shift their focus when necessary and keep on trucking, inventing ways that work to make their dreams a reality.

Before transformation could occur in the lives of these women, the old ways had to be dismantled. Kali, the Hindu Triple Goddess of creation, preservation and destruction, symbolizes this dismantling process which is so often a part of feminine spiritual lore. In the United States, people tend to emphasize the creation and preservation aspects of the motherhood dimension, but push aside the scary faces of death and transformation. This power to dismantle and transform contains the energy for bringing forth new models of cross-cultural relationships that value the feminine on par with the masculine and embrace diverse cultural styles.

Research shows that as many women and cultural minorities enter the work place, they often ally with each other. The shared experience of oppression may create a bond that leads to mutual understanding. In *Changing Woman Changing Work*, I addressed the feminine tendency toward inclusiveness, the capacity to contain paradox, connection with the Earth and attunement with indigenous cultures, respect for intuition and openness to holistic ideas rather than the stark ideal of realism based on rational thought. This approach is opposite to the rather straightforward, competitive, power-oriented stance of the stereotypical career-oriented individual. And, as such, a powerful feminine presence finds certain alliance and comfort with a multicultural perspective.

Balance, interaction, crossing edges and building new paradigms invite re-vamped images from old traditions. Though, in public, the men of the Southwestern Tiwa cultures are the speakers and decision-makers, family connections descend through the mothers'

lines. When I met Sharon Dryflower Reyna, a member of that culture, I had no doubt she was her own woman.

"There's some of me in that drum," Dryflower said with a
laugh on the day we met in San Francisco, where I bought a small,
irregularly shaped drum from her. Standing tall and dignified, she
handed it to me with great care. "There aren't many woman drum-
makers. My father was well known for the drums he made, but he's
getting on, and although I work mainly in clay, I'm interested in preserving that skill. I'm also committed to helping other women get
their art into the world."

Dryflower and others from the Taos pueblo in New Mexico
had a booth at a Native American Art and Craft show at the Academy
of Sciences in Golden Gate Park. People from all over the country
participated in that show, and my sense was that few of them sold
very much of anything at all. As I wrote a check for the drum,
Dryflower made friendly conversation.

I sensed she might be interested in the *edgewalkers* project,
and I told her about my research. She reached under the table and
handed me copies of two articles about herself—describing her life as
a single mother and Native American artist, along with some of her
personal philosophy. A few months later, we arranged to meet at her
home in Taos.

I called Dryflower after checking in to a nearby motel, and
she gave me directions to her house at the pueblo. The warmth in
Dryflower's voice and her easy laugh reminded me of her openness
the day we'd met at the art show.

The sculpture in her yard made Dryflower's house easy to
find the next day, and I pulled my rented car up behind hers in the
carport. I stepped onto the gravel and Dryflower opened her front
door. She was smaller than I remembered. She smiled at me, said
hello and spread her arms and hands to show me she was covered
with clay. Her apron, her face, her hands—were the color of fresh, red-
dish-brown earth.

"You're working!" I said, curious.

"Come see," she beckoned as she held open the door.

Inside the stuccoed adobe home, I saw four huge pottery pots
in progress. The big brown rounds completely filled the floor of her
living room.

"This is my friend," she said, introducing me to a tall, blonde woman. "She lives in town, but she's helping me out here today."

"You women are making some major pots," I offered.

"They're not pots," Dryflower said, faking upset. "They're turrets."

I couldn't understand what she was saying.

"Turrets! Turrets!" she repeated until I got it.

"Turrets," I pattered like a parrot.

"They're turrets for a temple. They're going to go on the four corners. We're making them for a women's organization that's building a temple to heal Mother Earth," she said as if it were an everyday occurrence to be building temple turrets in her living room.

"It's in Nevada," Dryflower's friend added.

"They needed these turrets," Dryflower said, "and we wanted to help, so we said we'd do them."

"Is this Taos clay?" I asked, seeing the trademark mica flecks shining in the walls of the huge globes.

"No, it's commercial," Dryflower said. "They make some with mica. It will look like Taos style pottery."

Where was the temple? Who were the sponsors? How would they fire the huge pots? How would they transport and install them?

Dryflower laughed at my questions, but politely.

"It's a project sponsored by a woman's foundation. It's for building up Mother Earth. They have this little temple next to the Nevada test site—the nuclear test site. The land is here, the shrine is here and here's the Nevada test site." Her squared hands outlined geography for me. "It's because there's so much damage to the earth. We as people, we as individuals, don't know how much harm we're doing to Mother Earth. Every second we're hurting Mother Earth. We're taking away. We're not giving back. So this is a way to give back a little. I'm going to put some medicine in the middle and we're both putting our prayers in here. It's a labor of love—something that is important."

And so we talked while they worked away shaping and pounding the turrets, magically growing round pots with square pieces, using the methods that had built pottery at the Taos pueblo, and others, for centuries. They would travel to the nuclear stained desert on a mission to be part of a healing process for Mother Earth, a mission central to the people of Taos pueblo for centuries, too, but probably never in this particular form.

The scene in Dryflower's living room, the big pots, the two women shaping and pounding them, painted indelible images of cooperation in my mind more than any of the words that passed between us. From common ground, literally, these women were constructing an offering they believed would make a difference. Consistent with both Dryflower's Tiwa and her friend's Buddhist traditions, the goals of healing Mother Earth transcended the specific convictions of their religions or cultural backgrounds.

Later, as the two friends were testing the moisture content of the still damp clay and talking about firing up the wood stove and mobilizing hair dryers to speed the process, they surveyed their work with satisfaction. "I told her last night," Dryflower said, "You know what? Your grandchildren can go to this temple and pray there—and know you built part of it."

Dryflower's sense of the future, her willingness to be optimistic and invest her energy in that optimism, the idea that the grandchildren yet to be born would visit the temple and care about their grandmother's hands shaping the clay spoke volumes. Dryflower's thinking on this subject is consistent with her deep roots in Tiwa history more than with her American pragmatism. But getting the turrets to the temple without the efficient car parked in her carport would be a much greater challenge. Both are important.

As I left Dryflower that day, we stood by the sculpture in her front yard, talking, saying good-bye. I asked Dryflower if there were ever times when she felt like giving up on her traditional connections.

"Many times. If I'm doing something that's fun and just having a really wonderful time, and I have to stop to come back here because there's a responsibility I have to carry out, I think, 'It's tough being Indian. I have to leave now. No. I can't stay. I'm committed.' If I were Anglo, or if I were Bannock, or something, I wouldn't have to go. I'd just dance all night long, and I wouldn't have to get up and take baskets to the kiva."

But, she does get up to take the baskets to the kiva.

"I'm the matriarch in my family. Of the extended family, I'm the oldest woman in line to take that responsibility. When somebody's sick or some ceremonial thing needs to be done, it's up to me to do it or find someone to do it. And when my uncle was governor of the pueblo, he would ask my opinion about things. I respected him because he was willing to listen to a woman's voice. Talking about social issues helped."

Her translation of the work she does as a ceramist, both traditional and contemporary, into a feminist project aimed at honoring Mother Earth, the temple in Nevada, is a natural transition between feminism and multiculturalism. Even though she honors the tradition of her people and would not stand up in a village meeting to argue a point because women in that culture do not do that, she knows her power and is willing to use it in her own creative way.

"It's not just the United States I'm concerned about," she told me. "I think it's beyond that point. It's the world. We need an attitude change about racism because the world is so little. I'm just a piece of sand. But I see far beyond that—to people in Australia, Tibet. You see? We're all interwoven," and she held her hands to make a cup, echoing the roundness of the pots on the floor, and the shape of the globe.

Women who are true to themselves, who challenge the role expectations held for them by traditional culture or religion confront the paradox of multiculturalism and feminism. Men who support them demonstrate profound courage. Such challenges require resilience, strength and the capacity to withstand disapproval or even condemnation.

The women whose stories fill this chapter do not see themselves as doing anything spectacular, but merely taking on what needs to be done in order to live their lives productively. Some principles that they feel center them follow.

Look at the big picture.

Sharon Dryflower Reyna: We need an attitude change about racism because the world is so little. I'm just a piece of sand. But I see far beyond that—to people in Australia, Tibet. We're all interwoven.

Carol Parrish-Harra: To sustain real love for people, you have to sustain a bigger picture of hope or vision than yourself.

Gail Christopher: The essence of my work is helping others to get in touch with their wholeness and extend that to those around them. We have to have gender balance as well as balance among people of color.

Be willing to confront.

Carol Parrish-Harra: You have to be willing to be the bad guy, which is the hardest part of all in the spiritual field. Women aren't prepared for that.

Mary Lee Daugherty: And then, when Gloria Steinem saw [the book], she said, 'My goodness, Mary Lee, is this feminism?' I said, 'Gloria, it's all the feminism that rural women can stand.'

Use your own experience to test reality.
Gail Christopher: I've worked hard to stay ever-constant to my self-esteem in the face of these conflicts, always mindful of the need to value myself, not to seek that value from others.
Carol Parrish-Harra: The experience of life is different than theory. *Edgewalkers* will challenge theories rather than letting them define life without question.

Tolerate internal struggle.
Gail Christopher: I have survived tremendous internal struggle. *Edgewalkers* have had to work through self-hate and can extend a sense of self-respect to others.

Adhere to your principles and see where they go.
Mary Lee Daugherty: That book [that got me fired] opened the door for me to go to Harvard and teach for two years as a research associate in feminist studies.
Sharon Dryflower Reyna: Just to educate myself, I learn about [other religions], but it's not anything I really want to get into...I am an Indian and I have my own beliefs.

Find ways to embrace change that include all people.
Carol Parrish-Harra: If women become so angry they hate men, they hurt their own sons.

Honor Mother Earth.
Sharon Dryflower Reyna: Every second we're hurting Mother Earth...taking away...not giving back. So this is a way to give back a little.

Carol Parrish-Harra, Gail Christopher, Mary Lee Daugherty, Sharon Dryflower Reyna as well as Aicha Barki and Loretta Sanchez are all self-made women from traditional backgrounds, which, for the most part, define their roles as subservient to men. They have challenged some of the old beliefs that were handed to them, yet stay connected with selected aspects of those belief systems, moving on in ways that support their power and independence as women. Painful as it has been for them at various times in their lives, they tolerate the uneasy paradox of multiculturalism and feminism, making their way through uncharted territory, showing that it can be done. These women and others who negotiate the feminist/multicultural edge support a strong feminine presence, make their unique contributions, and offer role models. Their voices are no longer silent.

part three

BREAKING BARRIERS ON THE EDGE
Personal, Cultural, Spiritual

"*There's a hunger for every mystic to manifest in the finite all that they know in the infinite. And, of course, it's impossible. That's the edge. They're inside the bubble and outside the bubble at the same time.*" Max Rein *a computer programmer and spiritual teacher has come to understand a particular kind of transportation.*

Adesha Rein picked up. "And yet, the mystic has one foot in heaven and one foot on earth. The bliss of his reality is not everybody else's reality and so that's painful at times."

At an individual level, *edgewalker* stories, like those of Max and Adesha, spell hope and possibility. As these efforts, and those of like-minded people come together, change can flourish.

The deepening multicultural morass in the United States and elsewhere in the world can easily seem overwhelming and disheartening. Issues so complex they defy easy solution, or maybe any solution at all, make cynicism and withdrawal, if not outright hostility, a typical approach. This dark swamp challenges me to search for solid—or mystical—ground, however remote it may be, upon which to build.

In this section we view some examples of individual *edgewalkers* at work and reflect on their spiritual underpinnings. From here, it's possible to find paths through and around some of the barriers that block positive change.

seven

WEAVING DIFFERENCES WITHIN
One by One

One of my missions in the world is to get people to accept paradox. We have so much inner
and social conflict because we don't think
something is true until we've resolved all of its
contradictions. Which means amputating half
of any reality and turning it into something
we made up.

John Perry Barlow, Co-founder: Electronic
Frontier Foundation; Grateful Dead Lyricist

"I was raised in a Chinese household. My mother was ethnic Chinese, born in Hawaii. My father was from China and worked in Chinatown, Honolulu. Certainly Chinese culture was passed on, but living in Honolulu, Hawaiian culture influenced me in so many ways. Still, white American culture had the greatest impact on me." Loreen Lilyn Lee, an executive assistant in Seattle, names the cultural tugs and pulls she's had to contend with inside herself. To make life even more complicated, conflicting worlds around her vie for her attention and loyalty.

"While living in Hawaii as an Asian, I wasn't a minority. However, I was aware of and influenced by the messages of the media and the commercial world. White people definitely had the power. White was beautiful. Blondes had more fun, you know. Clearly the dominant culture does impose its standards on everything. And with that imposition comes a feeling of having to choose. Come along and assimilate, or go on your own and expect to be poor or unloved or whatever. And I bought it. I believed them! I wanted to assimilate and be something I wasn't.

"I reached a point in my life a few years ago where I decided I didn't have to choose. I can live in all of these different worlds simultaneously. I read a book, *Borderlands - La Frontera: The New Mestiza,* by Gloria Anzaldua, a Hispanic-American woman who described herself eloquently and passionately. She said, 'I am everything. I am Mexican. I am American. I am Indian. I am a woman. I am a lesbian. I am a teacher. I am a writer. I am all of these things at once.' She told such a compelling story. It opened my eyes, giving me an option I had never heard before. Instead of being fragmented and having to negotiate between worlds, jumping from one to the next, I have different layers of myself that are inseparable. Each is always present, even though one may be more dominant in a given situation.

"I come in contact with a lot of ethnic people, a lot of biracial or multiracial people and there is a discussion or discourse about labels. For instance, multiracial or biracial people might say, 'I'm half-Japanese and half-white.' That half part is problematic because they're saying, 'I'm not whole anywhere.' When I talk to children, I say, 'You are a hundred percent white *and* a hundred percent Japanese.' They are complete. They have different ethnicities, but they are complete people. They can claim it all. They don't have to be disloyal to any part of their background.

"Language is important. How you describe yourself, or let others describe you, is critical to self-image. People need to know they have options. Don't buy into labels other people give you. Or their standards of beauty and success. Choose your own words to define who you are.

"Maybe growing up in Hawaii made a difference. Openness is the Hawaiian way. But I try to include others mostly because I've been excluded, and I know how it feels. It hurts."

The pain she has suffered sharpens Loreen's sensitivity to the validity of pain in other people. In getting along with others, she uses what she has learned through living with her own internal conflicts. Because *edgewalkers* accept the differences that exist within themselves, Loreen and other people who have worked through similar challenges are not afraid of or offended by people who are different from themselves. The biggest step is becoming aware that there are differences in world views and that these views determine the way you feel about yourself and other people.

Loreen has wrestled with the inconsistencies in her life choices. Chinese expectations of industry, loyalty and devotion to family and ancestors differ from the Hawaiian concepts, which are more relaxed, and from industrious white American pragmatism that highlights individuality. Loreen's decision to embrace them all gives her unique options. Loreen is interested in her own cultural complexity and has worked hard to understand it.

Without conscious attention, the tendency is to slide into one cultural view and ignore the others. That approach may be simpler, but is not too satisfying because it does, in fact, neglect a significant portion of one's personal reality. Unless we have some reason, as Loreen does, to view the world through particular lenses, we take for granted that our own view of the world is the correct one. It is not always possible to know when we're looking through the wrong lens, or any lens at all for that matter.

Patricia Nell Warren, novelist, publisher and gay activist, knows about different world views from personal experience. According to Jim Marks, editor of the *Lambda Book Report*, a review of gay and lesbian literature, Patricia's novel, *The Front Runner*, published over twenty years ago, is a fundamental text read by almost every gay man and many gay women when they come out. As a woman writer dealing with gay men's fiction, Patricia has been criticized for "exploiting" a group she doesn't belong to by writing about them. "I do what every writer does," she says. "I use my imagination and my power to empathize and see things through others' points of view. I feel that it's important to continue to write about men from a woman's point of view. I wish there were gay men out there writing about lesbians."

Earlier in her career, Patricia worked as a writer and editor for *Reader's Digest* and as a freelance writer for publications including

Track and Field News, Runner's World, Atlantic Monthly and *Modern Maturity.* She also wrote several books of Ukrainian poetry.

Patricia Nell Warren's novel, *One is the Sun,* spins a grand tale about one of the last Native American medicine women to actively lead her people. Both the novel and Patricia's personal quest in writing it explore the impact of different world views. In the opening pages of the book an old *métis* (mixed race) man said to a naïve researcher who was seeking ancient wisdom, "Many of our scholars today have this problem constantly. When they study the so-called primitive peoples, or the peoples of ancient times, they believe that they understand the 'circle' mind. But they underestimate that their own thinking is square. So they translate everything through the square. Do you understand?"

His wife added, "Here is a practical example. Today, many people have a thinking that is influenced by the fax machine. A person can fax a letter from San Francisco to Berlin in minutes. But that person must fight to imagine a time when a letter took six months to travel that far."

Patricia, who created the old man and old woman to get her story on its way, fights to imagine those homespun times in the past as well as more harmonious times in the future. She spoke to me of her own mixed background. "I am an example of an American who is part Native American. People think of Native Americans as enrolled tribal people who live on the reservation, practitioners of today's version of tribal culture as they see it. But there are a lot of us out there who do not live on the 'rez' and were not raised that way but who still have significant amounts of Native American blood."

In *One is the Sun,* Patricia wrote about both Native American and feminine spirituality, about how people from different cultures successfully mesh—and some of the consequences when attempts at blending fail. Earth Thunder, the central character, was a real person. During a ten-year vision quest, which began as background for *One is the Sun,* Patricia discovered that she had grown up right on top of Earth Thunder's medicine camp. The camp was located on the very same Montana ranch where Patricia and her brother spent their childhood running around old mounds, finding old arrowheads and stone tools, all reminders of the people who had inhabited the land before them.

It was the Native American philosophy she wrote of in her novel that we talked about in depth. Earth Thunder, the novel's central character spoke:

"'And so,' Earth Thunder's voice cut like a skinning knife, 'both of you say you hate this people and that people. You're liars! All winter, you sat in my lodge eating my soups that were made with salt from a half-breed trader and cooked by your half-breed sister named Curlew. Yes! Yes! And the salt was made by white-skins at the Big Salt Lake. Did you know that? Black Willow, you do your beautiful beading with beads made by white-skins in a far land, across the Big Water, brought to you by half-breed traders. Comes Far, you carry a thunder-iron made by white-skins. But you say you hate them? Liars! Dogs!'"

Earth Thunder's story confronts complexity, calling attention to the ways her people relied on others outside their tribe, even though they hated admitting it.

Patricia described her novel writing venture this way. "I had been going back and reading classical anthropology about native peoples. Because of my background in Native American ways, I knew something was off in this literature. After I'd re-read the anthropologist George Bird Grinnell and the writings of a number of other people, I began to realize something important. It was one of those realizations that doesn't come to you in a big flash, but slowly. I began to see that so much of what is written about native peoples and their ways was written by white men, educated in the Judeo-Christian tradition. How in the world could they translate what they were told by native people who had a very different view of life? You can't accurately portray a culture based on circles with square language."

She chose writing a novel as a way to explore this interaction—the interaction of circles and squares—hoping Earth Thunder's story would touch more people than an academic work might. "The problem is," Patricia emphasized, "that our culture tries having squares without circles, and it doesn't work."

Patricia's words emphasize the prevalence of *cultural splitting* discussed in chapter five. The mainstream tends to underrate the legitimacy of the "circles," the "others," discounting the possibility that feminine, spiritual, holistic, even shamanic energy add riches to modern culture. If it can't be understood from a scientific perspective, it doesn't exist.

Patricia talked about the "Circle of Law," one of the concepts she had learned while researching Native American life, of government that isn't hierarchical. In this model, eight segments of the culture—Mothers with Children, Healers, Soldiers, Educators, Young Artists, Workers and Hunters, Law Dogs, Council Chief—sit around the circle that makes decisions for the community. Each segment has equal input, or can veto an idea. She summarized, "With this kind of government you have a basis for renewal, change and a broader base for dealing with problems."

Without the Circle of Law's government, making a difference at a personal level is another option. Patricia shared a story that is a variation on the theme of participation. "I had a really extraordinary conversation a couple of weeks ago, returning from a book tour back East. On the plane, I saw a Middle Eastern-looking woman with a small baby sitting by herself. I know many people don't like to sit beside babies because they prefer quiet, but I made a beeline for her and sat down in the next seat.

"'I hope you don't mind the baby,' the young woman said.

"'No, no problem,' I told her, and smiled.

"The moment came when the baby's diaper had to be changed. 'I was raised on a ranch,' I said. 'Don't worry about me. Change his diaper. Kids dirty their diapers. That's part of life.'

"The woman said, 'Ah, the trouble with the United States is that there are so many attitudes that are just not real—like the attitudes toward children!'

"So we began talking. It turned out she was from Saudi Arabia and married to an American, whom she described as part Haitian, part Native American and part African-American. She, on the other hand, was a very devout Muslim. They live in the San Fernando Valley, but she has hardly any friends different from herself because she feels many of the people she has met have attitudes about people from the Middle East. She said, 'You are one of the first women outside my group I have actually talked to.' We discussed religion and what was going on in the world. Though strongly committed to her own religion, I found her tolerant and open-minded. We talked about women and about the importance of openness. She's an American citizen now, and all of her family is here, yet all of her tradition is still very much part of her.

"To me, the gift in that story was that here's a woman from a part of the world that so many people in America see as hard line, but the real human being sitting there with me was open to talking about herself, her son and her fear about the prejudices towards Muslims she would encounter. And we agreed that no matter what your belief, it's important to participate."

Loreen and Patricia know and accommodate their inner conflicts and use what they have learned as building blocks in their relationships with others. Wendell Fishman, introduced in chapter three, has had similar experiences. A jazz musician, computer assistant and substitute teacher, he calls himself a "fittie"—fifty percent this, fifty percent that.

"Since I was a young child, I viewed myself as having each foot in two different worlds. My mom is black, grew up in Oakland. Dad is white, a Jewish New Yorker from the Bronx. They met in San Francisco in the sixties. They're a pretty fiery combination. I've always thought of myself as in-between, a balancer, a bridge type, finding the common denominators between people and situations. Being half-black and half-white, I have a unique perspective where my black side can look at white people and my white side can look at black people.

"Being a fittie is incredibly painful at times. When I got back from a trip to Africa, it took me months, maybe even a year, to get myself together. As an *edgewalker*, I've definitely had waves of insanity. I'm an emotional person. I go through periods of depression, but even when there's a dark tunnel, I believe in the light. My parents gave me a good foundation for believing in myself. I remember once as a kid crying really hard because I didn't get my way. My dad helped me understand this by saying, 'You know, Wendell, sometimes the world makes sense. But only sometimes.'

"One of the things we need to work on in this culture is our listening skills. When I got back from Brazil last summer, I noticed Americans interrupt each other a lot. I've noticed my parents' different communication styles. Some of that difference is a black/white thing. A lot of times it's like hearing it and feeling it. A black idiom would be 'I feel you.' My mom is not the most verbal person, but she definitely makes herself clear. My dad, meanwhile, is an English teacher—verbose, with an incredible vocabulary—a great speaker, a very good lecturer. And sometimes they'll miss each other on that level."

He continued, "I was substituting in a class for tenth graders with bad attitudes and had to fill out an evaluation for the school district on suggestions for making the students' day more productive. I asked them for suggestions. Their reaction was that everything is boring.

"'Is it math that is boring? Or is it high school?' I asked them.

"That started a discussion, out of which I was able to get them to take a look at whether and how high school could help them get where they wanted to go."

Then Wendell shifted to another key, "My philosophy of rhythm—not just a song, but a whole sense of time, helps me think about the process that they were going through. Rhythm is connected with things like location—like physical space and time. What are you doing tomorrow? Can you give me directions to Taco Bell? Melody is connected more with emotion, a series of notes, telling me where I'm going, like a little journey. There are many ways to get from one note to another. As I progress as a musician, I find my melody, like I find my life path. At that level, I think all human creatures can share music, and so many of our young people today are wandering aimlessly out of touch with their inner melody."

Wendell stopped and looked at me directly and seriously. "You asked me how *edgewalkers* can help? When people see me talking to white people or black people—just going in between—it helps."

Satsuki Ina *goes in between* from several perspectives. She's a professor and therapist who has helped her students and clients address issues of ethnic identity.

Satsuki has been fiercely attached to both her Japanese and her American heritage at different times in her life. She has made a film in which people like herself who were children in the internment camps during World War II talk about their experiences and feelings then and now. I knew Satsuki twenty-five years ago when we both worked at California State University, Sacramento, and she went by her Anglicized name, Sandy. Although we've seen each other a few times over the intervening years, we haven't had any in-depth conversations until we met to talk about *edgewalking*.

"I was born in Tule Lake maximum security internment prison during World War II. My family was interned for a total of four years, and so I was born there and was two years old when I left. Part of that time, my parents were separated. The authorities took my dad away from Tule Lake in the middle of the night when my older brother and I were just babies. For several reasons, he had been identified as a dissident, although neither he nor my mother were. He was born in the U.S., as was my mother, and educated here. But both had some education in Japan, so they were very suspect. They were both bilingual, and my father had been very active in the Buddhist church, which probably also pinned him as a potential dissident. And he was into physical fitness, so he would organize these physical fitness programs. The authorities saw that as preparing the men for military action.

"My mother was left in the prison with us. My father was moved to Fort Lincoln, North Dakota, and he was in a German Prisoner of War prison where soldiers captured in Germany were brought over to the U.S. It was an incredible process for him, because the Geneva Convention governed the German camps. There was external law that required certain standards of living, unlike the internal prison camps where he left his wife and children. There was nothing governing those internal camps, so sanitation and dietary requirements were very different. My father was living without his family in a place where they had requirements for leisure time and 'meaningful activity,' even a beer garden. As part of his 'meaningful activity,' he learned from the German soldiers how to make shoes.

"After my father had been identified as a dissident and taken away, nobody else wanted that to happen to them, so other people at the Tule Lake Camp isolated my mother socially. I have looked at a lot of this, just in terms of my own therapy, to see what it was like for me as an infant. In my mother's diary she writes, 'I don't know if today is the day. They are going to line us up and shoot us.' She lived with that level of fear when she was in the camp.

"After leaving the internment camp, we moved to Ohio for three years, and then back to California. My parents would always get wound up when they had to look for a place to rent, never knowing what they would face. While we were in the camp, all their belongings had been vandalized. I've seen photographs of the police watching as warehouses containing their belongings were raided. We left the camp with very little except our bags and train tickets.

"In California, I grew up in a ghetto with blacks, Asians and Mexicans. My parents insisted we do well in school, and I did. They were loving, supportive, encouraging. They took any kind of job they could to support their family, including menial jobs, and did everything possible to make a home for us. My father was a traditional Japanese man—pretty remote and very sexist toward my mother. But, I think because of the internment experience, he was the one who was most responsible for me seeing myself as different. He was the one who said, 'You can be anything you want to be, if you work hard.'

"My father is from Samurai lineage, and Mother was from a farming family, a class difference which he took seriously. He was very scholarly. He was a poet, one of the few Japanese American poets ever published in the Japanese journals of haiku. He was a Japanese art collector—doing all this on the side. He taught haiku to other Japanese people.

"In his daytime job, I thought he was the white man's flunky. My parents worked together doing window decoration for jewelry stores. My experience is so vivid seeing my father in the evening and on weekends as a teacher—very revered. We would go to gatherings where people came because they knew my father was going to read his poetry. By contrast, then, he would have to travel to different places, like Sacramento, to install window displays during the hours businesses were closed. The managers would let him in, and they would call him 'Jimmy.' They'd say, 'Jimmy, come here! Fix this! Come over here!' I remember how patronizing they were of him, and he would scurry around and say, 'Yes, sir.' I was so angry with him. I hated him.

"I remember their boss. My parents worked for some of the best stores in San Francisco, and I think their bosses valued them. But, by the way they treated him, I could tell that they had no idea about my dad's intellectual life.

"While we were still living in San Francisco, one day, their boss pulled up in his big, fancy car and came to our door. It was close to Christmas, and he brought this beautiful doll and said, 'Look, it's for you,' and handed it to me.

"I wanted that doll. I'd never seen anything like that before. It was a Toni Doll and had all those curls. Oh, I wanted that doll so badly. But I didn't take it.

"My parents were humiliated because, by their Japanese standards, I was so impolite to refuse the gift. Having humility, not inflating yourself, not causing conflict, all part of Japanese culture, had worked well for them as survival modes, especially after the war and the internment. They weren't going to challenge anything. They were grateful to have jobs.

"He left the doll. I remember it sitting in the living room on the couch. I was so angry. I wanted it so much. The next day it was gone. My parents did something with it. I knew they were angry at me, though. But that was the end of it. We never talked about it after that. It was too complex. I never, at that point, would have been able to explain why.

"Now, at fifty-three, I'm comfortable with my identity. Once, I just wanted to be part of the mainstream—minimize my differences and belong. In elementary and high school, I felt ashamed of my parents because they had accents. Because of them, I look this way. I used to not like how I looked—wished I had a bigger nose, eyelids that didn't fold over and naturally curly hair. Some of that stayed with me through college. Once my children were born, I came to realize how beautiful both my children and my parents were. Then I went the other way, registering the losses that my family suffered because of the internment. I felt angry about the racism and the discrimination and the oppression. At that time, I didn't want to be around any white people.

"That lasted while I went back to college and was the reason I got involved in the Educational Opportunity Program. I wanted to help minority students survive in the college environment. It was my job to educate my children to succeed without giving up who they are. The pain for me came from trying to maintain my Japanese identity and not lose my uniqueness. Then I watched my children struggle with their own denial, their own reaction to being discriminated against. Sometimes it feels impossible to explain it. For example, to my husband. He's white. And wonderful. And he wants to understand.

"When I'm teaching a multicultural counseling class, a good part of my emphasis is on helping the white students find their own ethnic identity so they can have a ground from which to appreciate cultural differences. It's a strength to be able to walk that edge. And it's not an edge that only people of color learn to walk, but is a transferable skill that can be generalized if it's viewed as a creative process. It helps people to become more resilient, more willing to have less black-and-white thinking. Walking that edge can teach tolerance. It's a very Buddhist thing. When I have a sense of increased tolerance, I have less internal pain, not quite so much angst. I can accept differences as richness rather than right or wrong.

"Until now, no one has ever asked me such a significant question, 'How did you raise your children to survive in two cultures?' My parents did it unconsciously and erratically. But, from my own experience, and what I learned from my parents, I try to be much more conscious.

"The metaphor for me used to be two paths. You go this way, that way, or down the line. That doesn't work. My way of thinking isn't about paths anymore. It's more a woven tapestry. I'm not as clear where one strand ends and the other starts."

Satsuki has "woven" two cultures within herself, both personally and professionally. Like Loreen Lilyn Lee, Patricia Nell Warren and Wendell Fishman, she lives with paradox, sees the world as complex and doesn't back down.

It seems to me that none of these individuals were born *edgewalkers*. They all have felt lonely, dealt with discrimination, resolved conflict within themselves, tolerated tension and disagreement with family and friends, and have created ways to learn from their pain rather than just passing the pain on to someone else. They have come to see themselves as *edgewalkers* and therefore speak to the idea of facing the differences within themselves as well as those between other people.

As I looked at the patterns with which *edgewalkers* weave their intricate cultural textures, I strove to find common themes that all of us could use in understanding others and ourselves. Beginning with the most straightforward and ending with the most challenging, the following are markers that point the way.

Attention to cultural influences.

Loreen Lilyn Lee: I was raised in a Chinese household... mother was ethnic Chinese, born in Hawaii...father from China and living in Honolulu, Hawaiian culture influenced me...white American culture had the greatest impact on me.

Wendell Fishman: Since I was a young child, I viewed myself as having a foot in two worlds. Being half black and half white, I have a unique perspective where my black side can look at white people and my white side can look at black people.

Embracing one's heritage.

Satsuki Ina: I think because of my father's internment experience, he was the one most responsible for me seeing myself as different. He was the one who said, 'You can be anything you want to be, if you work hard.'"

Using self-knowledge to test reality.

Patricia Nell Warren: I knew something was off in this literature...I began to see that so much of what is written about native peoples and their ways was written by white men, educated in the Judeo-Christian tradition. How in the world could they translate what they were told by native people who had a very different view of life?

Moving through pain.

Wendell Fishman: I'm an emotional person. I go through periods of depression, but even when there's a dark tunnel, I believe in the light.

Satsuki Ina: The pain comes for me from trying to maintain my Japanese identity and not blend. Then I watched my children struggle with their own denial, their own reaction to being discriminated against. Sometimes it's lonely trying to explain it. For example, to my husband. He's white. And wonderful. And he wants to understand.

Using what you have learned about yourself to reach out.

Patricia Nell Warren: Because I believe in reaching out to people different from myself, I made a beeline and I sat down by the young Middle Eastern woman with the baby.

Loreen Lilyn Lee: I try to include others mostly because I've been excluded, and I know how it feels. It hurts.

Satsuki Ina: When I'm teaching a multicultural counseling class, a good part of my emphasis is on helping the white students find their ethnic identification so they can have a ground from which they begin to see why it's so cherished to have this ethnic identity. It's a strength to be able to walk that edge. It's not an edge that only people of color learn to walk, but is a transferable skill that can be generalized if it's viewed as a creative process. It helps people to become more resilient, more willing to have less black-and-white thinking. It teaches tolerance.

Allowing for paradox.

Loreen Lilyn Lee: When I talk to children, I say 'You are one hundred percent white and one hundred percent Japanese.' They are complete. They have different ethnicities, but they are complete people.

Patricia Nell Warren: I do what every writer does...use my imagination and my power to empathize and see things through others' points of view...it's important to continue to write about men from a woman's point of view. I wish there were gay men out there writing about lesbians.

The *edgewalkers* in this chapter dare to face their personal chaos and make peace with paradox. They untangle and weave again within themselves the filaments of contrasting cultures. C.G. Jung wrote that, "ultimately every individual life is at the same time the life of the species." From this perspective it is clear that people who tirelessly seek out their cultural roots and expand their self-understanding offer models for improving cross-cultural relationships.

If we can grasp the strands of our cultural heritage, weave them into a proud mantle, whether the colors clash or blend, we do not need to amputate half of our social reality. As people around the globe learn to work effectively with bold textures and colors, we can celebrate differences rather than splitting them off and trying to hide them. Loreen, Patricia, Wendell and Satsuki point the way to problem solving on a much broader level than their personal experience. What they do as individuals, we must do as a society.

eight

EDGEWALKING SPIRITS
The Universal Connection

One of the most surprising commonalities
that had surfaced among many of the people
we met was an acknowledgment of that connectedness to a mystical aspect of life. And,
ultimately, it was the longing to connect to
that Mystery... that kept us on the road.
Shainee Gabel and Kristin Hahn
Anthem, An American Road Story

A spiritual connection, personal and yet universal, seems to be the center from which we may reach out to those with whom we have differences. And each of us can make these connections when we open, as have the *edgewalkers*, to the possibilities around us. As individuals, when we harbor a reservoir of inner peace or spirituality, differences in other people don't seem so frightening. And, it is from this center that we may touch that same peaceful, spirit-filled place in them.

"There's another vision of life, a perspective of Earth as a provider, just from resources, not by putting a title on some acreage and being a self-made person. If you look at the western hemisphere or any other area in the world, you find that vision sustaining and giving life for this generation as it has in the past and will for future generations." The speaker, Frank LaPena, is an artist and university professor. From Wintu-Maidu origins, he participates in the tribal ceremonies of his people as a singer-dancer and dedicates himself to researching and supporting tribal tradition.

"You have access to that larger vision in ceremony. They say that religion functions to put you in touch with the sacred and with the spiritual—except as you notice, when you get into religions, they become very formal, institutional, and they grow rigid and exclusive as well. So I'm talking about ceremony that embraces it all. Being part of a larger system is the purpose, or one of the purposes, of ceremony, putting you in touch with your sacred self. We are of more than one dimension. Everybody has a spirit. You won't understand unless you have some opportunity to access a system that gives you that comfort and connection."

Many *edgewalkers* with whom I have spoken acknowledge a unifying spiritual energy that connects all people. Their ancient wisdom places all of us at a cultural cusp, a gateway that could open our world to social patterns never before realized. It is a sense of shared connection—unacknowledged, but central—that flows through common human experiences which transcend cultural, ethnic and political differences.

Since before history was recorded, human beings have looked for meaning in something bigger than the individual or the tribe, a connection with the other side. Today, a resurgence of traditional religions and inventive, searching New Agers, among others, speak to the same urge: the need to embrace both awe and adversity, to find relief from existential anxiety in a higher power, either in this life or through faith in one after death.

In some societies, the shaman or spiritual leader advises about tribal matters, is a healer, communes with the spirits and lives outside the norms of the group. She or he mediates with the other world, provides a channel, access to the mystical or something bigger than human experience.

Maybe shamans are the ultimate *edgewalkers* in a spiritual sense. They go into trances, have visions, travel to far away places, shift shapes and do their healing in an altered state. They then come back and live their everyday lives. It may be this connection with a primal life force and bridge with the numinous that allows for newness and change. *Edgewalkers* carry this energy into contemporary life.

Scholars Joan Halifax and Mircea Eliade, studying shamanism around the globe, identify common practices and symbols among people separated by time and space. Siberian shamans, African shamans, and Navajo shamans are more alike than different. This commonality seems relevant to any search for inter-tribal or inter-group connection. In his book, *Dreaming With Open Eyes*, art historian Michael Tucker explored the legacy of shamanism in contemporary art. He sees the universal aspects of shamanism as the force or spirit that contemporary abstract artists from diverse nationalities and cultural backgrounds strive to express. As Frank LaPena pointed out, "That spirit still prevails."

Meditation, myths, dreams and art offer pathways into universal connection. Even though in our practical, technical culture, such ethereal methods seem not quite applicable to every day life, bookstore shelves offer an ever-changing stream of material on these subjects. Somebody out there is interested.

In the fall of 1991, the Sacramento Psychological Association invited Donald Sandner, a Jungian analyst from San Francisco, California, to present a day-long workshop which he entitled "Psychotherapy and Shamanism: Is There Common Ground?" Don searched the world for links between ancient practices and modern life.

In the workshop brochure Sandner wrote, "Psychotherapy is not shamanism nor are its practitioners shamans, mainly because they do not conduct their activities in altered states of consciousness or ecstatic trances. But depth psychotherapy has two important features in common with shamanism: both seek direct experience of the inner world of the psyche, which is considered by both as separate from the outer world—and real; and both are largely concerned with subjective healing."

This "inner world of the psyche," touched by the shaman or the psychotherapist, and in the case of the *edgewalker*, maybe both, facilitates the process of making sense of conflicting worlds. And subjective healing both values and affirms the experience of the individual.

Sandner's words continue: "Shaman and psychotherapist both make use of powerful symbols drawn from myths, visions and dreams, and they use a holistic approach, treating the patient as a unified entity made up of body, mind and soul. Seen in this way, depth psychotherapy may be one of the modern branches of the ancient shamanic tree rooted in the beginnings of human life."

Finding the common threads that weave through both shamanism and psychotherapy, even when it is an imperfect fit, offers a sense of universality, not just with disparate cultures throughout the world, but back into time and into the future as well. Spiritual healing, the goal of both practices, is common to all people.

One of my favorite forms of spiritual healing is spending time outdoors, taking in the wide-open spaces or trudging up a wilderness trail. In 1984, my husband Dave and I, went hiking in the magical beauty of Yosemite National Park. The trail to the top of Yosemite Falls is relentless. It ascends steeply. Little level. No down. Two thousand vertical feet in three miles. That day, we unexpectedly stepped on a path that led far beyond the day's walk.

I was unaware that for a first-hand view of the falls plunging over the precipice, we had to push on farther and scramble over water-slick boulders. Instead, we struck up a conversation with some young men who were catching their breath before they made their final effort. Max Rein introduced himself, and, as we chatted, told us that his brother was visiting from Pennsylvania for the first time in years, a reunion. Touched by Max's openness, I impulsively pho-tographed the two men as they stood by the distant rail. When we returned home, I printed that shot along with some others and sent them to Max.

A week later, I got a note from Max saying that his teacher, Adesha, was so moved by what I did she was inviting my husband Dave and me to visit them for a weekend, no expense to us, to Evergreen, their retreat outside Laytonville in far northern California. Max warned us there was no electricity, but said they had indoor plumbing and a comfortable place for us to stay. We decided to go. Finally, after hours on the freeway and a couple miles on a dirt "road," we spied Evergreen on its crest ahead of us. Max, Adesha and her husband Mark, Max's other brother, awaited us.

We slipped into Evergreen as if into a warm, scented bath. Adesha taught us a little about meditation. We sat. With a twinkle in her eyes, Adesha explained, "You don't have to be perfectly still. If a mosquito gets you, or you have an itch, scratch it. Don't worry."

We returned to Evergreen a few times over the next year.

Three years after meeting Max, Adesha and Mark, Dave and I were shocked to hear that Mark was dead. He had been murdered in the home he and Adesha shared in Santa Rosa. Sadly, the next time we saw Max and Adesha was at Mark's memorial service.

After that, we lost track.

On February 8, 1993, I had a dream, part of a longer one about a group of Hopi dancers inviting me to join them, but I would have to play the role of Jesus. I turned that invitation down, saying I was just an ordinary woman, and then the dream continued:

> I received a phone call from Max Rein, who lived down the street. I went to his house to see what he wanted. He proudly showed me a peace pipe sitting on a sandstone hearth. The whole floor was stone. He also showed me a novel that he had written. Part of the cover was torn off, and the book was slick with lots of pictures, featuring a two-page spread of pipes, including the one he showed me. Max was very proud of this picture and told me it was from a dream and he was amazed to see it in this book...

In real life, I wondered where Max was, whether he and Adesha were still working together and what had happened in their lives. Christmas brought a card from Max with a return address. I wrote to him and told him about the *edgewalkers* project. He wrote back, "While the *edgewalkers* you describe are multicultural, the *edgewalkers* of greatest interest to me are those who walk the edge between the world as we know it and the purely spiritual world. These individuals are *edgewalkers* of the highest order, encompassing the definition you offer as a matter of course in their evolution. They have moved beyond a level of self-actualization, living continuously in cosmic consciousness and beyond."

I remembered Adesha as a friendly, humorous person who didn't seem on the surface to be a mystic if we were in line together at the supermarket. And yet, when I asked her about her name, she told me it came from God. I arranged a meeting to talk with her about walking the edge between the spiritual and the mundane. She and Max agreed to meet with me at my office.

After brief but warm greetings, Adesha began. "The mystic has to deal with the world as it is. They experience another realm and hope to bring that message into the mainstream. People aren't realizing their whole potential, only their body and their mind, not their higher self. It takes body, mind and spirit to make that person come alive. There's a need for the ones who have experienced this to bring that knowledge back into the mainstream.

"When I was twenty-five I had an experience of illumination. I was working, doing my housecleaning, and I got so tired, I stopped to rest, put my head on the table. I left my body. Became light. In that experience I had everything I ever dreamed that I would want—the most glorious feeling of bliss and peace. So when I came down again, I knew what I wanted. I knew I would not be complete until I could have a similar feeling without 'leaving' my physical body. I searched for many years after that, and I found it through meditation."

Adesha spoke about some other experiences and about her shift from self-consciousness to cosmic consciousness. I asked her what it was like to talk with people like me who aren't in that place.

"Because of the level of awareness, the level of perception of the whole is so much greater for a person in cosmic consciousness than for a person in normal consciousness, the relationship is redefined. It is possible to express love in ways not understandable, or necessarily perceptible, to others.

"This level of consciousness is available for everybody. Each person has that connection with the universe, and all they have to do is open up to that inner part, which is already in place. After one of the experiences I had, I was afraid the feeling was going to leave, but it hasn't. It is there all the time. But the mystic, the spiritual person, has to maintain the *edgewalk*. You just merge over to the other side. You merge that part of life with this part of life."

Speaking of her grief about Mark, she said, "When you saw me [at the memorial service] I was in denial. It hit me later. Not only profound grief as a wife, but also because Mark would have been a great, great teacher. Already, he experienced states of cosmic consciousness intermittently. I have no anger. I came to an understanding. It was his time to go. God uses all of us in this great play."

The universal connection Adesha described—a place in each of us that holds peace and harmony, a place from which we can connect with each other—makes *edgewalking* possible.

It is not Adesha's experience *per se*, or her view of it in particular that is central to our focus on *edgewalkers*, but the importance of the search for connection with cosmic consciousness. The openness that allows that connection, however it is defined, allows for connection with other individual people. Adesha's view is that we can move, as she said, "from self-consciousness to self-actualization. Then you can have independence and interdependence. Both are needed.

When you understand we are all part of that great energy, it makes you not so self-centered and self-conscious. You can go out and embrace others with a sense of oneness. You sense and feel connected with that more than separateness. You are not so different."

Here, Adesha echoed the feelings of Sharon Dryflower Reyna saying, "I appreciate those differences between me and whoever I'm with and whoever I'm near. I never break down and say 'your culture—this culture.' I feel one. I know the difference, but I feel oneness."

Or, as Gail Christopher said, "We can extend to others compassion we have for ourselves. *Edgewalkers* have had to work through self-hate and can extend to others what boils down to love."

Steven Wong, psychoanalyst, filmmaker and teacher in a workshop I attended, offered his view. "At first, I learned about being American, then about Lakota shamanism, and now I'm exploring Chinese shamanism. At some point, I anticipate cultural barriers will fall away as I reach universal connection."

The capacity to "have peace and harmony within" makes contact with someone different less frightening. Whether we move back and forth between this world and the other world, or between one culture and another, the process is similar. It is the ability to move back and forth that is important—that requires flexibility, openness, courage and a certain loss of self-consciousness.

People see or seek God, the divine or The Goddess in countless ways. The search for something beyond human understanding pushes some more powerfully than others. It may be through this search—this universal human experience—that we find a frame big enough to hold us all.

C.G. Jung described the *collective unconscious* as the realm in which emerging issues occur to lots of people simultaneously in one way or another. Jung's theory is that there are inherited feelings, thoughts and memories shared by all humanity. The collective unconscious is composed of *archetypes* or primordial images that correspond to experiences such as confronting death or choosing a mate, and manifest themselves symbolically in religion, myths, fairy tales and fantasies.

Most of the *edgewalkers* I have interviewed expressed a spiritual basis for their willingness, interest, capacity and commitment to deal with difference and interpersonal/intercultural conflict. A few are connected with organized religion, but most are not. They described themselves as "spiritual, but not religious."

Perhaps the highest goal of organized religion is to contain or protect spiritual enlightenment. If that only was pragmatic, we might all be connected in a gentle radiance. The problem is, as with other protective forms, the container often becomes rigid and interferes with the experience. So, even though they may be seeking a similar goal of spiritual enlightenment, individuals create a variety of paths for that purpose.

Reverend James Leehan is a priest at St. Paul's Episcopal Church in Indianapolis, Indiana. He is a friend, and for that reason I hesitated to interview him. Then, it became clear to me that, as someone who works within the institutional church and manages to be an *edgewalker* at the same time, his views are especially enlightening. Both a spiritual and practical person, he works in his own way to mobilize church resources to make a difference.

I interviewed Jim in the backyard of my Sacramento home on a windy summer day. Still wearing his bike shorts and sweaty T-shirt after a long ride, his lanky frame filling a sizable chaise lounge, he presented a distinctly unpriestly appearance. When I transcribed the interview, though, wind chimes ringing their random tunes behind our conversation added ethereal footnotes to his message.

Beginning his adult life as a Roman Catholic priest, Jim served as a campus minister, both in the Roman Catholic and, later, Episcopalian faiths. Currently, he works as a minister and a therapist. For the past two years, he has committed much of his considerable energy to Paths Crossing, a church program which endeavors to repair some of the damage Christianity perpetrated on the Native Americans.

First, I asked him to define how he saw himself as an *edgewalker*.

"For most of my life, I have been in different settings than the one I grew up in, a small farm community in North Dakota. As a young seminary student, I was home only in the summer, and then I moved into urban areas for college and graduate studies. Even after ordination as a priest, I worked most of my career as a campus minister which is both of the church but not in it, in the university, but not of it. In either community you are not in the mainstream norm."

Jim explained that seeing relationships such as these between the similarities of theological thought and secular philosophy, and learning to translate from one discipline to another, from one cultural orientation to another, allowed him to interpret the church to the university and the university to the church. "A fair level of independent thinking went into this work. There weren't too many places I could look for validation for what I did. I had to decide whether it was valid on my own, or within a fairly small community."

These skills serve him well in his present job. He told me about the program he was excited about, "Paths Crossing is an organization—being generous—in the Episcopal Church that matches Native American Episcopal congregations with Anglo Episcopal congregations in a partnership relationship rather than a mission-service relationship. Native Americans who were getting tired of the Anglos coming to the reservation and doing nice things for them then going away, with little real communication or sharing involved, initiated the program.

Jim said he became aware of the organization accidentally, but it advocates something he feels is important. As a campus minister, he has worked with secular political action organizations that were not specifically Christian or religious, but the resident religious folk carried them through. He recalls an experience with a sister city relationship between Cleveland and a repatriated refugee community in El Salvador called *Segundo Montes*.

"That community dictated what they wanted, which was not to have the gringos come in and tell them what to do. In fact, while they were even in the refugee camp in Honduras, they influenced the United Nations High Commission on Refugees to do things their way. When Doctors Without Borders came in to do their medical treatment, the refugees insisted that the doctors teach them to do basic medical procedures. The physicians said, 'No, we aren't allowed to.' The refugees then said, 'We don't want you in our camp.' And they literally kicked the doctors out of the camp for a substantial length of time. When the physicians returned they said, 'We can't teach you, but you can certainly watch us.'"

Jim explained the appeal of Paths Crossing is that Native Americans brought it to life so that what is being done for them serves their greatest needs and fosters communication, contact, understanding and reconciliation.

"The two communities—the Anglo and the Native American—have definitely been at odds with one another for over five hundred years. Both sides have been violent toward one another. As we took over their land, they fought back. As we massacred them, they fought back and massacred us in some cases, considerably fewer cases, of course. There is a lot of animosity, misunderstanding, bad feelings and lack of information—how little is known about real Native American history. We need to address that kind of misunderstanding—the untruths that exist, the lack of knowledge.

"Here's an example of the kinds of small steps we can take. In the Episcopal Hymnal there is a hymn that is based on a Dakota chant, and is actually the hymn that the Indians being executed at Mankato, Minnesota, at the end of the Dakota conflict in 1861 sang on the way to the gallows. But the Minneapolis papers said they went to the gallows singing an Indian War chant. Of course, they were singing it in Dakota, so the listeners couldn't understand it. It was really a Christian hymn.

"So last fall when representatives from our partner church visited St. Paul's, we included that particular hymn in our liturgy. That is a favorite hymn of the Indian community. Our choir director decided it would be good to put some drums with the hymn. They occasionally do different things other than the organ in our services. That didn't feel right, even to me. It wasn't until later in the afternoon that we were able to ask our visitors, 'How was that?'

"They graciously said, 'It was a nice gesture, and we understood what you were trying to do, but first, your choir needs direction on how to drum. They don't know how to do it. And secondly, you need to understand that we would not be able to use a drum in our services in our church in Minnesota, because many of our elders grew up in boarding schools where anything Native American was beaten out of them. They still feel that a lot of that is unacceptable. Our young people might want to use a drum in our services, but our older people cannot.'"

Jim went on, "Because of our earlier contact with people in our sister church, Melissa and I understood the drumming thing, but most of our congregation has really had to work to understand the difficulty. Of course, we have people at St. Paul's who don't like having anything other than the organ, so having a drum in the service is objectionable to them. Looking at it from that perspective, people understand our visitors' objections a little better. However, for our Indian friends, it was not merely a question of aesthetic preference but a deep cultural conflict."

Jim, like *edgewalkers* in other settings, explained that as a campus minister he often found himself in a bind between the institutional church and the programs he deemed important. He would do enough of what the church required to get support for the activist work he engaged in. His skill at walking the edge made it possible to maintain balance, but he found that process lonely and stressful.

"I was never totally comfortable with the mainstream church. I went through seminary at the time of the Second Vatican Council—at a time when things were up for grabs, being questioned and new things were being developed. My experience of the church and what it meant did not emphasize 'this is the only way to do it.' There are various ways that things can be done.

"Going through seminary in that formative period during the Civil Rights era, and then getting out into ministry and campus ministry at the time of the Vietnam War, it was clear that a lot of people were hurting and their needs were not being addressed. I related most directly to that community. It seemed to me that what church was supposed to be about was addressing the needs of people at the point of their pain. What is the best way to do that?

"Part of what I think the Native Americans are teaching us in the mainstream church is that they have had to deal with a lot of adversity and find a spiritual basis for operating, much more so than people in the mainstream. We have our hardships, deaths of children and that sort of thing, but it is not deaths of a whole village. So, how people respond to adversity and maintain their sense of faith, hope and direction is different, given different experiences. How do we learn from one another?

"I may qualify as an *edgewalker*, but it's a whole lot easier to walk from the mainstream into the marginal culture because I can always go back. And I do go back.

"I've learned how ignorant I am about Native American history, even though I grew up in parts of the country where that history was talked about. Through willingness to expose my personal ignorance and ask questions, I learned more than I ever anticipated."

Lee Mun Wah, another man who brings his personal commitment into social activism, extends a deeply spiritual service in a very secular way. Through training, consultation and his documentary films, Mun Wah addresses racism head-on.

A man who participated in one of Mun Wah's groups for Asian men told me it changed his life by helping him embrace, for the first time, his Asian heritage as beautiful and powerful. Mun Wah and I arranged a meeting to follow a four-hour workshop for a business in Sacramento.

Just to escape the 110-degree heat bearing down outside that day, I stepped inside the room as people began to leave the workshop, some with tears on their cheeks. I waited in back while Mun Wah talked with those who approached him. He listened to each attentively, talking, laughing and sometimes hugging them. Unhurried.

I asked him if he wanted to take a break before beginning our interview. He laughed and said no, "I've learned to pace myself."

We got down to business. I asked him how he sees himself as an *edgewalker.*

"In the work that I'm doing now, because I'm also Chinese-American, I feel that there are many roles in which I go back and forth. I try not to do it just in reaction. When you said 'mainstream,' my first thought was that the mainstream is European-American dominated. Many things are beautiful about this culture, but I have always felt a missing sense of spirituality.

"When I was doing my Asian men's group, particularly when I started about ten years ago, the men often would say to me 'Mun Wah, what we're doing in this room is not applicable to the outside world at all. I can't do this in the workplace.'

"'Why not?' I said, remembering something Robert Kennedy said in a speech. And I thought, *Why not?* But then I couldn't prove myself to them in many ways.

"None of them saw themselves as leaders. When one of the Japanese men told me that Jesse Jackson was coming to Japantown to speak, I asked him, 'Why is Jesse Jackson coming to Japantown to speak? Why aren't the Japanese people speaking? Why aren't you speaking?' He said to me, 'I don't have good enough English, and besides I'm not as charismatic as Jesse Jackson is.'

"I went home, and I decided something was missing in the seminars and workshops we were doing, so the very next week, I totally changed their focus. I wanted people to see that the mentors they are looking for are themselves and each other. So that became the premise. They began to do some things differently. And that's why I filmed *The Color of Fear.*

"What we do in this country is we have a competition for winning—for what's right and what's wrong. I can go very much with the Buddhist belief that there are many truths, but we have to be willing to hear them. We have to go inward and reflect on what's keeping us from listening, what's keeping us from understanding what another person is experiencing.

"Working with racism is volatile. People want to know how I can keep going into rooms like this. It's because I don't see people in the room as enemies. I see them as people who are afraid. Someone once told me we live by two forces—love and fear. When I can substitute the word fear for hatred and racist beliefs, then it helps me have more compassion and more humanity for someone I'm working with.

"One thing I learned from the sixties is that we were looking for one person to save us. When Martin Luther King, John F. Kennedy, Robert F. Kennedy and Ghandi were assassinated, I think that for me, I began to realize that we had to believe that each of us carries the seeds of leadership. I really encourage individual responsibility when people ask about the solution to racism. I say, 'Well, it's just three inches away.' When people begin to practice openness within themselves and with the person next to them, it begins the linking in the room."

As we talked, I became more clear about Mun Wah's deep determination and commitment. He had just completed a long, controversial workshop, which I am sure required much of him, yet his clear eyes and animated face betrayed no fatigue. The Color of Fear, the title of his powerful documentary, let me know he is conversant with fear. I asked him how he deals with his own.

"By being scared," he replied. "You know, in a little while, I'm going to meet the man who killed my mother. That's scary. And recently, when I received threatening calls and some hate letters, it scared me. When I go to the Deep South and meet members of the Ku Klux Klan, it scares me. All the time, it scares me. I talk about it. I cry about it. I get angry with it, feel it.

"I remember the night when my mother was murdered, in January, 1987. My brothers and sister were angry I didn't get a gun and bars for my windows. I told them fear didn't seem so tangible in that way. It felt like it was more in my heart than it was an entity. I wasn't too sure who was imprisoned, the persons I was protecting myself from or the fear that was imprisoning me. I didn't want to live my life like that. The only cure for fear is to trust again, which includes the possibility of getting hurt—being devastated again, being left. The only way I can allow love to come back into myself and to love other people is to trust them. That has helped me."

From different perspectives, Frank, Adesha, Jim and Mun Wah open themselves to the mystery of life and bring their energy to bear on the tangible world. Energetic, open, and easy to talk with, each sees the world differently and each lives a spiritual life. Their presence, even more than what they say, communicates the sense that they are part of something bigger than each one of us separately and that we are all in it together. Here are some themes they share.

Acknowledge the spiritual vacuum in modern life.

Adesha: People are not realizing their whole potential, only their body and mind, not their higher self. It takes body, mind and spirit to make that whole person come alive. There's a need for the ones who have experienced this to bring that knowledge back into the mainstream.

Lee Mun Wah: When you said 'mainstream,' my first reaction was that the mainstream is European-American dominated. Many things are beautiful about this culture, but I have always felt a missing sense of spirituality.

Seek ancient threads in contemporary life.

Frank LaPena: So I'm talking about ceremony that embraces it all. Being part of a larger system is the purpose, or one of the purposes, of ceremony, which also puts you in touch with your sacred self. We are of more than one dimension. Everybody has a spirit.

Donald Sandner: Seen in this way, depth psychotherapy may be one of the modern branches of the ancient shamanic tree rooted in the beginnings of human life.

Move between personal self and cosmic connection.

Max Rein: While the *edgewalkers* you describe are multicultural, the edgewalkers of greatest interest to me are those who walk the edge between the world as we know it and the purely spiritual world. These individuals are *edgewalkers* of the highest order, encompassing the definition you offer as a matter of course in their evolution. They have moved beyond a level of self-actualization, living continuously in cosmic consciousness and beyond.

Steven Wong: At first, I learned about being American, then about Lakota shamanism and now I'm exploring Chinese shamanism. At some point, I anticipate cultural barriers will fall away as I reach universal connection.

Engender personal peace and harmony.

Adesha: There's room for the ego, but it has to be in its proper place. If you re-adjust the ego a little bit, then you open up to this other part, a great dimension that gives you peace and contentment.

Lee Mun Wah: We have to go inward and reflect on what's keeping us from listening, what's keeping us from understanding what another person is experiencing.

Allow connection with others through spiritual enlightenment.

Adesha: I identify with them in a different way. They don't know it. I see God in them. I see that I am speaking with part of God, so I identify with them on that level. I think, 'This is God in Nina. Or this is God in Max.'

Jim Leehan: How people respond to adversity and maintain their sense of faith, hope, and direction is different, given different experiences. How do we learn from one another?

Gail Christopher: We can extend to others compassion we have for ourselves. *Edgewalkers* have had to work through self-hate and can extend to others what boils down to love.

Lee Mun Wah: Work with racism is volatile. Someone once told me we live by two forces—love and fear. When I can substitute the word fear for hatred and racist beliefs, then it helps me have more compassion and more humanity for someone I'm working with.

Embrace cosmic consciousness.

Adesha: This level of consciousness is available for everybody. Each person has that connection with the universe, and all they have to do is open up to that inner part, which is already in place. After one of the experiences I had, I was afraid the feeling was going to leave, but it hasn't. It's there all the time.

Sharon Dryflower Reyna: I appreciate those differences between me and whoever I'm with and whoever I'm near. I never break down and say 'your culture—this culture.' I feel one. I know the difference, but I feel oneness.

As I reflected on their messages, I realized that if Mun Wah and Adesha can "allow love to come back...and trust..." it helps me, too. Frank's connection with native tradition, Adesha's cosmic consciousness, Jim's ability to see and communicate common themes, Mun Wah's commitment and endurance in addressing racism encourage us to walk their steep path, listen more intently, or feel less hostile to the person around the corner consumed by prejudice. As I see their faces and hear their voices, I feel more courageous and can stand at the edge of differences I come to on my own path with greater resolve. I can learn to build bridges that I wouldn't have if I hadn't known them.

nine

DOUBLING THE ODDS
Creating a Community

> Ultimately, in great leaders and the organiza-
> tions surrounding them, there is a fusion of
> work and play to the point where, as Robert
> Frost says, "Love and need are one." How do
> we get from here to there? I think we must
> start by studying change.
> Warren Bennis, *The New Paradigm in Business*

For *edgewalkers*, community, "that place where love and need are one," can be looked at three ways:

1) To some extent, people who live astride two cultures have more in common with each other than with those in their culture of origin or the mainstream. They report constant pushes and pulls, feeling comfortable and able to make friends in various settings, but rarely feeling completely "at home," either in their cultures of origin or in the mainstream.

2) In order to preserve the remnants of their culture, or to provide respite in a challenging social environment, some *edgewalkers* work diligently to restore or support their alternative community lives.

3) In one way or another, *edgewalkers* work as translators between their cultures of origin and the mainstream, weaving the strands of both into the national community.

Because it has to do with openness, compassion and building relationships, *edgewalking* is all about community, but not necessarily in the usual sense of an identifiable group or place. I think of a "community" as a town. In *Webster's Unabridged Dictionary*, "town" is the sixth, not the first, definition. "Community" is from the Latin *communis*, meaning common. Regarding *edgewalkers*, I feel *Webster's* fourth definition, "common character; similarity; likeness; as, *community* of spirit," is less confining than a geographical definition and offers opportunity for contemporary perspectives.

Laura Munoz works in international marketing for a multinational corporation, translating not only language, but culture for her employer. When she first came to the United States from Mexico as a teenager, she found, to her surprise, that her Americanized cousins were not particularly supportive. Neither did she fit in with the more separatist Spanish-speaking Chicanas she met at school because she wanted to move into the mainstream. Her first feeling of community in this country was among other "foreigners" from France, Asia and the Middle East in her English as a second language class.

"When you mix in a culture," Laura said, "you have lots of obstacles. You don't know what's right or wrong. Those obstacles made me strong though, and I would tell myself nothing could stop me. Soon I could step back, analyze my old culture as well as my new one. And, by becoming friends with people from other parts of the world, I felt a sense of belonging that was bigger than either Mexico or the United States."

Laura is not the only *edgewalker* who expressed that she has more in common with "foreigners" who share cross-cultural experience than with those in either of their cultural groups. Surviving the initiation rite of moving into strange territory, leaving behind the comfort of the familiar and learning new ways creates bonds among others who have been through the same thing. This sense of belonging, based on common experience rather than location or cultural similarity, is an expansive element *edgewalkers* bring to the new global frontier. From their perspective, it becomes possible to visualize community as a network where people move from culture to culture easily enough, without sacrificing their own uniqueness.

Adrianne Mohr, of San Francisco, said, "I can move from one group to another without needing a big passport. I come from an extremely conservative family of Republicans. I do very alternative work, massage and therapeutic bodywork. A lot of my clients are much like my family of origin, but I can introduce them to the alternative healing that I do in a way that doesn't frighten them. I can translate different possibilities in the world to different people."

Adrianne is a single parent; practices *capoeira*, a Brazilian martial art; teaches parenting at a Buddhist retreat; and, despite a difficult family history and major value differences, she is on good terms with her mother.

"My mom is Catholic and my dad, who's now deceased, was Jewish. They downplayed their religious differences, like it was not that big of a deal. But I feel like those communities are really diverse. My mom wanted me to be a nice Catholic girl, and I came out with a Jewish cultural personality. Even though I went to Catholic Sunday School and had values that slid into that culture, I have much more of a strong matriarchal Jewish presentation. How do I put a strong Jewish mother together with the Virgin Mary? They co-exist inside me.

"There never was a moment in my family when I felt like I belonged. It was a big joke that when I was three months old I screamed during the whole Thanksgiving dinner. I think I had just realized what I had gotten in to. I never felt like I was a member of that family, ever. And I tried for years and years and years.

"My sense of community comes from a feeling I have, several communities of which I'm part. I went to an event this weekend where I had always assumed that the women were martial artists and had day jobs so they can play their martial arts. A lot of them are professional dancers. It turns out that several of them are Ph.D. candidates and two are tenured professors. I have more in common with them than I thought. That group is starting to feel a lot more like my community.

"I think community is a feeling. The politics have to be there when I think about who my community is. Because, also, my community is the *vipassana* [a form of Buddhist meditation],—a community of teachers—none of the people there would likely have anything to do with my *capoeira* friends. And yet, I have people I grew up with here in San Francisco who would never have anything to do with those two groups. They would never cross tracks.

"The unifying principle is such a felt sense. I think about it being the family I never got. I don't feel like I've yet found one community where all of my interests can be addressed. I often assume that if I were somewhere and only interested in one thing, then I would have a group of people who all like to bowl, and I would too, and we'd all like to watch the same television shows, and then we'd all be set."

Several *edgewalkers* wistfully allude to this Norman Rockwell image of community in which similar people engage in similar activities, creating a sense of comfortable homogeneity. And then they quickly discount it as a real possibility.

Adrianne portrays the *spirit* of community—not necessarily a physical place, rather something she carries with her. She also does what many *edgewalkers* talk about. She creates community for herself and for others. Building community, or *feeling* a sense of community as Adrianne described, may be a substitute for blood relatives for those whose families of origin confine, reject or crush them. Friends and professional or spiritual colleagues assemble groups based on common interests or values and offer support to each other.

Rachel Guerrero, Chief of Multicultural Services for California's State Department of Mental Health, talked about her indigenous roots, "going deep to claim the person you are," and taking her sense of community with her wherever she goes. She is very conscious, though, of community as personal support.

"At this point, I would say I have three communities in my life. I have people at work friends and colleagues—who are Caucasian. I have a community of Latinos who are my friends and colleagues. And then, I have a community of spiritual people.

"I need this support. As a woman in Sacramento, I have to make a conscious effort to get support for my ethnic side. So many of the white people that I work with don't understand why there is a Black Firefighters Association, why there is a Latino Social Workers Association. It's not that people want to separate from everybody else, but we need a place to come together as people of color and talk about support mechanisms for continuing to have passion for our work, for moving the agenda, for creating harmony and acceptance of diversity. All people of color deal with those issues in their jobs."

For many *edgewalkers*, creating community for personal support also has a political side, what Rachel called, "the agenda—trying to create harmony and acceptance of diversity." This image is in direct contrast to one in which community grows from similar people doing similar things. Rachel points to a process in which people who are different from each other can find harmony and support in their common endeavors, despite those differences.

Community building doesn't necessarily arise from harmonious communication. "The dominant culture makes you believe that they are all white," Rachel says. "But the dominant culture is made up of all kinds of diversity. It is an issue of power. People of color are not major power brokers in the dominant culture. We are part of the dominant culture, though, and we want to have our voice. Our voice is different from yours. There are different ways of looking at and solving problems. The white dominant way is not the only way."

The focus on individualism, mobility and work life has more effect on life choices and more status than family in many cultures. This may be truer of *edgewalkers* than anyone, because they relinquish some of the comforts of conformity to their family's traditional ways. The initiative required to leave the comforts, or discomforts, of home, may include motivation to connect with others who may or may not fit the original family mode. With the disintegration of the family as the basic building block in our culture, a sense of community becomes increasingly important, another paradox in the dialectic of cultural transformation.

A book of photo essays, *The Family of Man* came out in the early nineteen sixties—black and white photos of all kinds of people in different settings that communicated very powerfully that we are all in this life together. This idea of the human family hangs in tension with the competitive, rolling-stone style that dominates our country today.

Sharon Dryflower Reyna talked with me about her family, her village and how she stays connected with her traditional culture at the Taos Pueblo. For her, community building centers around preserving tradition.

"In our culture, we have large extended families interlocking." Using her circled thumbs she demonstrates, "A patriarchal society. Now, since my aunt died, I am the eldest female on my father's side. Father had seven brothers. Each has daughters. It's my responsibility to take charge of things that need to be done for the family. If my uncles need something, I do it for them.

"Sometimes I feel really torn. If I'm busy someplace else, I have to leave what I'm doing and go to the village and take care of something. When I go back there, it's like going back two hundred years. When I'm there, I wear my village clothes and get in that frame of mind. Sometimes it's hard. I'm an explorer. For example, tomorrow there are going to be dances. I put my cousin in charge of doing things for that. She's the next elder. She's my apprentice, like I was my aunt's apprentice.

"Everyone is organized around the grandparents. They are the core. I refer to my father's parents and brother and sisters in one way, and my mother's parents, brothers and sisters in another. We are all connected, not just in-laws, but family."

Dryflower sees herself as someone who is comfortable in both cultures—not just one or the other. She attributes this to the fact that her family was open and supportive to her.

"My family is well educated—uncles and cousins with master's degrees, uncles who have been school superintendents and teachers. They encourage me."

"I don't have choices. When push comes to shove, there's no doubt. It's unspoken—this is your commitment. This is your life. This is what you were raised to do. This is the part that makes the culture whole. And if I don't do my part, then it narrows that circle and creates a loss. Like you're weaving a basket, and if you leave one piece of willow out, it throws it off. And so there is no choice. And it's tough."

Although she acknowledges the pressures involved and that the connection may not be perfect, Dryflower's family remains important to her—central, in fact. She feels strong ties both to the village that demands conformity to age-old tradition and to her friends and colleagues outside the pueblo walls.

Edgewalkers are catalysts for change and, as such, move between cultures and link possibilities that transcend family or town. They support interaction rather than isolation and, in some cases, take an active part in building community. Often their building of a community, like Dryflower's, has to do with preserving traditional roots or honoring the remnants of their culture of origin.

Ron Eller and Mary Lee Daugherty in Appalachia and Frank LaPena in his ceremonial work with his Wintu Tribal community engage in similar activities. Rufus Burrow on a seminary campus creates community for other African-Americans in a challenging environment.

Rufus told me, "My basic sense and values came from my parents and elementary school teachers, all of whom were African-American. I took those values seriously as a child and I still do. One of the things I discovered when I came to this campus early on was that if I was going to make a difference, I had to come up with ways to save myself long enough to do so. That's the way I feel today about all the African-American kids.

"Lorraine Hansberry characterizes them as 'young, gifted and black.' One of our graduates, a very bright African-American woman, found herself dedicated to working with this phenomenon of inter-community murder and violence among young black boys. All the while she was working on her degree, she lived in one of the tough areas of the community and worked with those kids. I used to say to her, 'That's extremely important work, and we need people to do that kind of work. You are going to be a good teacher. But, somehow we're going to have to figure out ways to save you long enough to do that. You can't get yourself killed!'

"I felt that way about myself when I first came here. I have felt that way about other African-Americans who have joined the faculty since I have become more established."

Rufus created a safety zone, a place where people with similar needs find support. This safe harbor provides for Rufus, his colleagues and their students the respite that families theoretically offer, or have offered in the past.

Families have traditionally been building blocks for community, where people with like backgrounds, values and interests band together for the benefit of all. Even though, for many, this perception may be more myth than fact, it is a powerful myth. When the focus is on individuality, mobility, future orientation and breach with tradition, a climate is created in which, for many, community supplants family. As *edgewalkers* separate from their culture of origin and stretch to embrace mainstream life, families can be hostile to them. The ability to create community becomes a survival skill.

Loreen Lilyn Lee who is Chinese-American, grew up in Hawaii and now lives in Seattle. From her teenage years, family pressure for conformity conflicted with her desire to engage the larger community.

"Family is very strong in Chinese culture. The individual does not act without the family's approval, and I have done many things in my life without family approval. That's how I've gotten to know myself, and it has been difficult. Growing up in a culture where family is everything and the lineage goes back thousands of years makes it tough. My brother and mother still go up to my grandparents' grave every year, and they do ritual. They bring food, and they do ceremony. It's pretty wonderful when I look back on it, but the American in me is saying 'I am my own person. I have to make my choices.' I'm actually both Chinese and American and have to find my own way. I have chosen to do that."

Loreen maintains connections with her family, but lives apart from them. She feels she is considered different from the others. She deals with a familiar trade-off—pain of distance and alienation—for staying true to herself. Over time and with persistent effort, she has salved some of the old wounds.

"Part of living between cultures, Chinese, Hawaiian and Asian mainstream, is that I've learned to be flexible to the situation. Whatever sensory internal devices I have are on a depth of perception that people who associate with a more monochromatic population do not get a chance to develop—an appreciation for all different kinds of people. I'm not going to pretend that I'm without my biases, but I'm more willing to catch myself because of my experience."

George Esquibel's experience has been anything but monochromatic, and has taken some interesting twists and turns. A ceramist, he teaches art at Sacramento City College, was a founding member of the Royal Chicano Air Force, a well-known group of artist/activists, and is intermittently involved with Chicano student causes on campus. He serves as a translator between cultures, both supporting the well-being of Latino culture in the mainstream and working with Chicano students to become more effective in the mainstream.

"I was raised in a foster home with a German family, and so I have seen both sides. What makes me head for the indigenous now is the fact that I was out of it for a number of years and I want to find it again. I'm from a very large family, and we're trying desperately to create what was supposed to be there.

"I'm part Indian, Navajo from the Las Vegas, New Mexico, area. Unfortunately, the Spanish side won out in the early years because when I was young, my mother used to tell me that the Indians were dirty. When we would go to Santa Fe to the Fiestas, she was afraid I was going to be kidnapped by one of the Native Americans, even though she was half Native American. The Spaniards had created a division and they wanted to have a superior position. Our family has a lot of broken ties.

"I'm glad I learned the Anglo side of the world—the main culture—because that is a very complicated and necessary part of life. A lot of Chicanos get mad at me for trying to introduce them to this. You look at some cultural traditions—like Chinese foot-binding—and know that everything about a culture is not necessarily good to carry on. The Chicano, or the Mexican, has a lot of traits, I think, in the background that are not good. One of them that particularly bothers me is not meeting deadlines."

To confront your culture of origin about customs or behaviors that don't make it in the mainstream doesn't increase your personal popularity. This is community-building from the mainstream direction and, unpopular as it may be, is a necessary step. In the past, alternative cultures were expected to melt, to disappear completely. George takes a more moderate step in trying to point out to students that they aren't doing themselves any favors by hanging onto certain behaviors.

Decisions about what to preserve and what to change are not easy. George continues, "And yet, I wonder if we are better off for crossing over. I'm sad to see examples of where the Mexican culture is diluted so much that it may not have many remnants of the old culture. A state like California may be disastrous to imported cultures. I see that in the H'mong, the Vietnamese—how difficult it is for them to control their children when they get here."

Today, millions of people have roots outside their national borders. Even if the family has been there for a few generations, it lives outside its social context. It is the rose in the lettuce patch. Regardless of its beauty, it is often seen as a weed.

The capacity that *edgewalkers* have to stay connected with who they are and also move into different environments "without a big passport," as Adrianne Mohr puts it, offers optimism in the spirit of community. The horrendous issues we have today that can loosely be called "social breakdown," can be better addressed by the communication skills, flexibility, openness and creativity of the *edgewalking* process than by a "family values" mythology based on unrealistic expectations that families can never meet.

Edgewalkers break ground in building connections based on *cross-cultural experience* rather than just on *cultural similarity*. That does not necessarily mean they abandon traditional ideas of family or community, but they may redefine their relationships with those groups. Here are some themes they bring forward in their discussion of community.

Acknowledge and share with other *edgewalkers*.

Laura Munoz: By becoming friends with people from other parts of the world, I felt a sense of belonging that was bigger than either Mexico or the United States.

Adrianne Mohr: The unifying principle is such a felt sense. I think about it being the family I never got.

Loreen Lilyn Lee: Whatever sensory internal devices I have are on a depth of perception that people who associate with a more monochromatic population do not get a chance to develop—an appreciation for all different kinds of people. I'm not going to pretend that I'm without my biases, but I'm more willing to catch myself because of my experience.

Create or connect with community for cultural support.

Rachel Guerrero: So many of the white people that I work with don't understand why there is a Black Firefighters Association, why there is a Latino Social Workers Association. It's not that people want to separate from everybody else, but we need a place to come together as people of color and talk about support mechanisms for continuing to have passion for our work for moving the agenda—trying to create harmony and acceptance of diversity. All people of color deal with those issues in their jobs.

Rufus Burrow: One of the things I discovered when I came to this campus early on was that if I was going to make a difference, I had to come up with ways to save myself long enough to do so. It's the way I feel today about all the African-American kids.

Weave alternative cultures into national community and vice versa.

George Esquibel: I'm glad I learned the Anglo side of the world—the main culture—because that is a very complicated and necessary part of life. A lot of Chicanos get mad at me for trying to introduce them to this. You look at some cultural traditions—like Chinese foot-binding—and know that everything about a culture is not necessarily good to carry on.

Loreen Lilyn Lee: I'm actually both Chinese and American and have to find my own way. I have chosen to do that.

Edgewalkers are leaders in change, creating community locally and beyond, taking the opportunity to create connections that transcend ethnic, cultural or spiritual barriers. Although they rely on colleagues and people from their own cultural groups for support, and, in some cases, work hard to maintain the integrity of traditional communities, *edgewalkers* take their *spirit of community* with them wherever they go. They move beyond the safe enclaves of their cultural groups into the borderlands of difference and change. Moving into that place "where love and need are one," they build relationships with people different from themselves, creating community that is bound by neither time nor place.

ten

STEPPING FROM THEORY TO PRACTICE
A Limitless Capacity for Healing

Do you see the world as a mural
that's both a painting and a sculpture?
With images of people jumpin' right atchya
Beautiful eyes of black, brown, green, and blue
every single color, skin tone, shade and hue.

Respect another one's culture
Respect another one's culture
> Basho Fujimoto, "Travels over Land and Sea"
> from Free Association's CD, *Freequality*

By their very lifestyle, *edgewalkers* "respect another one's culture." They develop a high degree of *cultural competence*, know about cultural differences, acknowledge those differences to self and others and promote mutual understanding.

The focus of this chapter is on the next step, expanding *cultural competence*, making a commitment to respect one another's culture beyond an individual level to a broader, organizational one. A huge step, to say the least. Developing *culturally competent* mainstream businesses and organizations, organizations that *de facto* understand and include and work with cultural diversity as a major focus rather than an add-on, will change our culture.

At work, school or in some other group you belong to, you have undoubtedly seen failed attempts at taking this step. You have probably heard, if not experienced, deep cynicism about "political correctness." Depending on your own orientation, you may have been subjected to tokenism, "special programs" or blatant racism.

Do you believe no next step is necessary, that anyone possessing ability and willingness to work hard can get ahead? Get in to see a physician? Gain access to needed services or educational opportunities? Or, that we should achieve a colorblind society, making *cultural competence* gratuitous?

Without the direct experience of racism or discrimination, it is next to impossible to appreciate the invisible privilege that goes with life in the mainstream. The hard question boils down to this: Should you or I, who have worked hard to get where we are, share our hard won (or inherited) privilege with those who, because of their gender, economic status or ethnic group, find themselves outside looking in?

The answer to this question has deep roots in social history. Economist Adam Smith, generally credited with originating the theory of supply and demand, actually wrote his first book, *The Theory of Moral Sentiments*, 1759, about "civility." Smith's central thesis is that for a society to thrive, people must treat each other well. Mid-nineteenth century philosopher John Stuart Mill approached the idea of a successful society with a concept he called "the greatest good for the greatest number." In other words, the more widely wealth and privilege are shared (Mill even included women), the better off everyone will be.

It makes good sense to share education, wealth and privilege as broadly as possible from the most basic, practical point of view. Society's current momentum toward deeper *cultural splitting* between an affluent upper class and an ever-burgeoning underclass is just plain dangerous. Gated communities are no safeguard against desperate people who have little optimism about their own lives, let alone concern for the lives and property of others.

The question must also be asked from the other side. Why should people who continue their lives in one country, sheltered in the traditions of their ancestors from another land, brave the challenges of learning new ways, new languages and changing their views of the world? It is possible to get by in a cultural pocket without engaging the mainstream, and elders often make that choice. The benefits of mainstream life—a sense of inclusion, access to material well-being, impact on the political process, being hip—all have more appeal if they are truly available.

Softening barriers to mainstream life and a simultaneous step forward by diverse people has small but notable success in organizations. Not all attempts at creating *cultural competence* fail, and where they succeed, they demonstrate not only compassion, but an affirmation of cultural values.

Rachel Guerrero, Chief of Multicultural Services for California's State Department of Mental Health, is the first member in her family to receive a college degree. Warrior that she is (the meaning of her last name), she earned an advanced degree, a license and began work in county, then state, mental health. Through the years, making hard decisions many times and surviving endless downsizings and reorganizations in her department, Rachel has held varied job assignments.

Without abandoning her Latina (Mexican/Toltec) identity, Rachel shares a perspective grown from her roots in the Los Angeles area, years in state government service and participation at the national level as well.

Arriving at my office for our interview directly from work downtown, Rachel brings huge notebooks and an array of pamphlets, which she turns over for me to dig into later. With her business suit, she wears an aura of exhaustion and energy that is standard attire for people who chronically take on major responsibility. After accepting a cup of tea and settling onto the sofa, she began with a note on her personal background.

"In college, I limited how much I talked with my family about my experiences in the dominant culture because they would think I was trying to be better than they were, a fear I see now as distance between them and me. Not that they ignored my accomplishments, they were extremely proud. My parents cried at my graduation, just as proud as other parents. But it's very painful because they don't understand the experience you're having, the complexity of being in two worlds. And it's true. All the work I've done, my personal therapy, this business of being a public speaker—they still don't really understand what I do.

"I had done a keynote for about six hundred mental health and other service providers in Los Angeles. I was at the podium with city council people and other dignitaries. I talked about Pico Viejo, the east Los Angeles *barrio* where I grew up, and about cultural diversity. My talk was well-received. People came up to me and were very complimentary. After I finished, I stayed at the conference a while, and then I drove over to spend some time with my parents.

"They asked me what I did, and I said, 'Oh, I went to a conference...' They said, 'Oh, you talked!' Then, my mother said, 'It's time to make dinner. Rachel, make the chili.'"

Rachel paused, and I thought about what that moment in time must have been like for her. As she described her abrupt comedown from the excitement of being a well-received keynote speaker to her familiar job as chili grinder, I marveled at what it takes to make the transition. Rachel told this story in her typical calm, semi-ironic manner. Although her flashing hazel eyes sparked with anger at times, nothing about her tone or appearance belied her pain or said "victim."

Rachel chose to blend in and do what she needed to do on that particular evening. She continued the story, "So I went in and toasted the chilies in the traditional way, ground them with a heavy, old, black volcanic rock mortar and pestle, a *molcajete*. Later, I wrote a poem about it."

Rachel, and others like her who intimately understand this process of moving between the mainstream and another culture, advocate *culturally competent* organizations, programs and service delivery, complex as that agenda may be. Rachel, using the *molcajete* to grind chilies for her mother, is *culturally competent*. Even though she might have more efficiently used a Cuisinart, she modified her actions to fit her mother's view of the world in order to remain part of her family's culture. Since she grew up in this household, she knows the rules and expectations and can, if she chooses, do what it takes to be part of the family.

"I use a *molcajete* in my own home," Rachel tells me. "I like the symbolism, the way it connects me with my grandmothers and that place in Mexico from which my family comes."

Because she loves her family and wants to spend time with them, Rachel is willing to accommodate their rules and expectations to a point. She also chooses where to take a stand and assert her differences. This cultural sensitivity is infinitely more difficult for an organization, a school or a hospital for instance, than for an individual, but it is necessary. *Cultural competence* begins at an individual level, but a *culturally competent* organization is more than a collection (or smattering) of *culturally competent* individuals.

The project Rachel describes (Child, Adolescent Service Systems Project or CASSP) offers firsthand knowledge of a broad, capable effort to create social change at institutional levels. The project is an effort to move mainstream agencies to address *cultural competency*. Agencies need to do the service delivery equivalent of grinding the chilies in the *molcajete* in order to reach their clientele. In order to produce this outcome, the agencies themselves must become *culturally competent* at all levels, from policy-making, administration and service providers, through consumer services.

Rachel's discussion demonstrates how essential it is for people involved in service delivery to operate within the context of their clients' cultures. At the most elementary level, if a counselor goes to a Latino, African-American or Asian home, that counselor is likely to make little headway if she digs into the official part of her visit right away. The social part, creating an environment of trust—having tea, listening, meeting extended family in the home getting acquainted with the children—has to happen first and takes time, probably more time than a managed health care organization budgets. In the best of circumstances, though, real change happens. The child who needs treatment receives it, and the clinicians expand their knowledge. Hopefully, the outcomes are what the child and family need.

Depending on the skill of the counselor and the support the agency can give, it is possible to establish cross-cultural relationships and deliver services effectively where they are needed. To be successful in this area, an agency must be willing to make a long-term investment for an incremental strategic approach to achieve *cultural competence*. It must be a planned approach that includes all aspects of the organization. *Cultural competence* is a systemic viewpoint and capability, not a department, a program or an addition.

Rachel offered some background on the CASSP project as she explained. "In the mid-nineteen eighties Georgetown University produced a lot of monographs and other documents regarding the philosophy for children's systems of care. Among other things, they were interested in how agencies throughout the country provide mental health services to people who need them."

The big notebooks Rachel loaned me include laboriously constructed definitions and guidelines for *cultural competence*. The committee's research describes agencies throughout the country that provide service at many levels of effectiveness, give examples of agencies that are culturally competent and make recommendations for training.

The organizational context from which the CASSP project emerged did not have easy beginnings. The ethnic people on the planning committee, mostly psychologists and social workers from various states, were securely centered in their own ethnicity and were advocates for people of color. Nevertheless, when the first document appeared, it ignored culture and ethnicity in the delivery of services, offering only the usual passing reference to race culture.

Rachel explained, "The people of color in the audience walked out of the national meeting saying 'you are ignoring the important part of what we think will make a difference in helping families.' Ultimately they sat down with the director who listened and acknowledged the problem, and together they reworked the plan. Out of that process the Ethnic Resources Advisory Committee was born.

"And so this dynamic group continues," Rachel said. "They had completed the first document defining *cultural competence* in 1986 before I joined. They have since launched many other projects and continue to do training around the country.

"I have seen this process happen over and over again as I work with other organizations. The ethnic professionals protest the omission of attention to cultural competence. If the administrator hears them and stays open to working toward a solution, something new happens. It takes both sides to make progress. Otherwise, the same old stalemate continues."

Rachel looked dead serious as she explained that the group's research revealed that too many children of color with emotional problems are found not in the mental health system but in the juvenile justice system. Teachers, counselors and other authority figures are likely to see minority children who have emotional problems, or even serious mental illness, as troublemakers. Consequently, the children receive discipline rather than treatment, and a vicious circle continues. This injustice is not just a matter of money or power, although those factors apply. It emphasizes how important it is to have good mental health services that people see as helpful and truly understanding. This is where the *cultural competence* of administrators, policy makers, teachers, law enforcement officers and clinic staff members becomes instrumental.

We only have to count the prison population to see that the percentage of non-white inmates far exceeds their percentage in the general population. It is economical in both human and financial terms to treat children with emotional problems before their incapacity and desperation drive them to social violence and a life in jail.

Rachel pointed out that the high-level ethnic professionals on the advisory committee from all over the country practice what they preach. "They have done their personal work—found ways to channel their rage—so *we* can work together in ways that are *culturally competent*. Sometimes we have strong disagreements, but we make room for each other as we try to solve the overwhelming problems that all of us face on a daily basis in our jobs. There is a common ground of experience for professionals across ethnic groups.

"You don't have universal agreement on *cultural competence* among people of color," Rachel said. "All of us know and meet African-Americans and other ethnic people, for instance, who are very acculturated to dominant ways and want to minimize their color and ethnicity. They would say, 'Don't treat me differently.'

"I have white people ask me as a trainer, 'How come sometimes you want to be all the same and sometimes you say honor diversity?' Often they urge me to talk about similarities rather than differences. There are similarities and they are important. But to minimize differences misses the point. The differences make us who we are and we need to honor them, find ways to deal with them, rather than pretending they don't exist or trying to make them go away."

Being *culturally competent* means getting personal. Rachel pointed out, "What we are trying to do in some of our training is teach people to find out what a particular person's ethnicity means to them. What is their experience? How has it impacted their life? How are their values different from the person's providing the service?"

Using your best *edgewalking* diplomacy, you have to ask, breach social convention and find out how someone feels about who they are, how they think and feel. You can't anticipate what they want or need by what ethnic, social or occupational category they occupy. If you are a service provider, you can't just give them what you think will be good for them and expect it to work.

Rachel continued, "Some people like to talk about the nineteen sixties and the civil rights movement with the idea that we are all the same—that we should move toward being culturally blind or culturally accepting. This homogeneous approach hits the core of disqualifying a person's ethnicity, a tie most of us hold on to and one that has served us well. This approach asks us to give up our history, mythic stories, ancestors. I don't think so!"

Rachel brought the conversation home to her own identity group. "When I do training with Latinos, some of them get very nervous because they're afraid I'm going to shove my theory of how they should be Latinos down their throats. What I'm trying to communicate is that it is important to look at your relationship to your culture. We didn't all have the same experience. Much of dominant culture wants to deal with everybody in the same way, lump Latinos into one group with statements like, 'twenty percent of the Latino community feels this way or that way,' without looking at all the specific nationalities. It takes more work. There's such diversity many don't want to acknowledge within the cultures. That's what makes it so hard. Especially since, if we want to influence the dominant culture and embrace *cultural competence* as a way of doing business, we have to do it in a consistent way—saying it together so we don't become isolated as individuals or particular cultural groups."

Rachel pointed out what Coco Fusco and other *edgewalkers* have emphasized. You can't generalize about cultural groups anymore than you can "mainstream," "white Americans" or "feminists." But you can ask for information and then listen to the answers.

Considering the differences between different subcultures of Mexican people, not to mention between people of Colombian, Cuban and Mexican descent, the idea that Latino communities can get together and negotiate any kind of completely unified approach seems preposterous. Each has a much different history. The difficulty gets even messier between groups—African-Americans, Native Americans, Asians and people of mixed race. And yet, it is important to find ways for groups to come together around messages they can agree on. The message of *cultural competence* is one that has broad-based support.

It is one step for mainstream people to accept *cultural competence* as worth developing. Equally important is *culturally competent* communication within and between all groups. Getting clear about your own good reasons to move beyond *cultural splitting* into mobilizing your effort to become *culturally competent* helps.

CASSP's Ethnic Resource Committee emphasizes the importance of switching from old-fashioned paternalism to a more complicated model for service delivery—partnership. As Jim Leehan described the Paths Crossing project a few chapters back, he pointed out the profound difference between patronage, "We who have plenty will help those with less, so we can feel better about ourselves," and partnership. His dramatic example of the refugee community in El Salvador who refused medical help, rather than accepting it on a paternalistic basis, demonstrates how important it is for people to utilize services in their own context.

There is no denying that the failure rate is staggeringly high for countless special projects that were funded and initiated to provide a wide variety of services to particular populations in the past three decades. The reasons are complex, but the consistency cannot be ignored. History has hardened cynicism on all sides, making it ever more difficult to undertake yet another attempt, not only for the people who fund the projects, but for those who have spent years working hard only to see another failure.

"Real change is happening, though," Rachel said. "Part of it has to do with political power. No one can get elected in this state without ethnic support. That power is behind policy change. California is the first state to require all county mental health departments to put plans in place that show how they are working to achieve *culturally competent* policy, administration, providers and consumer services.

"I had to work hard to talk one of my colleagues into working with me on this project. 'I just can't do another one,' she protested. She did it though, and when she retired, she said, 'I can retire happy, knowing that this change has the strength of law behind it and will make a difference.'"

Culturally competent agencies produce better outcomes, making them more cost effective. In the most practical terms, if your agency is *culturally competent* at all levels, you are less likely to get sued because a service provider—counselor, police officer, teacher—does a racist thing to a person in the community. The clients you serve will stay in treatment and become more able to care for themselves, rather than ending up in the criminal justice system.

Rachel summarized some of what needs to be addressed, "When you are minimized, discarded, experiencing feelings of racism, if you aren't solidly centered in the idea that 'I have total pride in who I am and nobody's judgment of me is going to throw me off the edge,' you can become eaten up by anger." When rage becomes overwhelming, it is nearly impossible to maintain openness toward others.

"You have to do your own deep work and be able to claim the person you are. I see this in the advisory committee," Rachel said. "That group is my best example. They are able to harmonize difference because they know from experience that power struggles don't work. That means being able to manage your own personal rage, caring enough about the community that you continue to feel you have to do this job."

The Ethnic Resources Advisory Committee to CASSP talks about cooperating and sharing power. They take a different approach to goal orientation than is common in business and government. Rachel emphasized this important difference that is at the heart of *edgewalking*, "The process and the friendship is just as important as the product. The relationship building is part of what we do every day."

From this perspective, relatedness—long-term relationships and commitment in terms of partners in business—is more important than money and power. "Nina," Rachel said, "if we were working on this book together, developing the relationship would be a very important part of this task. And in the end, the task would get done." This approach challenges the hard-driving business style that is typical in the mainstream, but the *edgewalker's* sword cuts both ways.

When the mainstream can find a way to learn from the composite groups that fill that country's mosaic, as well as support and include those groups, the country will be richer for it. In our jubilance, we forget that some of the cultures that are uprooted and struggling in the particular countries they've adopted have been around in other locations much longer. Traditions and practices for supporting those who are ill or having difficulty are significant building blocks in those cultures. When practitioners from the defining culture can coordinate care with families or cultural healers rather than removing the client from all that is familiar around her or him, the treatment may actually work rather than causing even greater problems.

It takes people like Rachel and the others who move back and forth from the establishment to their own cultures to interpret the needs. "People have the same basic needs," Rachel said. "They differ in ways of meeting these needs. That is what we must keep teaching. There is not just one way."

Valuing difference and understanding that people hold different values is fundamental to gaining *cultural competence*. Those differences require understanding and respect. Otherwise, from the dominant perspective, we hold the misguided view that we are being good people by providing services, and ethnic clients are just ignorant not to accept them in the ways we offer them. We have to grasp how much it is to the advantage of the whole country to move policy making out of the constricted view of the mainstream and increase the vista. More than that, a certain arrogance about our way of doing things blinds us to the potentially negative impact our way may have on others. That arrogance also convinces many that it is the only way that works. Unfortunately, we have many examples of how the mainstream style doesn't work.

Sometimes we know we don't know. Then we have the opportunity to push ourselves, do a little *edgewalking,* and ask questions that will clarify the situation.

Culturally competent agencies respect difference, try to stay on top of their own work process making sure that at all levels they are consciously working toward *cultural competence,* include a staff of ethnic and culturally diverse people and endeavor to know what they are doing in regard to the people they serve. Such agencies view minority groups as distinctly different from one another and as having numerous composite groups, each with important cultural characteristics. Further, *culturally competent* agencies understand the interplay between policy and practice and are committed to policies that enhance services to diverse clientele.

I asked Rachel if there were places where she had seen the power structure change. "The places where I've seen the power structure change the most is where the administrator is a person of color who really believes in the importance of *culturally competent* work. I have also seen change where the administrator, even if not a person of color, offers strong support for progress toward *cultural competence* from the top and throughout the organization. In fact, there is a lot of lip service. People don't know how to make the change. They hear us talking about it, but they still don't really understand it.

"Now," Rachel continued, "many of us are assuming a much more radical position to push for *cultural competence.* When a conference organizer asks us to come do a one-hour workshop on cultural diversity, we say, 'No. You need to have it throughout your conference, as a keynote address or a presentation in your plenary session.' We all keep learning from each other. We're becoming much sharper and tougher. The whole group assumes responsibility way beyond what is required by the job. 'This is more than a job, it is a lifetime commitment to make life better for those who follow us and for those seeking services,' my colleagues say. They don't do it for the money. They do it because they care about the issues."

Rachel's warrior passion came through in her voice and her demeanor as she told me, "There are so many layers—your own evolution and your development as a person. One of the things that binds us as a group is that we all have acute awareness of the effects of racism. Most people at the table have experienced it head on. Most of us feel racism and cultural incompetence is something that needs to be addressed in this country and that we have to stop pretending that it is not present. We really are a pluralistic society and that means embracing diversity. Even though we are a nation built on diversity, much of the public policy denies that reality. A passion to heal those wounds, to make change and make a difference unites this group."

Creating programs and policies to heal wounds is a long-range effort. Creating *culturally competent* organizations happens in small increments. Rachel pointed out, though, that change happens all the time at a personal level.

"People see the *edgewalker* in you and call on you in informal ways to support them. Not long ago, a Latina woman in my office called me over to talk, started asking me something about being Latina and not being married. And she said, 'How do you deal with that?' I said, 'It's not a problem at all. You mean all the relatives who give you a bad time?' I asked. She replied, 'Yeah!' And I said, 'I claim who I am with them and let them know that I'm really happy with the choices I've made in my life. Why would it matter to them?' I just gave her an example of how I've dealt with this very Latino sort of mentality that you're not okay if you're a Latina woman—not a whole person—if you haven't married and had children and how I'm able to do that. That was a very informal way to demonstrate how to create competency in both these worlds."

Rachel's personal story and the work she has done at county, state and national levels, illustrate the need for and outline a process of building *cultural competence*. However, efforts at creating *cultural competence* are not limited to ethnic groups. The process of taking services to marginalized people who need them in their environment is similar for other groups as well.

The book, *A Tradition That Has No Name: Nurturing the Development of People, Families and Communities*, by Mary Field Belenky,

Lynne A. Bond, and Jacqueline S. Weinstock, describes an action research project, "Listening Partners," that the authors began in 1985. The study includes socially isolated, low-income mothers of preschool-age children who live in rural Vermont counties that report high levels of unemployment, domestic violence, child abuse and neglect.

This project's goals were to work with the women so they could appreciate their minds, which their culture does not value. As they developed that appreciation, they could "name, question and overcome the stereotypes that had left them feeling so diminished." The authors were also trying to demonstrate a theoretical point: "individuals' epistemologies or ways of knowing, provide a framework for imagining their relations to other, including friends and children."

This theoretical point is profound in terms of understanding *cultural competence*. In their study, Belenky and her associates worked with the women to help them expand their "ways of knowing."

"Ways of knowing," how people decide *which* information they will pay attention to, how they take in and process that information, "individuals' epistemologies," as Belenky and her co-authors call it, are central to creating *cultural competence*. In order for information or services to be useful, they must be accessible and seen as relevant to the people who use them. Staff must understand and follow through on what it takes to make them accessible to their client group. The staff has to be able to view the services from the point of view of potential recipients.

Like the group at Georgetown, Mary Belenky and her colleagues identify programs other than their own that are working toward *cultural competence*. Each of the projects has its own reasons for being, history, successes and failures. Cataloging these efforts, though they may be faint voices among a loud clamor of need, creates a growing body of information about what works and what does not work in developing *cultural competence*.

Through their research, the CASSP group listed agencies which provide *culturally competent* services. One of the criticisms they received is that too many of the agencies they cited are specialized: Asian Pacific Center for Human Development in Denver, or Institute for Black Family Development in Detroit, for instance. The point, ultimately, is for *mainstream* agencies, institutions and businesses, not just those serving special populations, to become *culturally competent*.

The following list, based on the Ethnic Resource Committee's guidelines and discussions with Rachel Guerrero and other *edgewalkers*, outlines some steps and values considerations for moving from theory to practice in *cultural competence*. Each item on this list is a complex undertaking and has many sub-steps that require commitment to personal development and, in some cases, understanding of conflict management.

1. **Define your relationship to your own culture**, whether you are a person of color or not.

2. **Move beyond blame and *cultural splitting*** by learning to hear and relate to values different from your own.

3. **Discover what an individual's ethnicity means to her or him** rather than assume that someone is a certain way because of identity with a particular group.

4. **Individuals must find it within themselves to communicate effectively in order** to cooperate in creating *culturally* competent policies and services by learning how to contain rage rather than dumping it on the listener(s).

5. **Harmonizing differences comes from deep personal knowledge that power struggles don't work.** Included here is the understanding that no one approach is the best for all tasks.

6. **Relatedness**—long term relationships and commitments in terms of partners in business—**is more important than money and power.**

7. **Changes in the power structure** are likely to occur more quickly when administrators are people who deeply believe in the importance of *culturally* competent work and endeavor to support steps toward *cultural competence* from the top and throughout the organization.

8. ***Culturally* competent agencies, institutions and businesses are cost effective.**

9. **Culture-specific characteristics of racial and ethnic minority groups** are accepted by *culturally* competent agencies, institutions, and businesses and acknowledged in identifying needs and planning services and products. They:

Value diversity,
Acknowledge difference,
Continuously conduct cultural self-assessment (personal
    and organizational),
Recognize dynamics of difference,
Institutionalize cultural knowledge,
Adapt policies, services, programs, and infrastructure.

10. Achieving *cultural competence* in dealing with diversity potentially makes some countries different than those with homogeneous or subordinated populations.

Because people have a propensity to seek out others like themselves and even make enemies of those who are different, efforts to cross boundaries and create cooperative projects in *cultural competence* are incredibly challenging and often feel like inventing the wheel. Despite all that, wheel inventions are emerging all over this country. Documenting such efforts and sharing information about steps that work create a resource bank for the intrepid souls who choose to commit their efforts to life's challenges out there on the new frontier.

The ideal of tolerating, even welcoming, differences underpins the view of new global cooperation. Achieving *cultural competence* moves us from the ideal (thinking about it) to practice (doing it).

eleven

MOVING AND
SHAKING ON THE RIDGE
From Regional to Mainstream and Back

> One day, a teacher pulled me aside and, after
> complimenting me on my classroom perfor-
> mance, suggested that I had what it takes to
> be "successful" but that I would have to over-
> come my roots and become "something
> more" than my people had been. I learned
> the hard way that it hurts to be a minority in
> a strange land. So I learned to adjust—to
> become bicultural and to hide who I really
> was and who my people were, except on every
> other weekend when we went "home."
>
> Ron Eller, Ph.D.
> Director, Appalachian Center

"As an adult now, I recognize that it is possible to live in two cultures and be from two cultures without giving up many of the
personal things that tie you to an older world. For me, strength in
family, some of the positive values those of us from the mountains
feel we have, offer great capacity to deal with stress. Close relationships to the land help us deal with the mass society and its emphasis

on technology. I am as much at home fishing, hunting or digging in my big garden as I am working on the computer, lecturing in a class-room or interacting on the Internet. From my perspective, both worlds have their stresses, but living in both allows me to escape the stresses of either at any particular time."

Miners, Millhands, and Mountaineers, Ron Eller's book about his people in Appalachia, presents facts, figures and stories about the life he works to understand, articulate and preserve. Located in a red brick house that has seen better days, The Appalachian Center at the University of Kentucky, where Ron works, is on a side street across from Limestone Avenue and the Law School. Both programs are on the same campus, but appear worlds apart.

Ron Eller and Mary Lee Daugherty, the two *edgewalkers* in this chapter, live and work on The Ridge, the Appalachian region of the United States that includes 406 counties in thirteen states, extending from New York to Mississippi. After attending college and pursuing other mainstream endeavors, these two individuals returned to their culture of origin, bringing back experience and know-how to their people, many of whom live in third-world conditions. Ron Eller and Mary Lee Daugherty struggle to preserve the uniqueness of the Appalachian area, believing that many of the traditions there offer the mainstream something of value that may be lost.

Ron said, "The reason there is a very strong Appalachian Identity today, what has been called a renaissance of Appalachian cul-ture, is that many of us from the region have transferred our personal struggles with living in two cultures to our understanding of the region as a whole. I think if you were to interview lots of others like me, you would find that what they have tended to do is to take their personal experience of having feet in two worlds, and their personal experience with mass society and its stereotypes, and have applied what they've learned to the larger Appalachian Region. We under-stand this as a way to maintain a sense of community. Really, it involves rebuilding a sense of community that many of us have lost—not old community but new community—that may have some char-acteristics of the old in a contemporary context.

"I think many of us tend to focus on how difficult that strug-gle is more than we tend to focus on the positive aspects of it. Most of us who are caught in the middle—we talk about this kind of thing constantly—tend to emphasize how difficult it is when you're not accepted, not fully part of either world but sort of spinning in between. You have to be constantly on the lookout to assure your family members and those in the traditional culture that you have not left them. When I was growing up, one of my grandfathers, the one who was a coal miner, would constantly challenge me, questioning me when I came back from college as to whether I was going to go hunting with him, or fishing, dirty my hands with real work, and the other grandfather the one who was the mountain preacher, constantly pressured me to 'read through them books' which from his perspective meant 'Don't allow that education you are going to get to reshape the way you think.' Read and gain what you can—but go beyond. They both knew I was passing into a different world.

"In their own ways, both of my grandfathers were afraid. In the mountains, we have a phrase that sometimes you 'get above your raisin'.' What that means in that very strong, traditional mountain culture with its leanings toward egalitarianism is that everybody is just as good as everybody else within a particular group setting. We tend to have a whole series of ways, that if someone tends to think he or she is better than the rest of the group, we try to hold the person down. That has often been a problem for us in the development of leaders. We tend not to want to develop leaders in the way that modern society often develops leaders. On the other hand, it has a very positive value of equalizing.

"It is hard when you are never fully part of the larger world too, and that is constantly brought home to you. I went to graduate school at Chapel Hill—best place to study Southern History—there was no place to study Appalachian History—after teaching high school for a couple years. As you know, one of the first things that they do in graduate school is have a reception for graduate students and faculty in order for the senior faculty to size up the newest crop of graduate students and see what they are all about. Well, we had this cocktail party where that occurred and, of course, I didn't know anything about cocktail parties. We didn't drink many cocktails in my house. I learned that what you do is watch everybody else and fit in by doing what other people do. So I was doing that, standing with a group, when a senior professor of ancient history came up and began a conversation with me. He popped the important question and asked, 'Mr. Eller, what is it that you hope to study while you are with us?'

"And so I said, 'I came to study Appalachian history, and I hope to write the history of my people.'

"He immediately put his hand to his chin, sort of stared off, and said, 'Oh, yes. I've seen the Foxfire Books. That's nice.' And immediately turned around, walking away to find someone who had a more academic, more legitimate purpose in being there, since my people weren't worth studying.

"What I faced when I went to graduate school was a dominant mainstream culture that said that Appalachia has no history, and that all mountain people did was sit in their cabins up in the hills until they were discovered by the rest of the country. The only things worth studying were the quaintness and the folk culture of the region.

"Of course, I ended up writing *Miners* and now that old view of Appalachia isn't so universally accepted. It is the kind of cultural assumption that many minority groups in the sixties and early seventies faced—women, Native Americans, African-Americans and others. History had been written primarily by white men, and primarily about white men from the perspective of the Northeast, and so those of us who came from different kinds of cultural experiences had to, in effect, rewrite history as a whole to indicate that our people also had one. In many ways, that was a history very active and interactive with what had been previously understood and known. But you never quite fully fit in and are never quite comfortable on all that ground. My family moved out of the mountains to Ohio in the fifties, and that's where I was able to go to school. During those years, I was constantly told by my teachers not to be who I was, and that if I wanted to make something of myself I had to become somebody different from who my people were.

"It was confusing. I learned then to live in two worlds. During the day when I would go to school, I would learn how to negotiate and deal with the mainstream experience. Then, in the evenings at home, and especially on the weekends when my family would go back home to West Virginia, I would be immersed in a different kind of experience with different music and different foods. So I learned to negotiate the world in two ways.

"People deal with this struggle differently. I even have family members—one sister in particular—who have rejected Appalachian identity, do not want to be 'hillbillies,' striving in every possible way not to be that. It's hard for me to figure out exactly what makes some individuals move in one direction and some in others.

"In a very general way, I think there's an element of concern for others in Appalachia to de-emphasize you as an individual, and place greater emphasis on you as connected to the group. Some people have that feeling more than others do. Those people tend to go into the ministry or social work or some kind of human service in comparison to others who tend to be more individualistically oriented in terms of their success. I don't necessarily say that from a derogatory perspective, but their sense of identity is shaped much more by how they see their own accomplishments as compared to how they fit into and relate to others around them. That is an individual personality trait as much as anything, but the kind of person who is oriented toward measuring success individually will tend to measure success by the national norms or national standards, by what is out there in the larger society that tells them they are successful. In modern society, that tends to be how big a house they have, what kind of car they drive, what kind of clothes they wear—materialistic things that bring one status in that environment. Some of us who are more attuned to having our sense of personal value reinforced by others and by how we relate to others, tend to be more conscious of community—who we're associated with, who we're tied to. That's not to say we don't experience the same kind of identity crisis, but our identities tend to be connected to the group rather than dependent more on individual accomplishments.

"A traumatic point for me was when my family outmigrated from West Virginia in the fifties. I was the oldest of five kids so I was more conscious of that transition than the younger ones. Shortly after we got to Ohio, I began being treated differently than the other kids in the class by teachers and began recognizing if I was going to be successful in school I had to change the way I dressed and spoke. My mother always wanted me to be successful, wanted me to graduate from high school—a family goal. Yet, at the same time, we were constantly going back home on weekends.

"I worked as a shoe-shine boy in my father's barber shop and would listen to all the stories about home from the other outmigrants from West Virginia, Tennessee, Virginia and Kentucky and became wrapped up in their stories and, at the same time, tried to be successful in school. It was a real struggle.

"I was able to get an academic and athletic scholarship to college. I was the first one in my family to go to college. The year I graduated from high school, my dad moved the family back to West Virginia, because he couldn't take the pressure of life and just didn't like it up there. He had made enough money to go back, buy a little house, and so he moved all my brothers and sisters home.

"I went off to college—had to put myself through with scholarships, worked in the campus post office twenty hours a week, then worked various summer jobs back home. At the end of my sophomore year, the college raised the tuition. I went in to see the dean, mainly to thank him. He told me not to worry, he was going to find a way to come up with the additional money, and he did. I got a Woodrow Wilson Scholarship that I shared with a black friend of mine from Alabama. It really struck me very, very hard. Here it was. My notion of going to college was that I was going to college to make it, to be successful on my own competence, and I was doing everything that those teachers in school had told me that I needed to do to be successful. And of course, my family was proud of me for doing it. But the conversation with that dean really pressed in my mind those hard questions of why was I the first one in my family ever to experience this. That led to my thinking, why did I have to hide who I was, the music I listened to and all of that? It dawned on me that I would be able to continue in college, not so much because I was individually successful, but because I was part of a minority group.

"And yet coming up in school, I was told not to be part of that group.

"It was devastating. It not only made me think about what I had experienced, why they had made fun of me, why I had to talk a different way. When you're young, it hurts you, but you don't understand it. That was the first point at which I began to want to understand why I was in that situation.

"And then I began to reflect more. I knew that my people were from the mountains in western North Carolina, where they originally settled. The Northern timber companies were buying up the timber in western North Carolina. My grandfather and his brothers had to leave the family farm, to work in the coalmines in southern West Virginia because they could no longer make a living. My grandfather's dream was that he was going to work for a few years in the coalmines, then go back home to the family farm and follow what the family had done since the Revolutionary War. But he never made it.

"Then my father had done exactly the same thing. He had to leave West Virginia and move to Ohio with the same kind of dream. And here it was. I was going to have to leave college—my personal dream which would have made me successful—and go back home. Grandfather had gotten me a job in the coalmine. I thought, *This is natural, just have to work a while then go back.* But what that dean said to me kept raising questions in my mind: *Why am I the first one to go to college? Why did my grandfather have to leave his home? Why did my father have to leave his home?* I thought, *To a great degree their dreams were not accomplished, but I'm going to be able, maybe, to accomplish mine.* It was all very confusing. It really made me want to know more about who I was. And that's how I ended up doing what I do.

"I really feel that I am put here to straddle those two worlds. I do what I do because I think I owe it to somebody else. I've often said in speeches that I give that at the time of the dean's conversation, I really felt I couldn't live with myself if I had gone off to become a lawyer or some individual profession. For me, there was something else I had to do. And so I have maintained that inner conviction for the last twenty-five years. I think there are lots of others like me in the region. It just happened that we came of age in the early nineteen sixties, and there were opportunities through national defense loans and national pressures to get minorities into higher education. Because of the media, there was an emerging consciousness of unity. We came of age at a time when that attention focused on us and pushed us in one direction or another. I know lots of people abandoned their Appalachian roots early in their lives. It's interesting; lots of them are becoming interested in the old culture now.

"It used to be that we would get heavily criticized in English classes about dialect and language patterns. People from the mountains would come to the University to become teachers. The faculty constantly had to teach the kids the proper way to speak—many of them still do. The local dialect was looked down upon. What we now try to do when working with teachers is tell them, 'Rather than criticize the kid who said 'hit,' instead of 'it,' point out that it's fine, but there is a way that you communicate in different settings so that both are valued.'

"Thirty years ago, that would never have happened anywhere. Anything local, such as dialect or anything that valued the local experience, would not have occurred in the classroom. The purpose of an educational environment was to get the kid out of that environment, put them off elsewhere by having them learn what the dominant norms were. What we have learned is that the transition put tremendous pressure on kids, and in fact we have a high drop-out rate and there are a number of reasons why. Those kids that tend to drop out are the kids from rural areas and lower income areas of the mountains, not the middle class kids who live in towns.

"Some of us were able to make that transition, to change our culture, in order to get out. Others could not make the jump and simply went back. Why should parents encourage their kids to undergo that transition in order to get an education? They will not only lose them physically to jobs that aren't available in Appalachia, because the kids have to get work outside the region, but they're liable to lose them emotionally because they become somebody else. The education system in the larger society—the assumptions in the larger society—just put horrible pressure and strains on these kids, not valuing who they are. When I went through that trauma in college and began looking into the history of my people, I began to recognize that for me, music was a very powerful, creative kind of thing. My family had lots of talent, and I became proud of what I had once been told to look down upon.

"We're only at the front end of a long-term continuing struggle. We still have not made effective linkages among ethnic and racial groups. My people in the mountains need to understand what they have in common with people from the Delta, the Chicano community in the Southwest, the Native American community and the fact that our histories are much the same in relationship to the larger culture. We don't share enough of that sense. Today, so much is affected by the media and by how, nationally, the media tends to portray groups in stereotypical ways because they want to commodify people— see distinctive groups as commodities—in order to target them for marketing purposes. The very process of commodifying people perpetuates divisiveness. I am as opposed to the 'apple butter' view of Appalachia as I am to portraying the area through images of the poverty stricken, benighted individual. Both representations are very shallow ones on which to build an understanding of a people, culture and all of what has happened to them. But those tend to be the primary ways the media pictures any of us.

"I have seen tremendous changes in the last thirty years in people's ability to react and to respond to different cultures. Our understanding, especially in the mountains, of who we are and the real growth of identity has expanded. I see that happening in every culture. Each culture has its own struggle. But then, there's the tendency for each of the cultures to abandon their internal struggle and become absorbed by the mainstream majority. We face that in the mountains, too.

"For us, assimilation is tricky because we're predominantly Anglo-Saxon, so it is easier to make the transition. Nationally, the struggle for us is about better housing, more adequate jobs, better health care, and all those things that improve the quality of life, and yet somehow finding ways to maintain a value system that is in itself different from the mainstream—in part, because we haven't had the same benefits.

"I'm on a national team which is assessing a program of the Ford Foundation called The Rural Community College Initiative. Ford is trying to work with rural community colleges in distressed areas to get those local colleges to be more responsive to the local communities rather than designing their curriculum to a national-urban model. They're working with job creation to fit local culture, and they've identified four distressed areas: Appalachia, the Delta, tribal colleges, and the Southwest Chicano communities. We hope not only to learn how to preserve our cultures—because some of these groups have been successful in ways we can share and learn from—but also how to encourage economic development that is sensitive to sustaining local values. I see this cross-cultural pollination emerging in several other areas, finding ways to make those conscious linkages across the country that really haven't been there before, through organizations like the Ford Foundation and others. I'm really encouraged by that.

"I can only share with you why I do what I do and what I hope will happen in the region that I care about and am part of. In America, as a society today we have become a scattered people and, to a great degree, have lost a sense of connectedness. I think we have reached a crisis of national identity, who we are as a people, that has become a personal crisis among individuals and families.

"The kind of freedom that emerged after World War II for more of us to pursue career opportunities and education has brought many benefits to many people. It has also come at a deep loss for many of us as individuals, loss of connectedness to family. We are scattered all over the place, don't live close to each other any more, have a high divorce rate, suffer loss of relationships between parents and children and are no longer rooted in religion, which tends to be reflected now in the re-emergence of right-wing fundamentalism. All of those things to me are signs that we as a nation are really in a state of cultural crisis reflected in individual stress.

"I tell groups that I work with that there are some aspects of our traditional Appalachian culture that can not only serve as a model to the rest of the country but that can effectively help us move into the post-modern world with more confidence. There are aspects of our traditional culture we don't want to hang on to—racism, sexism, all kinds of negative values that are part of that tradition, too. And we need to be conscious of that. But on the other hand, there are certain things in the way we in the mountains relate to each other that are very positive, and we now recognize the rest of society is searching for this kind of meaning.

"They want a greater sense of what a family is. Hillary Clinton's book, *It Takes A Village: And Other Lessons Children Teach Us* indicates a point of view which is not a new concept. That's the way kids were raised in traditional communities, whether they were Native American, Chicano, Appalachian or African. Everybody had responsibility for the children, an idea we ought to find a way to rebuild. One of the myths that came to be accepted in Appalachia was this myth of individualism. There was local color literature and academic writing that will tell you that Appalachians are such individualists that you can't get them to join an organization. Everybody in Appalachia wants to do his or her own thing. That is not an accurate reflection of the traditional culture. The traditional culture is very dependent on cooperation. Anybody who grew up in the region knows that every kind of work—getting Sunday dinner together for the family, men hunting, working on old cars, getting the tobacco in—shares a very collective sense of responsibility to the group. We work together that way, and the group as a whole succeeds. It wasn't until industrialization that our jobs got separated out from those group ties and the value systems began to emphasize individualism. A lot of what people from the outside interpret as individualism is actually resistance on the part of mountain people to absorbing outside values.

"One of the ways we work here is through community development, rebuilding local networks in the region. Some of the steps we teach and work with are:

> "*Taking initiative—moving beyond defensiveness.* So many of us from minority groups are used to being defensive about the assaults other groups put on us, we spend all of our time defending our culture. We don't take initiative to move beyond defensiveness, which is the very first thing a group has to do.

"*Storing collective memory.* Only when people understand what's happened before them can they appreciate their community. We have elders tell stories. Appalachians do it by Jack Tales and story tales, sitting around the front porch and sharing family stories. We sense we are a community because we preserve the stories in our past which contrast with a modern society's tendency to ignore the past and cast our eyes only on the future.

"*Focusing on what it means to be part of a particular group.* Private virtue versus public virtue. Participation. Developing a sense of vision.

"*Vision process.* Here we work with community members to dream about the future, about what might be, about our assets, as well as our deficiencies.

"*Leadership.* The most effective leader in mountain culture is the one who gets people involved and then disappears back into the group. It is a different kind of leadership than the modern, corporate-style power management practiced in urban areas."

Ron Eller has found a focus that allows him not only to embrace both his traditional culture and the mainstream, but to support others who engage the same process. He has become a cultural interpreter of Appalachia at a national level.

Another highly educated Appalachian has returned home to the same region with a mission. Mary Lee Daugherty takes a slightly different slant on community development.

"Pastors in rural communities are often the people who are in the transition areas of people's lives. They deal with life crises, death, accidents, divorce, abuse and murder. That's where people go. They don't go to the clinical psychologist in rural communities. There are none."

No stranger to the mountains, or to leadership, Mary Lee Daugherty is Founder and Executive Director of The Appalachian Ministries Educational Resource Center (AMERC), described as "the largest consortial effort to emerge in the history of theological education in the United States—an ecumenical program which provides critically-needed specialized education and training for seminarians preparing to minister in the small towns and rural churches of Appalachia and beyond." This organization is beginning its second decade. Harvard and Yale Divinity Schools are listed among the forty-eight sponsoring institutions that back the program, and thirty-nine other theological institutions have sent students as well. In Appalachia, economic decline has undermined the basic structure of local communities, often leaving churches and schools as the only remaining institutions which can offer help—and hope—to the people.

Mary Lee's schedule is challenging. She travels, teaches, lectures, raises money and maintains family connections. She agreed to meet with me on a Sunday evening in early June, although it was a concession on her part because new students were arriving that evening and she wanted to be there to greet them. A tornado had torn through Berea, Kentucky, the week before our interview, partially destroying the newly renovated headquarters building, invading the main building at the AMERC farm, and leveling the warehouse that contained much of Mary Lee's personal property. Nonetheless, the new group of students would proceed on schedule.

Mary Lee wrote a dissertation about snake-handling Pentecostals, earned a Ph.D., is an ordained Presbyterian minister, taught at Harvard, missionaried in Brazil for three years and traveled to India. Superwoman perhaps? She is a quiet force whose understated personal presence in no way communicates her power. She is not shy and not pushy.

"I was born in southern West Virginia in coalfield country. My dad's family had all been in the mining industry for at least two generations, maybe three. My mother's family, on the other hand, had come from an Indiana farming background, but were involved in the glass industry in West Virginia. My dad's family was old time Methodist, Holiness-Pentecostals, which is often the religious ethos of the working poor, also of miners. Whereas my mother's family, more the Scots-Irish Presbyterians, believed you should do everything decently, in order. They were much more pro-rational and pro-education. I had a foot in both worlds. That's a positive if you're going to continue to walk both roads. At least for me, I appreciated from the time I was very little the contribution that both made. Also, each taught me to despise and reject the other. There was always this tension, always the tug-of-war, even for me as a kid. That's both good and bad.

"Part of what I learned in Brazil about how to speak a new language was to become a child again—reading about the country's history and culture and listening to the music that makes up a way of life. I began to get clues about how to help people who are experiencing culture shock in their own culture, but don't recognize it as such, as they move back and forth.

"It was astonishing to me that clergy would come out of a seminary in New York City, or say, California or Minnesota or Georgia, and come into the mountains and never read a book about Appalachia. They wouldn't understand the difference between rural and urban value systems and yet they assumed they could do effective work. It was just mind-blowing to me. I reflected on how hard I had to work to make the transition into Brazilian society.

"I really began to work with seminarians coming into my own church in West Virginia from the various seminaries from the cities, taking on their first congregations in rural and small town communities. They would come very excited, and in eighteen months they were ready to go back to what they knew.

"There were no cultural amenities. Their wives or husbands had a hard time finding work and were bored. For them, the church was program and not people. And time was money and not people. There was no appreciation or understanding of the whole different value structure and way of life organized around kinship, family traditions and rural customs.

"There are subcultures within our own culture, and I wondered how we could train a whole group of people born and raised in suburban, urban and inner-city environments who find themselves entering all denominations and ministries. How could we demythologize what it is to live in a rural community and agricultural environment? How could we ease the pain of it, understand it and be sympathetic to it? That was the basis on which I began putting this whole effort and curriculum together. I really had to experience it in another culture like Brazil's, because even though I had been walking between the two cultures, I did not recognize that was what I was doing.

"The way you teach people *edgewalking* is by introducing newcomers to the demographics—introduce them to the major issues that the region is struggling with—political, economic, social, migration patterns and labor history—and help them to understand the people. And, if they've never been on a farm and they're going into an agriculturally related community, then they need a whole understanding of the struggle that farmers deal with—not just intellectually. We want them to get in the dirt and get grubby.

"We're trying to contextualize the whole learning process. The seminarians are here in Berea for half a week of intellectual input, films, reading and research opportunities. But the most powerful thing that happens to them is the going out, settling in the homes with mountain people, riding around the county with them and working side by side with them on the farm or in the community organization. You need to go out there and live with people and grub around with them, muck out a latrine with them, and sit around the table and just listen, listen, listen.

"Most people want to give in a positive way. I personally get a lot of joy in helping people experience that. In the early part of my ministry, I watched so many disasters in rural communities, churches, school systems and clinics when people simply could not decode the language of those they were trying to help.

"When new people come in—like tonight—I'm going to say to them they have a unique opportunity here this summer to do three kinds of listening. Most of us are so accustomed to telling, if we're educators or teachers, that this is a special opportunity. I ask them to:

> "*Listen to each other.* Because many of you who are Roman Catholics, for instance, may have never really talked to Pentecostals. You've probably never even known any, or African-American Christians, or Native Americans—here's an opportunity and a free space to do that.

> "*Listen to the people in the region.* Go as participant observers not to preach or teach. We give them a whole exercise in knowing how to identify the power structures and the power brokers and different sociological ways to look at a rural community, church, extended family. Very importantly, also, we divide

people up, twice a week in groups of no more than nine or ten, to let them reflect on what they've seen and how they feel about it.

"Listen to themselves—what I call the work of the Holy Spirit, or the call of vocation. What is this going to mean to you economically, socially to bring your children in here, your wife or husband? Can you make the transition or are you discovering this is not for you?

"All of the faculty, including myself, have lived in different cultures. We have all had third-world experience and been through the transition process ourselves. That helps us with our international students, as well. And we do like to have every culture and religion in our mix—not only Catholic, Protestant, Evangelical, Pentecostal Holiness, black and white—but also people and students from other third world countries. When we're doing the economic analysis, or the sociological analysis, many of them say, 'It's just exactly like this in my country.' We're not having to make the point as we talk about food parcels or sweat shops. The international students identify with that and recognize that this Appalachian culture has dimensions of the third world.

"As we celebrate diversity, we come to appreciate that minority people have to understand how to get their vote, how to work the system in order to gain enough power to be valued in the specific structure of the society they are in. Empowerment through community development work is absolutely critical to help people stand up and see that being black is beautiful, or being white and from Appalachia is beautiful. Being Asian-American is beautiful. There has to be the kind of self-respect the women's movement learned in order to celebrate women, to feel good about yourself, then you can make an impact and place for yourself in the structure. Unless we learn self-respect and develop the ability to give and take as a society, we're going to be ripped apart by violence."

This last sentence, delivered with a matter-of-fact punch, revealed Mary Lee as a practical woman whose spiritual mission is larger than her commitment to her church. She takes that commitment to the most practical level with a very earth-bound understanding of the people of her region.

Both Ron and Mary Lee work at building a sense of community in different ways and through different institutions. They share deep commitment to the people of Appalachia and creatively work to link the region to the country's mainstream while helping Appalachian residents maintain the integrity of their culture. "Spinning between two worlds," as Ron puts it, is second nature to them, and they see the importance of moving from regional life to mainstream and back. Also, they understand the sensitivity of the process and that it requires personal courage and involvement to make a difference. Here are some of the main themes they discussed.

Translate culture in and out of the region.

Ron Eller: People like me take their personal experience with having feet in two worlds and their personal experience with mass society and its stereotypes and apply what they've learned to the larger Appalachian Region. We talk about that as a way to maintain a sense of community. You have to be constantly on the lookout to assure your family members and those in the traditional culture that you have not left them.

Mary Lee Daugherty: Part of what I learned in Brazil about how speak a new language was to become a child again—to begin at the beginning to read history, listen to music, learn about the things that make up a culture. I began to get clues about how to help people who are experiencing culture shock in their own culture, but don't recognize it as such, as they move back and forth.

Know your special identity.

Ron Eller: It dawned on me that I would be able to continue in college, not so much because I was individually successful, but because I was part of a minority group. I really feel that I am put here to straddle those two worlds. I do what I do because I think I owe it to somebody else. I've often said in some of the speeches that I give that at the time I really felt that I couldn't live with myself if I had gone off to become a lawyer and done one of these individual professions. For me there was something else that I had to do.

Mary Lee Daugherty: I really had to experience it in another culture like Brazil's, because even though I had been walking between the two cultures, I did not recognize that was what I was doing.

Tolerate being different.

Ron Eller: Those of us who came from different kinds of cultural experiences had to, in effect, rewrite history as a whole to indicate that our people also had one. In many ways that was a history very active and interactive with what had been previously understood and known. But you never quite fully fit in and are never quite comfortable on all that ground.

Some of us who are more attuned to having our sense of personal value reinforced by others and by how we relate to others, tend to be more conscious about who we're associated with and who we're tied to.

Teach the value of regional or ethnic difference, rather than trying to force conformity to the mainstream.

Ron Eller: What we now try to do when working with teachers is tell them, 'Rather than criticize the kid who says 'hit,' instead of 'it,' point out that it's fine, but there is also a way that you communicate in different settings so that both our ways of communicating are valued.'

Mary Lee Daugherty: The way you teach people *edgewalking* is by introducing newcomers to the demographics, introducing them to the major issues that the region is struggling with—political, economic, social, migration patterns, labor history—and help them to understand these people. You need to go out there and live with people and grub around with them, sit around the table and just listen, listen, listen.

Learn from other cultural groups and share expertise in relating to the mainstream.

Ron Eller: My people in the mountains need to understand what they have in common with people from the Delta, the Chicano community in the Southwest and the Native American community, and the fact that our histories are much the same in relationship to the larger culture. The very process of commodifiying people into groups perpetuates divisiveness.

There is the tendency for each of the minority cultures to abandon the struggle and become absorbed by that mainstream mass. We face that in the mountains too. For us, it's a problem because we're predominantly Anglo-Saxon so it is easier to make that transition. Nationally, the struggle for us is about better housing and more adequate jobs, better health care and all those things that make a better quality of life, and yet somehow we must find ways to maintain a value system that is in itself different from the mainstream—different in part because we haven't had all of those mainstream advantages.

Confront undesirable aspects of a culture.

Ron Eller: There are aspects of our traditional culture we don't want to hang on to—racism, sexism, all kinds of negative values that are part of that tradition, too. And we need to be conscious of that.

Promote constructive change through community development.

Ron Eller: One of the ways we work here is through community development, rebuilding community in the region.

Mary Lee Daugherty: Empowerment through the church and community development work is absolutely critical to help people stand up to see that being black is beautiful, or being white and from Appalachia is beautiful.

Both Ron Eller and Mary Lee Daugherty opt to stay in the mix, tolerate complexity and translate one side for the other.

"Maybe it's easier for us because we're Caucasians in a predominantly Caucasian culture," Ron had said. Maybe. Both Ron and Mary Lee learned to talk right, dress right and use the proper fork, but neither has sacrificed their integrity in the process. Their efforts in helping their people deal with the larger culture, and in helping the larger culture relate to their people, grows out of their capacity to do both.

A storybook doll about six inches high, blue eyes staring straight ahead, a rubber snake wrapped around her neck and body, stands on the console to the right of Mary Lee's front door. The tiny, blue-eyed doll with her reptile companion represents a way of life that many in people in our country have not seen or heard about.

As Mary Lee pointed out, "Yet many people in our nation are struggling with different types of symbolic snakes of evil and transition. Perhaps in rural Appalachia the deadly snakes to be overcome are just more visible. As rural life becomes more complex and poverty continues to increase, this doll-like image may still have meaning fifty years from now as people continue to struggle against the evils that continue to oppress them."

part four

SCANNING THE FUTURE
OF *EDGEWALKING*
New Harmonies,
New Challenges

"**M**y parents shipped me off to a Japanese orphanage for the summers when I was in junior high, for their own idealistic reasons," Barbara Arnn, once a Japanese scholar, now an editor, told me. "I learned to scan, to recognize cultural patterns and then make choices across them. You have to decide either to meet the expectations of the other people in whose culture you are, disappoint the expectations, defy them or ignore them."

Scanning the future requires this same ability to perceive patterns and determine where each nation fits in the global scene. Rapid communication and transportation make any part of the planet accessible to any other part. It becomes tougher to shut out growing pressures from ballooning populations, competing economic needs, and clashing religious and political views.

This section includes a spiritual/cultural experience in the Yucatan, an example of *edgewalking* beyond national borders with an eye toward global connection. In my own country, the United States, I feel we face a transition as important as those faced during and after the Revolution for Independence. Although, so far, conflict in this time of change has not reached military proportions as it did in those times, the shift from a mainly Anglo power structure to a truly multicultural one challenges the existing social system, both the formal legal parts and the less obvious tacit agreements we take for granted. But it is in the concept of each of us as citizens of the world that *edgewalking* makes its most profound statement about the future.

twelve

CONNECTING GLOBALLY
Acting Locally

There's an intensity to interfacing differences. What new can be discovered? Created? And then a sense of having done something wonderful. What talents and skills help this process? What motivation?

Writing this book has had an incremental influence on me. I feel more open, yet less sure of how to go about looking for information, humble about the complexity of cross-cultural communication. And absolutely dedicated to getting better at it. Loreen Lee was honest enough to tell me that I was over-enthusiastic about recruiting her to talk about *Edgewalkers*. I puzzle over how to get to know people without being intrusive. Is it possible? That sense of balance—just the right amount of intrusiveness, leaving space for the other to choose—seems to be the secret.

Having a place to stand, to look at what's going on in countries around the world offers perspective. Beyond opportunities at home to practice *edgewalking*, it makes sense to explore other cultures, move outside the familiar when we can. I made that choice in 1995 when a friend told me about a trip to the Yucatan to celebrate that year's spring equinox—a Mayan Solar Initiation. I decided to go when I heard about the event, but I rationalized the trip—the expense, the time, how flighty and impractical it seemed—telling myself it would be an opportunity to meet and interview *edgewalkers*. The organizers anticipated four hundred participants from all over the world. At least fifty more than that showed up. I didn't do one interview, but my experience there embodies much of what I think *edgewalking* means.

I put myself in a situation that was unusual for me: trying to understand the ancient Mayans. It was a spiritual journey of sorts, but nothing that I could articulate. Yucatan. Jungle. Pyramids. Equinox. Ancient prophecies. I simply wanted to go. According to the Mayan calendar, that was a special time, ending a 520-year era of darkness and entering a new cycle of light.

Beyond deciding to go, the first bit of *edgewalking* I did was attempting to put myself in the situation emotionally. I love to visit mystical spaces—pursue the intuitive and seek magic. But I'm a practical scientist as well. My skepticism challenges me—follows me, nagging, so I rarely land clean on one side or the other. Trying to stay open to my experience, my conflict stays with me. I decided to live with that ambivalence rather than diminish it. Staying in this space between my North American pragmatism and some amorphous spiritual/cultural exploration is another *edgewalking* step. I resisted the pull to go one way or the other—to split and be cynical about the side I hadn't chosen.

From the information I quickly collected I could not tell whether the leader, Mayan Shaman Hunbatz Men, was truly a spiritual person or a charlatan. I wanted to find out.

March 20, 1995. Celesttina, my Canadian roommate at the huge glitzy hotel in Merida, Yucatan, and I stepped into the lobby to merge with a mass of figures. Most had followed the leader's request, as had we, to wear white each day we did ceremony. The sight startled me. I hadn't planned on joining a cult.

To my reaction, Celesttina said, "They are just a lot of people dressed in white."

At the first ceremony site, Dzibilchaltun, 450 "initiates" from around the world spilled from mammoth air-conditioned buses. German, French, and Eastern, as well as many North American syntax collided in the sunlight. I felt like I had stepped into a movie soundtrack. Then it registered. The tropical bird sounds were real. Piercing screeches, whistles and warbles. Soft air. Heat and dust—and diesel fumes from our monster buses.

Paying attention to those sensual cues—the heat, the bird calls, the moisture in the air, even the diesel fumes—rather than pushing them out of my awareness, helped me move into this environment psychologically. It felt different than where I lived and I wanted to understand it.

Dzibilchaltun is a National Archaeological Site, a ruin near Merida. At dawn, on the equinox, the sun rises so that it is framed by the small temple's doorway as you approach from the west. We weren't there in time for that sight. The hot, white sun was already well in command when we arrived.

Chatter, white clothes, a collection of stragglers and pushers, we moved as directed onto the ancient grounds toward the *cenoté*, a shallow oval of crystal water with steep limestone edges—the sacred well.

The leader, "Hunbatz," I heard people call him, directed us in his sonorous voice, "Keep moving, circle the *cenoté*, we are going to open the initiation here." Just the process of moving this many people over rough ground had a calming effect. The ghostly forms around the old well looked Biblical, holy somehow. Pallid reflections wavered in crystal water, sprinkled with lily pads. Little fish went to school. Today was no special day in their lives.

Hunbatz shouted directions. "Look at the sun. Raise your arms to the sun. Become the sun."

He began to chant. "Kin, Kin," (pronounced KEEN) seven times, sacred syllables chanted. Kin, Kin, Kin, Kin, Kin. Four hundred voices wove the chant that hovered, cloudlike, above the cenoté.

A breeze chilled the sweat droplets, now forming on my face. Sunlight bounced off my white shirt. I felt the presence of the past.

I saw my roommate meditating as she stood, waiting for the next move. I joined her. I was doing something several *edgewalkers* talked about—learning by observing. Nobody told me how to do this, but I watched others and figured it out.

I peeled my attention from the organizational dynamics and second-guessing the leaders. A psychologist accustomed to assessing human motivation, I wondered about people who had chosen to interrupt their regular lives to spend this equinox week in the Yucatan with Hunbatz Men. And me—my habitual way of looking at the world and thinking about it, my *unconscious structures of belief*, were getting in my way. I tried to stop them and tune in exclusively to what was happening.

The *cenoté's* blue skin, smooth and cool, attracted me. I allowed the water's calm to slow my zooming calculations and ease into images of those who walked this place centuries ago, seeking the sacred. I closed my eyes and invited the ancient ones. Stood. Breathed. Cleared. Inner spaces opened. My tears slid forward, cooled my face and echoed the water's presence in me.

OAAHNNNNK. OOOAAAHHNNNNNNK. The bass roar of a huge reed pipe, wood flutes, the timbre of a hand drum, bells. Music has sung all the time, I guess, but just then entered my realm. Old music. Modern people making it. Under the royal poinciana, outlined in dazzling backlight, the musicians sparkled. This was their place. It was my place, too.

"We are going to circle the cenoté three times," Hunbatz' direction interrupted my reverie, "and then walk slowly to the temple."

"That will take 'til noon," I heard someone behind me snap sarcastically. She was right.

I told myself that time was unimportant. I absorbed the sun, appreciated the breeze and decided to move slowly over the rise behind the musicians toward the temple path.

The way unfolded, pale dust hung head-high, stones under foot, white-clad pilgrims, flat, lemon-colored light. I moved deeper into the line, feeling for quiet. I drank in the sun, let it in, breathed, cleared my head and meditated.

Celesttina walked by me, silently. I appreciated her quiet and moved into it. We walked, too fast for meditation, but I let my mind clear, almost.

The small temple sits its hill at the end of a treeless boulevard. I knew more dramatic structures awaited us at Chichén Itzá and Uxmal, but I was here to participate, so I walked on and relaxed into the experience. We circled the base of the structure's hill on a rocky path, savoring the shady side. I shot a couple of good angles, finished a roll of film and stowed my camera in my backpack. Relieved in a way, I quit watching photographically, sinking more deeply into a meditative state. The ever-shifting group splayed whitely on the sun-bathed flat before the temple. Hunbatz directed the initiates to ascend the steep stone steps in groups of five.

About halfway up the hand hewn granite, the power of the place stunned me and I unexpectedly gasped for breath. Heavy, sweet air bathed me in awe. Tears started to fall again as I imagined sacred ceremonies held there. Inside, initiates hugged the walls, wept, meditated, chanted and drummed. Views from window openings skimmed the jungle in all four directions. I knew this place as sacred. I wanted to pause indefinitely but couldn't forget that four hundred people needed to move through before lunch. Being efficient, I left, went outside and waited for Celesttina. She took her time. I was beginning to understand.

Late afternoon, Chichén Itzá. Sun God, Great Spirit, overarching presence of the divine, Hunab K'u. It was ninety-five degrees Fahrenheit on the turf before the Temple of Kukulkan—*El Castillo* the Spaniards called it—the main pyramid at Chichén Itzá. Arms out, embracing the sun, the people held their hands over their heads, acknowledging the Great Spirit. Seven times they repeated, "Kin, Kin, Kin, Kin, Kin, Kin, Kin." Deep elliptical notes rose and fell—resonating through spaces between sound.

Tomorrow was the equinox. I was grateful for today's visit without the larger crowd. The previous year, thirty thousand showed up to see Kukulkan, sacred serpent symbolizing fertility and new life (Quetzalcoatl, in Aztec lore), appear and slide down the pyramid. For about a half-hour at the Equinox, the play of sun and shadow painted the snake on the north balustrade of the monument's side. This gift of Mayan astronomical genius was what we had come to see. Tomorrow, thousands would view the phenomenon.

Hunbatz assembled two native women and six or seven native men before our huge delegation seated on the west side of the pyramid. He introduced the newcomers as "The Supreme Mayan Council," and explained that even though foreigners could come to the pyramids and do ceremony, the Mayan people could not. The Mexican government controlled the anthropological sites and prohibited native religious practices there. He began a statement, using a hand-held, battery-operated microphone, honoring the council as the first contemporary Maya to celebrate the Equinox at this site in current times. After his first or second sentence, a booming roar issued from the "official" loudspeaker, drowning his voice, so only those seated closest could hear. Nobody moved.

Chichén Itzá, March 21, 1995. Forty-five thousand people assembled for the special equinox. Picnicking, milling, mostly subdued, the crowd swelled through the day. Our group of four hundred plus was there early, before the throngs arrived.

Strategically placing our busloads of people around the Temple of Kukulkan, we easily surrounded the pyramid's huge symbolic mass. We encircled it three times—letting the monument symbolize the body of Hunab K'u, and the group representing the spirit. Forming the circle wasn't difficult, but moving it was. Hunbatz, obviously frustrated that something so apparently simple could bog down, stomped his feet and yelled, "Walk, Walk! You are the spirit of Hunab K'u. Move!"

Finally, enough people stepped at the same time to grease the skids, and the sluggish human wheel turned. I chose my morning's dream theme, *Born before the time of dawn,* for meditation and let my mind travel into the emptiness of time before time.

The thermometer climbed its own pyramid. Thirst reached into my throat and grew. We were circling quickly now, holding hands, twisting my chronically sore shoulder so it hurt. I tightened my grip, pictured young braves hanging from high places with sticks piercing their pectoral muscles seeking visions in rites of passage.

Closing my eyes, I was in a different reality. The third time around, I traveled without effort through magical dimensions, new energy flowing through me. Carmine, ochre and flame swaths, bits of light flying off them, twined through my vision. Warmth penetrated my being. I felt at one with the sun, the breeze and the long gone architects whose holy geometry elegantly memorialized this site.

The ancient Maya predicted that a brother from lands way beyond the sea would come to awaken the people after a period of darkness. Dressed in colors of the sun, his visit would reconnect the Maya with an age-old commitment to their solar creator. He would restore cosmic knowledge to be shared with all members of the sacred human race.

Representing Tibet's exiled Dalai Lama who had been invited but did not attend, three red and gold robed lamas participated in ceremonies, enduring hours in the searing sun. At one point, these visitors stood with a group of Mayan healers and the Supreme Mayan Council to close a segment of the initiation. Hunbatz invited participants to file past them in a single line—to greet? Acknowledge? Be blessed? Request healing? I was not clear about the instructions, but I recognized potential for a special moment.

Waiting with an uneasy self-consciousness, I overheard an outspoken woman nearby ask, "What do you say to a lama in line? 'Is it hot under those robes? How's the family?'"

Her irreverence nudged me off balance at first, and then helped me think more about my next step. I decided I would just make eye contact with each person in the line—the healers, the monks and the Supreme Mayan Council.

That's how I began.

When I reached the first woman, who had earlier been introduced as a native healer, a *curandera*, the depth in her eyes and the softness of her face pulled me, and I spontaneously reached out to shake her hand. Then I shook hands with the rest and searched their eyes. Other ruins, jungles and the shifting crowd wove a background. These powerful ones stood firmly at the massive base of the pyramid. Each looked at me steadily, and I looked back. As I finished the line, I felt filled with light, as if I might spin to the top of the sun-painted monolith behind me.

I knew that each of those individuals was a real person, lived and breathed, and had limitations just as I did. But, in addition, each embodied his or her own spiritual connection, power, and willingness to participate with others from that place. Whoever they were, and whatever their motivations, they gave me something I will never forget.

We completed our ceremony before noon. Later that day, cross-legged on the stickery, short, warm grass before the Temple of Kukulkan at Chichén Itzá, waiting for just that moment when the hot spring sun would cast the magical serpent's shadow on the ancient structure, I was struck by how far I seemed from my usual reality. And how happy I felt being there. I looked up at the huge pyramid and tried to imagine it in its heyday. Thousands of others, most of them Mexicans, transported there in huge buses that now lined the nearby roadways like empty cocoons, waited for the shadow to reach exactly the right place. People in the crowd had been batting clear plastic water bottles in the air, giving the impression of oblong bubbles flitting around, but now a hush settled. The serpent was nearly complete on the balustrade of the pyramid. From my pragmatic side, it seemed slightly excessive that forty thousand people were waiting for a shadow. And yet, when the time came, conches sounded, bells rang, drums played, people chanted and I felt their spirit within me. It didn't matter that I was a middle-aged, middle-class psychologist from Sacramento.

I have unwrapped gifts from that spring's journey over the past years. The first two days shared there were just the beginning. Meditating in the sun, honoring the Maya and contemplating infinite time strengthened me. Feelings of deep connection with the past and future echoed those I had the year before, peering through tears at Upper Paleolithic paintings in Grotte Lascaux, France. Suddenly, I knew my significance—and insignificance—in time and space. And I felt hopeful, appreciating that humans seek and find meaning. Enduring art speaks through millennia.

I have developed a sense that *edgewalking* includes, for its participants, this placement in history—a sense of timelessness and continuity, as well as morality. From that perspective, it becomes easier to handle life's challenges.

The joy of ceremony in and around the Mayan ruins—holding hands with antiquity—lingered. Fascinated by such ceremonies and practices, I decided to make them mine, part of my everyday life beyond the zeal of special trips or seminars.

Edgewalking invites courage and creativity to synthesize the unfamiliar and exotic with the mundane. This balance has potential to give birth to a future for our world that is not possible otherwise. Learning to *edgewalk* holds the possibility of transcending a future locked in perpetual power struggles that become increasingly violent.

The people with whom I have spoken while writing this book have found ways to manage their personal diversity without abandoning its complexity. One of the challenges I have faced as I have tried to elicit the *edgewalking* process is to practice what I have come to understand as its principles. I have tried to look at what works and doesn't work as we impact each other at home, on the job, in the world at large. I want to know what characteristics *edgewalkers* share with each other, what constellation of personal traits sets them apart and how I can improve on those traits in my own journey.

It would be easy to think that *edgewalkers* are just unusually talented people and that they come by their competence naturally. Or that they were born into circumstances that forced their competence. To some extent that may be true, but a deeper look at their lives shows that they have their struggles and learn from them, just as the rest of us can. On the other hand, many people are born into multi-cultural or diverse circumstances who do not choose *edgewalking*.

Among the personal traits I have noticed in all *edgewalkers* are: high energy, curiosity and openness. As I asked questions of them, they voiced questions as well. How did I get interested in this subject? Who else had I talked to? And excitement: "That's me!" several exclaimed. "Nobody has ever asked me anything like this before. I never thought about it this way." Generally, they were not offended by an awkward question or comment on my part, but would help me out. They seemed to share a generosity of spirit, communicating in various ways, *we're all in this together*.

The *edgewalkers* I met see relationships among things and look at the big picture. They think holistically and abstractly as well as concretely. Although many are accomplished professionals or technicians, they see these skills as means to ends more than goals. They have a kind of patience which enables them to put up with lack of certainty better than many people, they don't have to know for sure what the next step is but can wait to decide. They have capacity to choose one (person, idea, activity) without judging others as wrong. They also seem to stay a little detached from immediate outcomes and are aware of a bigger picture.

Each in his or her own way touches upon a sense of the divine, something bigger than the individual. This reference is typically oblique rather than well-defined and does not have to do with organized religious practice in most cases. A feeling of humility seems to be part of this aspect.

In conversations about transition between cultures, the *edge-walkers* often pause, take their time, and then use examples to illustrate their experiences. They tend to be storytellers and to have thought about their lives. I walk away from them feeling touched, enriched and inspired.

Many of these characteristics are things that thoughtful people can practice and develop. Although many more lessons can be gleaned from the text, here are ten main *edgewalker* themes that emerge.

1. Self-knowledge is the key.

Self-understanding from both psychological and cultural points of view is an imperative concept.

As Jahi McCurtis says, "I grew from learning how to be white—I thought that was the only way to positive self-hood—to realizing that attitude had me all out of sync."

Not only understanding oneself, but using that knowledge to test reality as defined by others is part of this theme. From her background in native culture, Patricia Nell Warren recognized, "something was off in this literature...much of what is written about native people and their ways was written by white men, educated in Judeo-Christian tradition. How in the world could they translate what they were told by native people who had a very different view of life?"

The art of bringing that self-knowledge to bear on the culture comes together when we can learn about our ethnic or spiritual background and choose aspects of it to honor in everyday life. Then we can pay attention to *edgewalking* and stay true to something that is not taken for granted in whatever mainstream we inhabit through learning to express difference in a non-adversarial way.

Difficult as it may be, honoring one's complexities, rather than trying to simplify, comes out of profound self-knowledge. Self-knowledge is the basis in knowing and sticking to your principles in order to see where they will lead.

2. Acknowledge and work through your own pain and rage.

This theme was stated in various ways: *Move through your pain, reach the other side of rage, move beyond blame and cultural splitting.* In addition to painful issues of racism and discrimination of various kinds, the particular pain that *edgewalkers* describe as steps toward self-affirmation has to do with not fitting in easily with either culture with which they identify.

As Rachel Guerrero pointed out: "The people on the advisory committee, high level 'minority' professionals from all over the country, have done their personal work—reached the other side of their rage, whether through psychotherapy or some other method—so we can work together in ways that are *culturally competent*. We have learned to make room for each other as we try to solve overwhelming problems that all of us face on a daily basis in our jobs."

This may mean, in addition to dealing with one's personal feelings, learning about conflict management in a focused way. Although some individuals may have a natural talent for peacemaking, this process involves more skill than natural talent. If you work or live in a situation where you have the ability to influence group thought or process, it makes sense to become competent with technology that is readily available today for understanding and managing conflict. More than anything, this process requires the ability to overcome or resist temptations to *split*.

3. Personal flexibility and flair for embracing paradox permeates the *edgewalkers'* persona and discussions.

They say: Develop flexibility, stay flexible, pay attention when you step back and forth between cultures, find ways to embrace change that include others different from yourself, move between personal self and cosmic connection, promote flexibility and continuous learning, translate culture in and out of your region.

Although each of the themes listed here includes a necessary aspect of *edgewalking*, the business of flexibility and capacity to embrace paradox is the one that makes standing astride two cultures possible.

As Joey Garcia explained, "All this potential exists within each of us. It is like little doors opening inside—a door to understanding a particular pattern of speech, or way of seeing the world or relating to a person."

Multiple views have the potential to make room for all. When you get beyond two, adding another becomes easier. It becomes possible to move beyond the duality of yours or mine into an inclusive plurality.

Even though some people take great glee in ridiculing governance by committee and the consensus process has gone through its trials, $N + 1$ *is* richer than a single point of view. Knowing how to appreciate and facilitate group process in informal settings promotes the possibility of including multiple points of view. The skill is one of community building, rather than promoting rugged individualism. It's a shift the world is ready for.

4. Promote constructive change through community development.

Whether it is at the level of creating a support base for people of one's own identity group, such as Rufus Burrows discussed, or efforts to rebuild a region as demonstrated by Ron Eller and Mary Lee Daugherty, *edgewalkers* work to better the world.

Recognize commonalities, look at the big picture, value relatedness as more important than money or power—are some of the messages that come through *edgewalker* conversations.

When Mary Lee Daugherty says, "Empowerment through community development work is absolutely critical to help people stand up to see that being black is beautiful, or white and from Appalachia is beautiful," she speaks to a major element of *edgewalking*. The step away from homogenization and into respecting differences as part of the whole is a huge one.

5. Be willing to speak out.

Here is where courage comes in. Risk being alone, be willing to confront, encourage willingness to dissent, acknowledge the diversity myth, be clear that the underlying cultural assumption is white, acknowledge the spiritual vacuum in modern society, confront undesirable aspects of your own culture.

Carol Parrish-Harra put it bluntly. "You have to be willing to be the bad guy, which is the hardest of all for women in the spiritual field." It's difficult for men and women in almost any field because saying the unspeakably different thing often means losing the approval of peers or colleagues. Because *edgewalkers* carry conflicting cultures within themselves, they frequently find themselves in the position of saying things that are unacceptable to one group or another.

6. Use what you have learned about yourself to reach out.

Use personal experience with prejudice to understand the pain of others. Allow connection with others through spiritual enlightenment.

Loreen Lilyn Lee expressed it as clearly as it can be said. "I try to include others mostly because I've been excluded, and I know how it feels. It hurts."

This approach is one that sets *edgewalkers* apart from many other people who use their pain to justify excluding or demeaning others. For whatever reasons, they choose to use their personal experience as a platform for helping others. By doing so, they create a huge, human chain that connects people who would otherwise have little in common.

7. Embrace your own differentness.

As a professor, Satsuki Ina takes a direct approach in addressing this issue: "When I'm teaching a multicultural counseling class, a good part of my emphasis is on helping the white students find their ethnic identification so they can have a ground from which they begin to see why it's so cherished to have this ethnic identity. It's a strength to be able to walk that edge. It's not an edge that only people of color learn to walk, but is a transferable skill that can be generalized if it's viewed as a creative process. It helps people to become more resilient, more willing to have less black-and-white thinking. It teaches tolerance."

The melting pot no longer is the guiding philosophy for how to be an American. As it becomes more acceptable for people to acknowledge their differences and still be counted, the beauty of that complexity can emerge in our culture.

Seek your sacred path.

After his mother was murdered, Lee Mun Wah responded to the situation in a manner consistent with the way he lives his life. "I wasn't too sure who was imprisoned, the persons I was protecting myself from or the fear that was imprisoning me. I didn't want to live my life like that. I thought the only cure for fear is really to trust again, which has the possibility of getting hurt—being devastated again, being left. I felt like the only way I could also allow love to come back into myself and to love other people was to trust them. I don't know what any body else's process is, but I do know that has helped me."

Lee Mun Wah's sacred path is not about practicing a particular religion or proselytizing others. It is about opening himself and offering his energy as a channel for change.

Cultural change is three feet away. It happens individually. This is what Lee Mun Wah tells the participants in the powerful workshops he does in corporate, educational and government settings all over the country. It isn't necessary to take on the world. You only need to be present, attentive, and expressive with the person next to you.

The message from the *edgewalkers* is not about a particular path, but that we all share basic roots in humanity, and through those we can connect with each other.

Create something new.

Basho Fujimoto summarized the *edgewalking* process succinctly: "Our interest is not about taking traditional elements from our old cultures and mixing them altogether, making a nice, evenly distributed multiculturalism. It is more like taking just the consciousness of all of our heritage and bringing in one point and working with that to create something new."

Looking to the future, creating new forms, walking the edge, all contribute to innovative possibilities for pulling our world beyond dualistic conflict into a new era.

Edgewalkers living their views make a difference. Laura Munoz, sitting in my living room telling me about her experiences in Mexico and in Sacramento, sharing views on cross-cultural communication, emphasized her point much more richly than any other method can. I saw Laura. I heard her pain and her excitement. I imagined what it would be like to be in her job, with her knowledge. She was not a statistic. She was a person.

10. Make a point of getting to know people different from yourself.

Look around. Count the opportunities you have to do just that. Pay attention to your own reticence and see what you can do to soften it. Be sensitive to the possibility that others have the same hesitations, and see what you can do to make it easy for them to relate to you.

Under the surface, tension and resistance to change continue, despite real and token change at a more visible level. Our world has never before been home for so many varieties of people coinciding with such wonderful possibilities for cultural support. We have an opportunity to step forward in the evolution of human understanding or we can choose to continue hardening our dualities into perpetual conflict.

Participating in the Mayan Solar Initiation thrilled me. It affirmed my intuitive risk to step outside the predictability of my life to join a global community, if only for a short while. I could wear its magical colors wherever I went, and return to its powerful images when I chose. The radiance of sacred serpents, jungles, Mayan temples, and the sun's colors shone on my journey.

I had never voluntarily participated in a group with which I had less in common. People from all spectra attended that event, from practical community development workers to mystics in communion with inter-spatial beings. Each traveler sought his or her meaning in the activities we shared. What people did have in common was the sense of new-beginning, optimism about the human condition, commitment to a better world.

The ancient Mayan concept that ancestors arrived from the stars and inhabited not only Central America, but Greece, Egypt, Peru, India and other cultural centers created a new perception for me. Including the Tibetan Lamas (the Hopi had been invited, too) as leaders in the Solar Initiation spoke to a global view. It was *edgewalking* on a mythic scale.

I think about how to carry forth what I have learned here in my own life, and I have come up with four steps that I can manage on an individual basis. These personal efforts don't negate the value of pro-active commitments or inter-cultural activity, which are needed too. But as an individual, just being true to myself, I can have influence when I do the following:

1. Stay conscious.

Pay attention to what I see and experience, not what I think should be happening or what I've heard. Listen for feedback about my *unconscious structures of belief.*

2. Look for places with temptations to *split* and work to integrate those.

This is the most available, and perhaps most difficult, opportunity for personal (cultural) change. When I resist acting out my anger in one way or another, but move to promote connection, I am practicing what I preach.

3. Reach out when I have the opportunity.

Recently, in a bookstore, I started talking with an African-American woman who was looking for a book in the "Writing" section. As we spoke, she told me in some detail about a dream she had had where she was in a crisis situation and the people in the house where she went for help could not see her. Her comment affirmed my efforts to move through my protective reticence and speak with her.

4. Speak out when I hear others *splitting.*

This is a verbal form of walking the edge between two people who have just started fighting. But done judiciously, perhaps with humor, offering the possibility of a middle ground or something that does not force a choice one way or another can be genuinely helpful. Where this speaking out helps most is in a group situation where sides are polarizing. When neither side feels right, it probably isn't.

The sense of belonging and hope, of global connection and human possibility is part of what *edgewalking* offers as we, across the world, choose our path toward the future. By definition, that connection must be made with people who have more differences than similarities to each other.

Any one of us is in danger of falling off one side or the other at any moment, and from time to time that happens. Part of the nature of *edgewalking* is its uncertainty. But in a world suffering from many forms of divisiveness, risk-taking, building relationships on the edge, is something each of us can do in our own hometowns across the globe.

thirteen

BEYOND THE ENLIGHTENMENT
Patterns and Contradictions

The ideal, born of the Age of Enlightenment, that an individual's (man's) rights are inalienable, was once new thinking in political, personal and spiritual development. Today, this powerful idea at the root of Western society's existence is that edge from which both our magic and our troubles grow. The resulting rugged individualism inspires achievement, even conquest, but commitment to community sometimes takes a back seat.

Looking at the world through the eyes of the *edgewalkers* offers a new perspective beyond the Enlightenment. The challenge is to include our past vision with a new concept for the future. *Edgewalking*, the fine art of cross-cultural empathy, communication and economic-political inclusion, is a strong alternative to *splitting*, or ultimately, revolution.

Redefining, at a subconscious and visceral level, the meaning of our world's inhabitants as interwoven in the new millennium and thereafter, is what this book is about. I envision something close to the true spirit of democracy that I learned about in grade school. All men (meaning people) are created equal, as in we are all equal in the eyes of the law, no matter our country of citizenship.

I voted in a primary election recently. The garage around the corner where I exercise my right and privilege, available to people of my gender less than two decades before my birth, was empty. Three middle-aged women tended the voting booths and ballot box.

"The turnout is always light at primaries," one of them half-apologized as she saw me looking around.

So in America and in other countries as well, it gets to be government by the politicians, not the people. And certainly not people of color, or women, dissimilar to the overwhelming majority of politicians.

How can school children today, taught the ideals of brotherhood, respond to these ideals if they conflict with their experience living in prejudice, poverty or war?

And yet, the energy that flows from the enlightened of the past—those bloody grass roots that sustain life that is real, earth-connected and potent—offers an unacknowledged force for creating something new. Nevertheless, some people throughout our world are working to preserve the ecology, improving relations among identifiable groups, understanding and promoting the conditions for reducing violence and building bridges.

However, the contrast between building the world and building the world's people is the edge that emerges more and more clearly over time. The less noble aspects of our world built on conquest, eminent domain, slavery and genocide scream their presence. They spew into ethnic wars, street violence, corporate greed and grand scale hypocrisy or far as sexual morality.

The state of the art in organizational and individual psychology is such that we know about inclusive decision-making and conflict management. With time and resources, we can diagnose and treat many of the kinds of disorders that lead to violent, acting-out behavior. But the money goes into control rather than development. We have the potential to manage complex social problems, but seem shortsighted about investing in that potential on a large scale. The tendency is to react and do something about the symptom, like building more prisons, rather than investing in the complex, difficult work of providing *culturally competent* social and educational programs.

Places where a lot of poor Americans live jammed together, riddled with drugs and violence, are terrifying. I get scared traveling through certain parts of my own and other countries—especially at night. I haven't reached the point where I will stay home, but I can imagine that happening. However, we have the capacity to fix, or at least greatly improve these situations; yet, in many cases we don't.

This is especially sad in America. To have the resources and the philosophy that we are equal under the law and not act accordingly creates a painful contradiction. In countries where there is a blatant caste system or no enlightened, humanistic philosophy, the expectation is different.

And yet, the philosophy of enlightenment is out there and should make a difference.

Being a citizen of the world will mean being able to determine what you want in your life, figure out what it takes to get there, scrape together the resources you need, work hard to make it happen. A better life is not guaranteed, but the promise is there. Breaking convention along the way may be part of it. Staying within the law is also part of it, as well as respecting the rights, if not always the wishes, of others.

In America, we have typically visualized this pattern—for white men. The difference now is that it applies to me, a woman, and to people who have not typically had that access in the past. In the beginning, in college, I was often the only woman in the upper-division political science classes I took. When I finished my doctorate in psychology, affirmative action opened doors that might have stayed shut without it. That year, universities were looking for "ethnics and women" to fill positions.

The contradiction is that we still have many people in our country who do not have access to this path of upward mobility. Arguably, the people who are most blocked are those born into limited financial straits who, from the get-go, have fewer resources. Sorting out the cause and effect that sifts proportionately more people of color into this financially deprived status is almost impossible. People do get out. Several of the *edgewalkers*, Rachel Guerrero, Frank LaPena and George Esquibel relied on both their talent and their determination to make lives different from their backgrounds. And yet, they stay connected with their roots.

The delicate balance between freedom to be all that you can be and respect the rights of other people seems to be the heart of what it means to have a global perspective. *Edgewalkers* have a deep sense of this process and risk themselves to support others in their journeys.

But America, like other countries, also has an incredibly dark side. More Vietnam veterans have killed themselves since the end of that "guerrilla action" than were killed in the war, a terrible commentary on our lack of commitment to people who sacrificed for their country. The vestiges of colonial genocide still haunt the woods and plains where the first people lived before the Europeans arrived. Racism, classism and "attitude" hang on from the time that slavery was a way of life in the American South.

This shadow is similar in other parts of the world.

I see the homeless, their possessions stacked in and tied onto shopping carts, tread past my office in midtown Sacramento. The homeless, many of them mentally ill, are the hopeless underclass in the land of plenty. Again, this sight, with slight variation, is repeated in other countries. The old order can't hold. New is emerging, but its definition hasn't quite formed and resistance is strong. Civil unrest is one signpost of the problems that bubble and boil in the world's nightmare. But other events of less violent proportion signal conflict and uncertainty.

Laura Santigian is a scholar who's visited 140 sites in sixteen different states in the United States trying to get a fix on how citizens define what it is to be an American, particularly in the West. She is interested in whose stories are told and held to be important.

"I've done a lot of speaking and writing about an exhibit entitled *The West as America* at the Smithsonian in nineteen ninety-one. It caused a nationwide brouhaha," Laura told me.

"The Smithsonian hung these artworks—Western art and images of the frontier—and then asked some questions about the kinds of attitudes, particularly toward Indians, that were in the paintings. Some historians and a couple of Senators attacked the exhibit as un-American, wanted to diminish funding for putting what they called 'leftist propaganda' up on the wall. This exhibit looked at both the triumphs *and* the tragedies of westward expansion. It questioned the costs of westward expansion to the people who were already there. It looked at the kinds of ideologies that were expressed within these artworks that might give us insight into dealings with power as a nation-building entity.

"Near the exit of the exhibit, as is frequently the case, the museum supplied comment books for visitors to write in. These writings took on a life of their own as over three thousand people stood in line to add their comments. Those pages recorded a debate about who and what is American, whose stories can be told, and what is important.

"At the time, right around the Gulf War when patriotism was at a peak, 'Supporting the troops' was a defining force of what it means to be an American. So an "attack" on an American icon, the American West, in the Smithsonian Institution—which is as close to an American shrine as we have—created an explosion. The notion of Americanism was the core of the debate. Many people hold a strong notion that you can't acknowledge the problems in this country and still be a good American.

"We need to imagine an America that is every bit as complex as what faces us now, one in which we begin to understand that not one of us is free until all of us are free, that it doesn't do for us to say that when people try to hold on to their own racial and ethnic cultures that we're supporting the balkanization of America. If we want to build an America where people feel related to each other, then we're all responsible to each other. Dialogue about difference is essential."

At the most basic, personal level, *edgewalkers* offer views of cross-cultural cooperative possibilities and carry on "dialogues about difference." Fair or unfair, corporate greed, politics and international conflicts are realities that are here to stay. Takeovers, downsizing and moving manufacturing offshore for cheaper labor impact large numbers of workers and their dependents. But we can also impact life at an individual, personal level as more of us become experts at dealing with difference.

"I'm not offended when people make insensitive remarks. I try to create a teaching opportunity," Denise Senter of Indianapolis told me. "I assume they've had little experience with my African/Native American world, and don't know how to get around in that realm. Most of my experience with these conversations is good."

Denise is practiced at holding her own and absorbing the recoil that race innuendos invite. She was direct when I asked her how she does it.

"[I do it] by having conversations with people who don't seem that comfortable with me as an African-American woman, who may have come to certain conclusions about what my life is like or what my experiences have been. They may avoid talking to me, or they may reveal assumptions they've made in the way they talk that jar me. Instead of being put off, I take their actions as an opportunity to explore, and then invite them to share more about their ideas."

As the world's complexion changes, old assumptions about

who is an ideal citizen of a particular nation don't work. Our "structures of belief" need revision. Antiquated biases, prejudices and stereotypes can give way to a new sensitivity and skill at knowing people for who they are—not for their skin color, their religion or where their grandparents were born.

If we pay attention to those like Denise Senter who effectively confront racism in their own lives, we can find ways to hear America's and the world's pain differently. It will change the way we are. The challenge is to develop and incorporate new standards which each individual can hold as her or his own, standards that dissolve the duality between "them" and "us."

A broader range of acceptance can reduce the *splitting* that sets people against each other. Even though it is hard to maintain firm footing on the edge astride two cultures without slipping more to one side or the other, *edgewalkers* can show us the way to maintain our balance.

fourteen

WHERE DO WE GO FROM HERE?

It took two thousand years to build the temple at Karnak; they worshipped in it for two
thousand years and it's been a ruin for two
thousand years—and the state it's in now is
very impressive. What was it like with the
golden gates and the painted pillars?

David Hockney, *That's the Way I See It*

Sitting on the banks of the Nile, alone, artist David Hockney
reflected and wrote about his impression of Egypt—of how the
remnants of antiquity have a way of mirroring our personal insignificance and our shared humanity at the same time. *Edgewalking* crosses
time and space as well as cultures. By opening our hearts, as David
Hockney did, we receive gifts from the past and have the opportunity
to preserve them for future generations.

The fact is we do all live on the same spinning globe. Our
choice is to learn to get along or do ourselves in, one way or another.
The exciting news is that many efforts, like the Mayan equinox celebration, the CASSP Advisory Committee, Mary Lee Daugherty's
AMERC and others all over the world offer hope for the brighter of
the two options.

A handful of Native American artists from California traveled to Latvia in the summer of 1998. During the weeks they spent
there, they participated with Latvian artists to create cross-cultural
works—people from both sides of the world handling the same canvas, sculpture or ceramic. When I visited American Indian
Contemporary Arts in San Francisco to see the products of this *edgewalking*, I was not disappointed. The imagery communicates cultural
sharing beyond language barriers. There was no "blending" here.
Images from cultures of both the Latvian and Indian artists remained
intact, and in harmony, in the same work. The artists sparked each
other's creativity. And they visually demonstrated their compatibility.

Conversing with the gallery's executive director, Janeen
Antoine, I learned about another cultural exchange that has been
going on for some time. She invited me to view a video documentary,
If Only I Were an Indian, about people in Czechoslovakia who adopt
the practices and lifestyle of Native Americans. These aficionados in
Czechoslovakia, Germany, Russia and other Eastern Bloc countries
"become Indian" for varying lengths of time.

In the film there were three Natives from Manitoba, Canada,
who visited an "Indian camp" in Czechoslovakia. A man and two
women exited a shiny, white rental van, dressed in everyday western
clothing. As they walked toward a sprawling collection of teepees,
smoke from campfires streaked the horizon. Horses, dogs and partially bare bodied "Natives," painted, wearing feathers and ceremonial regalia, came whooping toward them. The Czech "Indians" welcomed their visitors. Over the week or so they spent together, they
shared recipes and cooking chores, made art and played music
together, talked endlessly, danced and were part of the ceremony.

The Czech "Indians" are people who, in their disenchant-
ment with the sparseness of their own culture during the communist
regime, found meaning in Native American lifestyles, which they
researched and interpreted to the best of their ability. Some of their
people have even come to North America to study Native language.
"Indians" in the various European countries may adopt the practices
of a particular tribe or tribal group, or they may be Pan-Indian, incor-
porating bits and pieces from assorted tribal groups.

The Native people from Manitoba in the film talked about
mixed reactions to the experience. On one hand, they were deeply
touched by the interest of the Czechs. On the other, they felt ripped-off,

that someone had taken their culture out of context and adopted it as their own. As the video ended, the Canadian visitors seemed to have formed close relationships with their "Indian" hosts.

This process of cultural imitation is not really *edgewalking*, because the people doing it abandon their own culture as much as they possibly can in order to *assimilate* another. What it does portray, however, is the permeability of international boundaries, irrelevance of time and geographical distance and the power of cultural sharing.

The European "Indians" dedicated themselves to learning about Native tradition, creating costumes, cooking Native foods, living under conditions typical of two centuries ago. With very limited resources, they manufactured carrying cases, "skins" for their teepees, special gear for their horses. Over the short period of time, they saw the value in a culture different from their own.

As the people from Manitoba dealt with their culture shock and their mixed feelings, they appeared to soften toward their imitators and formed personal bonds. *That* is an example of *edgewalking*.

The Czech Indians were reaching for something deep and indigenous, maybe the same mystical connection David Hockney described at the Pyramids. Or what Sharon Dryflower Reyna meant when she said, "I'm just a piece of sand. But I see far beyond that—to people in Australia, Tibet. We're all interwoven."

The next steps on the global frontier include listening to conflicting voices within ourselves. When we can find ways to hear our own pain with compassion, it will change the way we listen to others. The challenge is to open the little doors within ourselves, dissolve the duality between "them" and "us."

Like David Hockney, we can acknowledge that our civilization has come a long way. We have complex technology for conflict resolution and problem solving that is not built on force. It comes down to individual people tolerating difference, being able to compromise (sometimes sacrifice) enough to build mutually agreeable solutions. But for many people, the frustration of working toward peaceful solutions is too great.

Reverend Carol Parrish-Harra described the difficulty of going against the grain, proposing compromise when others want to fight. "The *edgewalker* role is valuable here, but most of the time it's sort of put down. They're seen as troublemakers, out of step. When you want to credit an *edgewalker*, you color them as a dissident artist, inventor, daring one, change agent, yeast in the bread. They are little, rough-edged, unpolished gems put into those places to help us advance—look at things we don't want to see, find answers we didn't know existed."

Those rough-edged, unpolished gems do make a difference. They are symbols of people who often push their ways in, seeming like outsiders to just about everyone, including themselves.

One such individual, Terry Cahn-Tober, a clinical psychologist on the Navajo reservation at the time we talked, came to the United States at the age of ten. She and her parents feel fortunate to have survived the Holocaust in Poland.

"Growing up in New York, I felt very much an immigrant. It was a strong identity and one I was proud of. We spoke Polish at home, and even to this day, I feel an immediate affinity with anyone who has a foreign accent. When I raised my own family in suburban Connecticut, that immigrant identity went underground. Despite the fact that my husband was also an immigrant, we outwardly lived the typical, assimilated, "middle America" way: three kids, two cars, house, lawn, professional career. None of my friends had accents. Yet, underneath it all, we felt different.

"My kids felt different too. We didn't buy them Alligator T-shirts or the latest style jeans. We avoided fads. This was because we knew that material possessions were fleeting things, not intrinsic parts of a person. Financial status, in my personal experience, could change in a moment. Before the war, when I was very young, my parents were well-to-do professional people. Hitler plunged them into absolute poverty. Various agencies supported us during the first year in this country after the war. However, my father, a physician, struggled hard to learn English and pass the medical boards. In a relatively short time, our socioeconomic status rose again. Up and down, down and up."

Terry reflected for a moment.

"As children of Holocaust survivors, we were on another edge. You'd hear things in our family that other kids didn't hear about, and it separates you out. Like the other day, a woman was talking about nineteen thirty-nine, going to the World's Fair in New York. I'm thinking, *nineteen thirty-nine is when the Nazi's invaded my town.*

"As both a child of Holocaust survivors and a survivor

myself, I lived on yet another edge. Conversations at our home were not like those other kids heard around the dinner table. My frame of reference was different.

"My experience in Poland was also that of an *edgewalker*. I was a Jewish child in a Polish (meaning Catholic Polish) country. When Hitler started persecuting the Jews, I hid under a false identity. I was a Jewish child who pretended she was not a Jewish child.

"I owe my survival to a wonderful Catholic family who hid me in their home for several years during the war. They were poor and uneducated. But they were rich in a truly religious sense. I grew to love them very much.

"Being away from my own parents was a mixed blessing—another edge. Of course I missed them a lot and cried for them. But life in my home had been filled with tension, both due to the war and to my parents' conflicts. The Catholic family was more relaxed. The mother, especially, was warm and loving. Not that they didn't have their own problems. The father drank, the four teenage boys fought. But I kind of enjoyed that rough and tumble, basic survival behavior in this family. There was none of the more insidious middle class patina over the hostility.

"Because of my experiences in different settings, I never felt 'real' in my family of origin or in my own family as a grown-up. I always felt like I was sort of floating someplace; I hadn't felt real since I left Poland. My desire to recapture that feeling was always there. I knew I wanted to be in a more third world type of place—a place that would bear some resemblance to the Catholic foster family that saved my life.

"And so, a few years ago, after my last child went off to college, I accepted a job as a clinical psychologist on the Navajo Reservation. And now I walk another edge—a white person in an Indian culture. The Navajo people have been wonderfully warm and accepting. Yet there is the edge—the line you can't quite cross. You can only get so close and no closer.

"It's been a fascinating experience to participate in this culture. Contrary to my East Coast psychotherapy clients who suffer from 'internal conflicts,' my patients here have real problems. You don't wade through 'defenses' and 'coping mechanisms' to reach their inner core. They talk to you straight from the heart. No bullshit.

"Just like my Polish foster family, people here are living at a survival level. Many still have no electricity, no telephone, no running water. But they're connected meaningfully to life in their families. Ask a child, 'And what did you do this weekend?' They went to help Grandma chop wood, haul water. This is still the way of life. The families, although they've been fractured and messed up, are still pulling together. Being with them brought some long-frozen feelings back. And those feelings make it possible to bridge our differences.

"We have similar histories. Our people were both marked for genocide. I can identify with their 'Long Walk,' a cruel forced evacuation of their land. On a personal level, there are similarities, too. After I left my beloved foster family, I had to spend two years in a convent boarding school. Indian children, too, were removed from their homes and forced into boarding school. They, too, were placed in foster care, with religious beliefs different from their own.

"Not long ago, I had an insightful experience with one of my Navajo co-workers. We walked into a dormitory at a boarding school. Little five- and six-year-olds were napping in a large room with many beds. I had a flashback. I was back again in that convent, alone and lonely. I started to cry. My Navajo friend put her arm around me. A bond formed between us. She could see that I'm not that different from her people.

"The Native Americans are, of course, *edgewalkers* too. They don't think of themselves as 'Americans,' in a mainstream sort of way. They identify with their own people: Navajo, Hopi, etc. To them I'm an Anglo, in some ways still their enemy.

"Life is strange. When I was a Jewish child on the Nazi chopping block, I would have given a lot to be called Anglo. They were not marked for extinction! But there, I was a Jew. When we came to the United States, I was a Pole. And now I'm an Anglo! In fact, I am part of all of these, even part Navajo now, and so I feel totally entitled to call myself an American. I am very patriotic. This country has been very good to me. It took me in and made it possible for me to live a full life."

Terry Cahn-Tober has integrated her own complex history. She's connected with the spirit of people who were in North America before "Western Civilization." She's in tune with that voice that speaks of nature, of planning for the well-being of eight generations from now, of a Great Spirit that touches everyone and everything. Since returning to New York, she reaches for the future as a volunteer at the United Nations, doing what she can to promote peace.

The role of the *edgewalker* in politics and the public forum is another inroad. The more we hone our *edgewalking* skills at a personal level, the more powerful we can be in organizational situations when we have the opportunity to speak out or to promote *culturally competent* decision making. Every day we have choices about *splitting*, being open or closed, working to understand someone different from ourselves who might be considered unacceptable by our friends.

When Whoopi Goldberg was in the South filming *Ghosts of Mississippi,* the story of Myrlie Evers' thirty-year struggle to bring her husband's killers to justice, Whoopi received a very different reception than Medgar Evers had. "People who wouldn't have let me in thirty years ago wanted me to rent their houses," she said.

Across the globe then, things *have* changed, given, not as much as needed, but progress slow and sure is undeniable.

But, asked if she faces racism, Whoopi was quoted in the *Cape Cod Times* as saying, "Racism is inherent in this society. So, yeah, I face it every day, as do gay people, women on welfare. It is there. It's just part of life. Classism, sexism, -isms. It's there and it always will be there." In addition to her ascension to stardom over the past ten years, Whoopi is a champion for the homeless, human rights and contributes her efforts to battles against AIDS and substance abuse. She is outspoken about racism. Whoopi herself makes a difference.

So can you and I. As we become more conscious of the edges we walk, we can take practical steps to soften the "-isms" that whirl around us. As Lee Mun Wah so succinctly stated, "I encourage individual responsibility when people ask about the solution to racism. I say, 'Well, it's just three inches away.' When people begin to practice openness within themselves and with the person next to them, it begins the linking in the room."

Like Terry Cahn-Tober and the other *edgewalkers* you know or have read about, each of us seeks self-definition. We try to make sense of our own history, learning and experience, but we also view ourselves through the eyes of others.

The *edgewalkers* about whom I've written stand in two places at once—honoring their own uniqueness and staying open to the uniqueness of others. Stability with openness must be the task of the new global frontier. Each of us can become edgewalkers, learning to stand firm and bend, receiving new input without forgetting who we are, conversing effectively across culture and interest groups and allowing minority voices, even if unpopular or inconvenient, to be heard.

Holding the core together has to do not just with what language people speak, nor their country of origin, or even their economic situation, but with connection of the heart. That heart connection is the optimal future for us all, no matter our country of origin nor our country of choice. It places value on the potential of an individual's life, embraces community and offers inspiration to make a better world. Hopefully, in what C.G. Jung termed the *collective unconscious*, it garners the creativity and the courage to pull this universe of ours into the new millennium where all its citizens feel themselves integral.

Our world's faces, languages, styles and identities are all shifting. Change is, and always has been, a major defining character of the future. Civilization is a work in progress. The struggle to walk the edges of the globe is much like the struggle to be an authentic person. It means searching our deep roots and finding new beginnings, acknowledging the bad with the good and paying attention not only to our inner experiences, but to those of other people as well.

Edgewalkers' voices at that new frontier invite all peoples to join in the dance on the edge. I pray we accept that invitation, reach into the complexity of our rich, cultural diversity and embrace all our brothers and sisters around the world.

NOTES

Part I: DEFINING *EDGEWALKING*
The Real Meaning of Treading Through the Morass

1. Frank LaPena was interviewed by the author, 17 November 1994 at California State University, Sacramento. In subsequent conversations he has discussed tradition, art and the *edgewalking* concept.
2. See also: Jeannine Gendar, "Painter, Frank LaPena," *Indian Artist*, Spring 1997, 50-57 and Lois Crozier-Hogle and Darryl Babe Wilson, "Frank LaPena: Tradition is the Evidence for the Truth of Life," in *Surviving in Two Worlds, Contemporary Native American Voices*, Jay Leibold, ed. (Austin: University of Texas Press, 1997), 53-60.

Chapter One: WALKING THE EDGE: A Two-way Street

1. Early 1940's, Winslow, Arizona.
2. The Hopi people have been much studied by anthropologists. See: Frank Waters, *Book of the Hopi* (New York: Penguin Books, 1977 edition); Frank Waters, *The Man Who Killed the Deer* (New York: Washington Square Press/Pocket Books, 1971); and Robert Boissiere, *Meditations With the Hopi* (Santa Fe: Bear & Company, 1986).
3. Some contemporary psychological theory emphasizes the importance of a *true self*, as opposed to a *false self* or *role* adopted to please others or to cope in a hostile environment. A huge body of work in *self-psychology, ego psychology,* and *object relations* deals with this theory. Prominent authors include: Rubin and Gertrude Blanck, Heinz Kohut, Otto Kernberg, Margaret Mahler, William Masterson, Robert Stolorow, and D.W. Winnicott among others. Books on related topics that provide overviews: James F. Masterson, *The Search for the Real Self: Unmasking the Personality Disorders of Our Age* (New York: Free Press, reprint 1990); Jay R. Greenberg and Stephen A. Mitchell, *Object Relations in Psychoanalytic Theory* (Cambridge: Harvard University Press, 1983).

4. *Splitting*, an unconscious psychological defense mechanism in which an individual sees the world all one way or the other. See Chapter Five, note 2.
5. Stephen Magagnini, "Getting Along," *Sacramento Bee*, February 1999, p. 21-25. "Over four days, *The Bee* articles explore how dozens of people from the Sacramento area bridge the racial and ethnic divide. Also we will explore some of the toughest issues remaining and share tips on embracing our diverse community," wrote Executive Editor, Richard Rodriquez.
6. Santo Domingo Pueblo, known for its jewelry makers and preservation of tradition, is approximately thirty miles west of Santa Fe, north of Interstate 25.

Chapter Two: BLENDING CULTURES: The Melting Pot Assumption

1. Gloria Anzaldua, *Borderlands - La Frontera: The New Mestiza* (San Francisco: aunt lute books, 1987), p. 86.
2. Amitai Etzione, *The Spirit of Community: Rights, Responsibilities and the Communitarian Agenda* (New York: Crown Publishers, 1993). See discussion on *multiculturalism*, p. 152-156.
3. California Department of Finance 1993 population projection series depicts the state's population in 1997: Asian 10.78%, African American 6.85%, Latino 30.30%, White 52.06%. The forecast for 2020: Asian 11.68%, African American 6.37%, Latino 40.99%, White 40.96%. See Laura McCoy, "Ethnic quilt woven with conflict," *Sacramento Bee*, 27 October 1997.
4. Daniel Gordis, *Does the World Need the Jews? Rethinking Chosenness and American Jewish Identity* (New York: Scribner, 1997).
5. Arthur M. Schlesinger, Jr., *The Disuniting of America: Reflections on a Multicultural Society* (New York: W.W. Norton & Company, 1992).
6. Joan Beck, "Get the Facts Straight and Start Dealing with Racial Realities in the Once-a-Decade Head Count," *Chicago Tribune*, 11 July 1996, p. 23.
7. Michael S. Teitelbaum and Myron Weiner, eds., *Threatened Peoples, Threatened Borders, World Migration and U.S. Policy* (New York: W.W. Norton & Company, 1995).
8. "We pigs are brainworkers here. The whole management and organization of the farm depend on us. Day and night, we are watching over your welfare. It is for your sake that we drink that milk and eat those apples." "Two legs good, four legs better!" See George Orwell, *Animal Farm* (New York: Plume, 1996).
9. David Hollinger was interviewed by the author in Berkeley, California, 28 June 1996. His book, *Postethnic America: Beyond Multiculturalism* (New York, Basic Books, 1995) offers an excellent discussion of options that are also beyond the *melting pot*. See also David Hollinger, *Science, Jew, and Secular Culture: Studies in Mid-Twentieth Century American Intellectual History* (Princeton: Princeton University Press, 1999).
10. From "Translating a Culture: Latino Writers Romancing the 'Gringo' World," with Kathleen Alcala, Ana Castillo, Benjamin Saenz and Victor Martinez, San Francisco Bay Area Book Festival, 9 November 1997. These authors discussed the dilemma they experience in being "put in a box" as ethnic writers, while at the same time valuing their cultural identity. See Victor Martinez, *Parrot in the Oven: Mi Vida* (New York: Harper Collins

Children's Books, 1996) for an authentic tale of transformation with cultural conflict emphasized.

11. Alan Cowell, "Like it or Not, Germany Becomes a Melting Pot," *New York Times*, 30 November 1997, International Section.

12. Jahi Anyabwile McCurtis was interviewed by the author in Indianapolis, 31 May 1996.

13. Judy Tuwalestiwa who lives in Kykotsmovi, Arizona, was interviewed by the author, 3 August 1997, at the time of her show "Cadences of Light & The Canyon Poem" at the Linda Durham Contemporary Art Gallery, Galisteo, New Mexico.

14. See Bradd Shore, *Culture in Mind: Cognition, Culture, and the Problem of Meaning* (New York: Oxford University Press, 1996) and Clifford Geertz, "From the native point of view: On the nature of anthropological understanding," in *Culture Theory: Essays on Mind, Self and Emotion*, Richard Schweder and Robert Levine, eds., (Cambridge: Cambridge University Press, 1984).

Chapter Three: MULTIRACIAL HERITAGE: A Refreshing, Confrontive Approach

1. Stephen Magagnini, "Multiracial Americans Seek Acceptance as Numbers Grow," *Sacramento Bee*, 12 October 1997.

2. Tim Rosaforte, *Tiger Woods: The Makings of a Champion* (New York: St. Martin's Paperbacks, 1997).

3. Basho Fujimoto was interviewed at his home in Davis, California, 19 March 1996.

4. Schlesinger, p. 138.

5. Ibid, p. 53.

6. Stephen Magagnini, "Census to Allow Americans to Claim Multi-Race Heritage," *Sacramento Bee*, 30 October 1997.

7. Magagnini, 12 October 1997.

8. Martha Minnow, *Not Only for Myself: Identity, Politics, and the Law* (New York: The New Press, 1997), p. 140.

9. Karen S. Peterson, "Interracial Dates Common Among Today's Teenagers, *Sacramento Bee*, 3 November 1997, A6.

10. Basho completed his internship with Kodo in Japan. He was not selected to join the touring group, but deeply values his experience with the group.

11. Free Association performs in northern California. Their first CD, *Freequality*, contains original music about mixed race, love, and life in many different modes.

12. Wendell Fishman was interviewed by the author in Davis, California, 5 April 1996. See Katya Bigel Azoulay, *Black, Jewish and Interracial: It's Not the Color of Your Skin, but the Race of Your Kin and Other Myths of Identity* (Durham: Duke University Press, 1997).

13. James Redfield, *The Celestine Prophecy: An Adventure* (New York: Warner Books, 1994).

14. Malik Johnson was interviewed by the author in Davis, California, 23 April 1996.

Chapter Four: DIVERSIFYING CULTURALLY: Unconscious Structures of Belief

1. Gene LePlane, interview with *Follow Me Home* director Peter Bratt, *San Francisco Frontlines*, August 1997. Other resources that deal with both sides of Bratt's statement, "White people just don't get it!" include: Stephen L. Carter, *Reflections of An Affirmative Action Baby* (New York: Basic Books, 1991); Ellis Cose, *Color-Blind: Seeing Beyond Race in a Race-Obsessed World* (New York: Harper Collins, 1997); Stanley Crouch, *The All-American Skin Game, or, The Decoy of Race: The Long and the Short of It* (New York: Vintage Books, 1995); Nikki Giovanni, *Racism 101* (New York: Quill, 1994); Lani Guinier, *The Tyranny of the Majority: Fundamental Fairness and Representative Democracy* (New York: The Free Press, 1994).
2. Benjamin Schwarz, "The Diversity Myth," *The Atlantic Monthly*, May 1995.
3. Miriam Acevedo Davis was interviewed by the author 31 May 1996, in Indianapolis, Indiana.
4. Arthur M. Schlesinger, Jr., *The Disuniting of America: Reflections on a Multicultural Society* (New York: W.W. Norton & Company, 1992).
5. Rufus Burrow was interviewed by the author in Indianapolis, 30 May 1996. See his scholarly, thought-provoking book, *James H. Cone and Black Liberation Theology* (Jefferson, North Carolina: Mc Farland & Company, 1994).
6. Coco Fusco who lives in New York was interviewed by the author in San Francisco, 11 March 1996. In addition to film work and articles, her book is *English is Broken Here: Notes on Cultural Fusion in the Americas* (New York: The New Press, 1995).

Chapter Five: SEARCHING FOR A CULTURAL MIDDLE: Beyond Color and Race

1. Barbara Arnn, who lives in Connecticut, was interviewed by the author in Santa Fe, New Mexico, 3 March 1997 and in San Francisco, 5 November 1998.
2. The concept of *splitting* is defined as the inability to synthesize contradictory good and bad self or other representations. John G. Gunderson, *Borderline Personality Disorder* (Washington, D.C.: American Psychiatric Press, 1984), p. 43-44. In it's extreme form, *splitting* is a core dynamic of the borderline personality disorder. However, in it's less pathological form, the *splitting* defense can occur in all of us when we feel threatened. James F. Masterson, *The Search for the Real Self: Unmasking the Personality Disorders of Our Age* (New York: Free Press, reprint 1990), p. 78-81. In *The Real Self, A Developmental, Self, and Object Relations Approach* (New York: Brunner/Mazel Publishers, 1985), p. 117-120, Masterson illustrates the *splitting* defense with the story of "Snow White and the Seven Dwarfs."
3. David Allen, *Fear of Strangers and Its Consequences: The New Thinking About Ethnic Strife* (Yonkers: Bennington Books, 1993).
4. Ruth-Inge Heinze was interviewed by the author in Berkeley, 25 July 1995. She has written widely on cross-cultural issues and shamanism. See *Shamans of the Twentieth Century* (New York: Irvington Publishers, 1991).
5. Rosalee Van Stelten, who lives in Calgary, reviewed an early copy of *Edgewalkers* and wrote a note about her mixed family background in response. She was interviewed by the author in Sacramento, 1 February 1999.

6. The task of the psychotherapist in working with a client for whom *splitting* is prominent is to help that individual develop the capacity to observe his or her own *splitting*. When an individual develops this level of competence, it becomes possible to recognize the process for what it is, a defense, allowing that person to make choices based on complex, rather than over-simplified, information.

7. Conversation with Marietta Davenport, Archaeologist, U.S. Forest Service, Fredonia, Arizona, April 1992.

8. Gail Christopher was interviewed by the author, 1 April 1996. In addition to diversity curriculum development and professional writing, her book is *Anchors for the Innocent: Inner Power for Today's Single Mothers and Fathers* (Chicago: The Human Capacity Press, 1993).

9. Carol Parrish-Harra was interviewed by the author, 11 April 1996. She is an international speaker and workshop presenter. Her publications include *Adventure in Meditation*, 3 vols., 1995-97 and *Reflections*, compiled by Maggie Webb-Adams (Tahlequah, O.K.: Sparrow Hawk Press).

10. Barbara Arnn. See chapter five, note 1.

11. Patricia Nell Warren, who lives in Los Angeles, was interviewed by the author in San Francisco, 10 September 1997. Her novel *One is the Sun* (New York: Ballantine Books, 1991) deals with *edgewalking* in early America between natives and European settlers of the Great Goddess persuasion. Patricia Nell Warren's story is in chapter seven.

12. Joey Garcia was interviewed by the author in Sacramento, 5 December 1994. It was from her that I learned about Hunbatz Men and the Mayan Solar Initiation Experience described in chapter twelve.

13. Satsuki Ina was interviewed by the author in Sacramento, 24 May 1996.

Chapter Six: MIXING OIL AND WATER: The Multicultural/Feminist Paradox

1. Katha Pollitt, "Whose Culture," *Boston Review DEBATE*, October/November, 1997. See also Katha Pollitt, *Reasonable Creatures: Essays on Women and Feminism* (New York: Knopf, 1994).

2. Susan Okin, "Is Multiculturalism Bad For Women? When Minority Cultures Win Group Rights, Women Lose Out," *Boston Review DEBATE*, October/November 1997. See also Susan Okin, *Women in Western Political Thought* (Princeton: Princeton University Press, 1992).

3. Yuri Kageyama, "Japan Quick to Approve Viagra—But Birth Control Pill is Still Banned," *San Francisco Chronicle*, 11 February 1999.

4. Youssef M. Ibrahim, "As Algerian Civil War Drags on, Atrocities Grow: In Raids, Islamic Rebels Have Made Women a Frequent Target," *New York Times*, 28 December 1997, International Section.

5. Mayan Solar Initiation and Seminar, planned and led by Hunbatz Men, Merida, Mexico, March 1995.

6. Carol Parrish-Harra is Director and President of the Board of Trustees of Sparrow Hawk Village, a spiritual community with an educational focus, in Tahlequah, Oklahoma. See chapter five, note 9.

7. Resources in this area include John D. French, Andrew Gordon, Alexander Keyssar, eds., *The Gendered Worlds of Latin American Women*

Workers: From Household and Factory to the Union Hall and Ballot Box (Durham: Duke University Press, 1997); Jane S. Jacquette, ed., *The Women's Movement in Latin America: Participation and Democracy, Thematic Studies in Latin America* (Boston: Unwin Hyman, 1989); Francesca Miller, *Latin American Women and the Search for Social Justice* (Hanover, N.H.: University Press of New England, 1992) and Silvana Paternostro, *In the Land of God and Man: Confronting Our Sexual Culture* (New York: E P Dutton, 1998).

8. Jeffrey Zaslow, "Straight Talk: Loretta Sanchez," *USA Weekend*, September 1997, p. 23, 26-28.

9. Phil Garcia, "Defeated by a 'Dragon Slayer' Dornan Sounds Off on His 984-Vote Loss to Sanchez," *Sacramento Bee*, 25 September 1996, A10.

10. Gail Christopher, See chapter five, note 8.

11. A naprapath (from Czech *naprava*, correction) practices a system of treatment based on the theory that disease symptoms are due to strained or contracted ligaments and disorders of the connective tissue and can be cured by massage. *Webster's New Universal Unabridged Dictionary*, 1983.

12. Mary Lee Daugherty was interviewed by the author in Berea, Kentucky, 2 June 1996. An ordained Presbyterian minister, she founded and is executive director of Appalachian Ministries Education Resource Center (AMERC). At the time of the interview, AMERC was eleven years old.

13. Nina Boyd Krebs, *Changing Woman Changing Work* (Aspen: MacMurray & Beck, 1993).

14. Sharon Dryflower Reyna was interviewed by the author at Dryflower's home at Taos Pueblo, New Mexico, 20 January 1996. Taos Pueblo is near the New Mexico town of Taos, two to three hours' driving time north of Santa Fe. The Taos Indians both accommodate tourist visitors and maintain tradition. See Nancy Wood, *Taos Pueblo* (New York: Alfred Knopf 1989). Dryflower's picture is on page 120. Also, for some examples of *edgewalking* between the Taos people and the United States government, see R.C. Gordon-McCutcheon, *The Taos Indians and the Battle for Blue Lake* (Santa Fe: Red Crane Books, 1991).

Chapter Seven: WEAVING DIFFERENCES WITHIN: One by One

1. Shainee Gabel and Kristin Hahn, "John Perry Barlow. Co-founder of the Electronic Frontier Foundation, Grateful Dead lyricist, contributing writer for *Wired*, retired cattle rancher," in *Anthem: An American Road Story* (New York: Avon Books, 1997), p. 237.

2. Loreen Lilyn Lee was interviewed by the author at Port Townsend, Washington, 15 July 1996.

3. Amy Tan refers frequently to this complexity from a Chinese-American perspective in her novels *Joy Luck Club* (New York: Putnam, 1989) and *The Kitchen God's Wife* (New York: Putnam, 1991). See also Pang-Mei Natasha Chang, *Bound Feet and Western Dress* (New York: Doubleday, 1996) and Laura Uba, *Asian Americans: Personality Patterns, Identity and Mental Health* (New York: Guilford, 1994).

4. Patricia Nell Warren, *The Front Runner* (Los Angeles: Wildcat Press, 1995, 20th anniversary edition).

5. Wendell Fishman, See chapter three, note 12.

6. Satsuki Ina, See chapter five, note 13.

7. Subsequent to the Japanese attack on Pearl Harbor, over 120,000 Japanese Americans were interned in United States prison camps. Over half were children. Funded primarily by the California Endowment, Satsuki Ina produced a series of workshops and a documentary film, *Children of the Camps*, aired nationally on PBS, May 1999.

8. C.G. Jung, *Psychology and Religion: West and East.* Collected Works 11 (Princeton: Princeton University Press, 1969), p. 146.

Chapter Eight: *EDGEWALKING* SPIRITS: The Universal Connection

1. Gabel and Hahn, p. 361.

2. Mircea Eliade, *Shamanism: Archaic Techniques of Ecstasy*, Willard R. Trask, ed., Bollingen Series LXXVI (Princeton: Princeton University Press, 1964); Joan Halifax, *Shaman: The Wounded Healer* (London: Thames and Hudson, 1982); Ruth-Inge Heinze, *Shamans of the Twentieth Century* (New York: Irvington Publishers, 1991).

3. Michael Tucker, *Dreaming With Open Eyes: The Shamanic Spirit in the Twentieth Century* (San Francisco: Aquarian/Harper, 1992).

4. Donald F. Sandner and Steven H. Wong, *The Sacred Heritage: The Influence of Shamanism on Analytical Psychology* (New York/London: Routledge, 1997).

5. Adesha and Max Rein, who live in Windsor, California, were interviewed by the author in Sacramento, 24 April 1996.

6. Richard Maurice Bucke, *Cosmic Consciousness* (New York, Dutton, 1969).

7. Steven Wong speaking at "The Sacred Heritage, The Influence of Shamanism on Analytical Psychology," a workshop sponsored by the C. G. Jung Institute of San Francisco, 31 May 1997.

8. James Leehan was interviewed by the author in Sacramento on 8 September 1998.

9. Angie Debo, *A History of the Indians of the United States* (Norman and London: University of Oklahoma Press, 1970); Jack Weatherford, *Native Roots: How the Indians Enriched America* (New York: Fawcett Columbine, 1991).

10. Lee Mun Wah, who lives in Oakland, California, was interviewed by the author in Sacramento, 9 August 1996.

11. Lee Mun Wah, *The Color of Fear* (Oakland, C.A.: Stirfry Productions, 1996), film.

Chapter Nine: DOUBLING THE ODDS: Creating a Community

1. Warren Bennis, "Learning Some Basic Truths about Leadership," *The New Paradigm in Business: Emerging Strategies for Leadership and Organizational Change*, ed. Ray Michael and Alan Rinzler (New York: Jeremy P. Tarcher/Perigee Books, 1993), p. 80.

2. Laura Munoz was interviewed by the author in Sacramento, 10 October 1995.

3. Adrianne Mohr was interviewed by the author in San Francisco, 1 June 1996.

4. Rachel Guerrero was interviewed by the author in Sacramento, 27 February 1996 and several times subsequently.

5. Edward Steichen, *The Family of Man* (New York: Museum of Modern Art, 1996). Also see Jerry Mason, ed., *The Family of Woman* (New York: Grosset & Dunlap, 1979).
6. Sharon Dryflower Reyna, See chapter six, note 14.
7. Ron Eller was interviewed by the author in Lexington, Kentucky, 3 June 1996, as was Mary Lee Daugherty in Berea, Kentucky, 2 June 1996.
8. Lorraine Hansberry's play, *A Raisin in the Sun*, first drama by an African-American to be a hit on Broadway, became an overnight success when it opened in 1959. Hansberry worked diligently on behalf of human rights until her early death at age thirty-four from pancreatic cancer.
9. Congresswoman Patricia Schroeder was fond of saying, "Family means the people who have to take you in at night."
10. Loreen Lilyn Lee, See chapter seven, note 2.
11. George Esquibel was interviewed by the author at Sacramento City College, 23 January 1995.

Chapter Ten: STEPPING FROM THEORY TO PRACTICE: A Limitless Capacity for Healing

1. *Free Association*, See chapter three, note 11.
2. Adam Smith, *The Theory of Moral Sentiments* (Indianapolis: Liberty Fund, 1984).
3. John Stuart Mill, *The Subjection of Women*, ed. Susan Moller Okin (Indianapolis: Hackett Publishing Company, 1989).
4. Rachel Guerrero, See chapter nine, note 4.
5. A few of Rachel Guerrero's lines:

   Latina women cross between cultures like some women change shoes.

   Thank you very much I don't accept your stereotypes, limitations, racist, judgmental expectations.
   I leave them all behind.
   I have shed your cloth of limitations, confinement and bias.
   I've wrapped myself in the beautiful multicolor, multicultural cloth of pride, optimism, empowerment, opportunity and change.

   I curse the narrow representation the media has of Latina women as prostitutes, lawbreakers, maids, uneducated homegirls addicted to drugs or a girlfriend of a gang member or criminal.

   Latinas are invisible.

   Presente! Aqui estoy siempre!
   We have voices that are strong steady and sure.
   I will survive.
   (September, 1995, unpublished)
6. Mareasa R. Isaacs and Marva P. Benjamin, *Towards a Culturally Competent System of Care*, vol. II of *Programs Which Utilize Culturally Competent Principles* (Washington, D.C.: CASSP Technical Assistance Center, Center for Child

Heath and Mental Health Policy, Georgetown University Child Development Center, 1991).

7. Nationwide, one-third of African-American men between the ages of 20 and 29 are locked up, on probation or on parole, up from one in four in 1990. In California, African-American males account for one-third of the state's prison population, but just 3.7 percent of the overall population. Stephen Magagnini, "Forum Looks at Blacks' Prison Statistics," *Sacramento Bee*, 21 February 1999.

8. Mary Field Belenky, Lynne A. Bond and Jacqueline S. Weinstock, *A Tradition That Has No Name: Nurturing the Development of People, Families and Communities* (New York: Basic Books, 1997).

Chapter Eleven: MOVING AND SHAKING ON THE RIDGE: From Regional to Mainstream and Back

1. Ron Eller, See chapter nine, note 7.

2. Ronald D. Eller, *Miners, Millhands, and Mountaineers: Industrialization of the Appalachian South, 1880-1930* (Knoxville: The University of Tennessee Press, 1982). In 1998, Ron Eller was appointed John D. Whisman Scholar for the Appalachian Regional Commission. He consults and advises at the national level on Appalachian issues.

3. Ron Eller, Rueben Martinez, Cynthia Pace and Michael Pavel, *Rural Community College Initiative, Access: Removing Barriers to Participation,* (Washington, D.C.: American Association of Community Colleges, 1998).

4. Hillary Rodham Clinton, *It Takes a Village: And Other Lessons Children Teach Us* (New York: Simon and Schuster, 1996).

5. Mary Lee Daugherty, See chapter six, note 12.

Chapter Twelve: CONNECTING GLOBALLY: Acting Locally

1. Mayan Solar Initiation, See chapter five, note 12.

2. *Dzibilchaltun*, according to Antoinette May, "the place where there are symbols inscribed on flat stones," is the oldest Mayan city in continuous use. Antoinette May, *The Yucatan: A Guide to the Land of Mysteries* (San Carlos, C.A.: Wide World Publishing/Tetra, 1993).

3. A *cenoté* is a natural well in the limestone that is prominent on the Yucatan Peninsula. The one at *Dzibilchaltun* is shallow with clear water. At Chichén Itzá, the *cenoté* is deep, murky, and a repository from which evidence of human sacrifice has been recovered.

4. Hunbatz Men, *Secrets of Mayan Science/Religion* (Santa Fe: Bear & Company, 1990).

5. Chichén Itzá and Uxmal are major archaeological sites in the Yucatan, where the buildings from Mayan civilization remain and, to varying degrees, have been restored.

6. Kukulkan, the fabled plumed serpent, is the Mayan deity of healing and magical herbs, the lord of hope and the morning star, a god of springtime and emergent life. See Antoinette May, chapter twelve, note 2.

7. Hunab K'u, the greatest god, the creator of the world, father of the divinities, the one god alive and true, and the deity responsible for the flood that

destroyed the four worlds that proceeded that of the Mayas. This was the supreme god, but beyond shape and substance so that he could never be represented pictorially. See Antoinette May, chapter twelve, note 2.

8. Barbara Hand Clow, *The Pleiadian Agenda: A New Cosmology for the Age of Light* (Santa Fe: Bear & Company, 1995).

Chapter 13: BEYOND THE ENLIGHTENMENT: Patterns and Contradictions

1. Laura Santigian was interviewed by the author in Sacramento, C.A., 1 October 1997.
2. Denise Senter was interviewed by the author in Indianapolis, 31 May 1996.

Chapter 14: WHERE DO WE GO FROM HERE?

1. David Hockney, *That's the Way I See It* (San Francisco: Chronicle Books, 1993).
2. Joe MacDonald, John Paskevich, Ches Yetman, Producers, Zemma Pictures, Co-producers, *If Only I Were an Indian* (National Film Board of Canada, 1996). The film's title is from one of Franz Kafka's stories, "The Wish to Be a Red Indian." Nahum N. Glatzer, ed., *Franz Kafka: The Complete Stories*, (New York: Schocken Books, 1971).
3. Terry Cahn-Tober, who lived in Tuba City, Arizona, at the time, was interviewed by the author in Santa Fe, 4 March 1997.
4. Emily Benedek, *Beyond the Four Corners of the World: A Navajo Woman's Journey* (New York: Alfred A. Knopf, 1995) is the life story of Ella Bedonie, a Navajo woman who moves between her traditional world and that of White American culture.
5. Michael Janusonis, "Whoopi Serious—About New Film and Social Justice," *Cape Cod Times*, 8 January 1997, C7.

BIBLIOGRAPHY

Allen, David. *Fear of Strangers and Its Consequences: The New Thinking About Ethnic Strife.* Yonkers, N.Y.: Bennington Books, 1993.

Anzaldua, Gloria. *Borderlands - La Frontera: The New Mestiza.* San Francisco: aunt lute books, 1987.

Azoulay, Katya Bigel. *Black, Jewish and Interracial: It's Not the Color of Your Skin, but the Race of Your Kin and Other Myths of Identity.* Durham: Duke University Press, 1997.

Belenky, Mary Field, Lynne A. Bond, and Jacqueline S. Weinstock. *A Tradition That Has No Name: Nurturing the Development of People, Families and Communities.* New York: Basic Books, 1997.

Benedek, Emily. *Beyond the Four Corners of the World: A Navajo Woman's Journey.* New York: Alfred A. Knopf, 1995.

Boissiere, Robert. *Meditations with the Hopi.* Santa Fe: Bear & Company, 1986.

Bucke, Richard Maurice. *Cosmic Consciousness.* New York: Dutton, 1969.

Burrow, Rufus. *James H. Cone and Black Liberation Theology.* Jefferson, N.C.: Mc Farland & Company, 1994.

Carter, Stephen L. *Reflections of An Affirmative Action Baby.* New York: Basic Books, 1991.

Chang, Pang-Mei Natasha. *Bound Feet and Western Dress.* New York: Doubleday, 1996.

Christopher, Gail. *Anchors for the Innocent: Inner Power for Today's Single Mothers and Fathers.* Chicago: The Human Capacity Press, 1993.

Clinton, Hillary Rodham. *It Takes a Village: And Other Lessons Children Teach Us*. New York: Simon and Schuster, 1996.

Clow, Barbara Hand. *The Pleiadian Agenda: A New Cosmology for the Age of Light*. Santa Fe: Bear & Company, 1995.

Cose, Ellis. *Color-Blind: Seeing Beyond Race in a Race-Obsessed World*. New York: Harper Collins, 1997.

Crouch, Stanley. *The All-American Skin Game, or, The Decoy of Race: The Long and Short of It*. New York: Vintage Books, 1995.

Crozier-Hogle, Lois, and Darryl Babe Wilson. *Surviving in Two Worlds, Contemporary Native American Voices*. Edited by Jay Leibold. Austin: University of Texas Press, 1997.

Daugherty, Mary Lee. *The West Virginia Edition of the Women's Yellow Pages*. Charleston: University of West Virginia, 1979.

——. *Women and Religion*, Supplement to *The West Virginia Edition of the Women's Yellow Pages*. Self-published: 1981.

Debo, Angie. *A History of the Indians of the United States*. Norman and London: University of Oklahoma Press, 1970.

Eliade, Mircea. *Shamanism: Archaic Techniques of Ecstasy*. Translated by Willard R. Trask. Bollingen Series vol. 76. Princeton: Princeton University Press, 1964.

Eller, Ronald D. *Miners, Millhands, and Mountaineers: Industrialization of the Appalachian South, 1880-1930*. Knoxville: The University of Tennessee Press, 1982.

Eller, Ron, Rueben Martinez, Cynthia Pace and Michael Pavel. *Rural Community College Initiative, Access: Removing Barriers to Participation*. Washington, D.C.: American Association of Community Colleges, 1998.

Etzione, Amitai. *The Spirit of Community: Rights, Responsibilities and the Communitarian Agenda*. New York: Crown Publishers, 1993.

Fernandez, John P. *Race, Gender and Rhetoric*. New York: McGraw-Hill, 1998.

French, John D., Andrew Gordon, and Alexander Keyssar, eds. *The Gendered Worlds of Latin American Women Workers: From Household and Factory to the Union Hall and Ballot Box*. Durham: Duke University Press, 1997.

Fusco, Coco. *English is Broken Here: Notes on Cultural Fusion in the Americas*. New York: The New Press, 1995.

Gabel, Shainee, and Kristin Hahn. *Anthem: An American Road Story*. New York: Avon Books, 1997.

Geertz, Clifford. "From the native point of view: On the nature of anthropological understanding." *Culture Theory: Essays on Mind, Self and Emotion*. Edited by Richard Schweder and Robert Levine. Cambridge: Cambridge University Press, 1984.

Gendar, Jeannine. "Painter, Frank LaPena." *Indian Artist,* Spring 1997.

Giovanni, Nikki. *Racism 101.* New York: Quill, 1994.

Glatzer, Nahum N., ed. *Franz Kafka: The Complete Stories.* New York: Schocken Books, 1971.

Gordis, Daniel. *Does the World Need the Jews? Rethinking Chosenness and American Jewish Identity.* New York: Scribner, 1997.

Gordon-McCutcheon, R.C. *The Taos Indians and the Battle for Blue Lake.* Santa Fe: Red Crane Books, 1991.

Greenberg, Jay R., and Stephen A. Mitchell. *Object Relations in Psychoanalytic Theory.* Cambridge: Harvard University Press, 1983.

Guinier, Lani. *The Tyranny of the Majority: Fundamental Fairness and Representative Democracy.* New York: The Free Press, 1994.

Gunderson, John G. *Borderline Personality Disorder.* Washington, D.C.: American Psychiatric Press, 1984.

Halifax, Joan. *Shaman: The Wounded Healer.* London: Thames and Hudson, 1982.

Heinze, Ruth-Inge. *Shamans of the Twentieth Century.* New York: Irvington Publishers, 1991.

Hockney, David. *That's the Way I See It.* San Francisco: Chronicle Books, 1993.

Hollinger, David. *Postethnic America: Beyond Multiculturalism.* New York: Basic Books, 1995.

Ina, Satsuki, producer. *Children of the Camps: The Documentary.* film, Sacramento, C.A., 1999.

Isaacs, Mareasa R., and Marva P. Benjamin. *Towards a Culturally Competent System of Care,* vol. II: *Programs Which Utilize Culturally Competent Principles.* Washington, D.C.: CASSP Technical Assistance Center, Center for Child Heath and Mental Health Policy, Georgetown University Child Development Center, 1991.

Jacquette, Jane S., ed. *The Women's Movement in Latin America: Participation and Democracy, Thematic Studies in Latin America.* Boston: Unwin Hyman, 1989.

Jung, C.G. *Psychology and Religion: West and East.* Collected Works, vol. 11. Princeton: Princeton University Press, 1969.

Krebs, Nina Boyd. *Changing Woman Changing Work.* Aspen, C.O.: MacMurray & Beck, 1993.

LaPena, Frank, ed. "Emergence: The Fourth World." *This Path We Travel: Celebrations of Contemporary Native American Creativity.* Golden, C.O.: Fulcrum Publishing/Smithsonian, 1994.

Martinez, Victor. *Parrot in the Oven: Mi Vida*. New York: Harper Collins Children's Books, 1996.

Mason, Jerry, ed. *The Family of Woman*. New York: Grosset & Dunlap, 1979.

Masterson, James F. *The Real Self: A Developmental, Self, and Object Relations Approach*. New York: Brunner/Mazel Publishers, 1985.

———. *The Search for the Real Self: Unmasking the Personality Disorders of Our Age*. New York: Free Press, reprint 1990.

May, Antoinette. *The Yucatan: A Guide to the Land of Mysteries*. San Carlos, C.A.: Wide World Publishing/Tetra, 1993.

Men, Hunbatz. *Secrets of Mayan Science/Religion*. Santa Fe: Bear & Company, 1990.

Mill, John Stuart, *The Subjection of Women*. Edited by Susan Moller Okin. Indianapolis: Hackett Publishing Company, 1989.

Miller, Francesca. *Latin American Women and the Search for Social Justice*. Hanover, N.H.: University Press of New England, 1992.

Minnow, Martha. *Not Only for Myself: Identity, Politics, and the Law*. New York: The New Press, 1997.

National Film Board of Canada, *If Only I Were an Indian*, film, Joe MacDonald, John Paskievich, Ches Yetman, Producers, 1996.

Okin, Susan Moller. *Women in Western Political Thought*. Princeton: Princeton University Press, 1992.

Orwell, George. *Animal Farm*. New York: Plume, 1996.

Parrish-Harra, Carol. *Adventure in Meditation*, 3 vols. Tahlequah, O.K.: Sparrow Hawk Press, 1995-1997.

Paternostro, Silvana. *In the Land of God and Man: Confronting Our Sexual Culture*. New York: E. P. Dutton, 1998.

Pollitt, Katha. *Reasonable Creatures: Essays on Women and Feminism*. New York: Knopf, 1994.

Ray, Michael, and Alan Rinzler, ed. *The New Paradigm in Business: Emerging Strategies for Leadership and Organizational Change*. New York: Jeremy P. Tarcher/Perigee Books, 1993.

Redfield, James. *The Celestine Prophecy: An Adventure*. New York: Warner Books, 1994.

Rosaforte, Tim. *Tiger Woods: The Makings of a Champion*. New York: St. Martin's Paperbacks, 1997.

Sandner, Donald. *Navajo Symbols of Healing: A Jungian Exploration of Ritual, Image, and Medicine*. Rochester, VT: Healing Arts Press, 1979.

Sandner, Donald F., and Steven H. Wong. *The Sacred Heritage: The Influence of Shamanism on Analytical Psychology*. New York/London: Routledge, 1997.

Schlesinger, Arthur M., Jr. *The Disuniting of America: Reflections on a Multicultural Society*. New York: W.W. Norton & Company, 1992.

Schwarz, Benjamin. "The Diversity Myth." *The Atlantic Monthly*, May 1995.

Shore, Bradd. *Culture in Mind: Cognition, Culture, and the Problem of Meaning*. New York: Oxford University Press, 1996.

Smith, Adam. *The Theory of Moral Sentiments*. Indianapolis: Liberty Fund, 1984.

Steichen, Edward. *The Family of Man*. New York: Museum of Modern Art, 1996.

Tan, Amy. *Joy Luck Club*. New York: Putnam, 1989.

———. *The Kitchen God's Wife*. New York: Putnam, 1991.

Teitelbaum Michael S., and Myron Weiner, eds. *Threatened Peoples, Threatened Borders, World Migration and U.S. Policy*. New York: W.W. Norton & Company, 1995.

Tucker, Michael. *Dreaming With Open Eyes: The Shamanic Spirit in the Twentieth Century*. San Francisco: Aquarian/Harper, 1992.

Wah, Lee Mun. *The Color of Fear*. Oakland, C.A.: Stirfry Productions, 1996. film.

Warren, Patricia Nell. *One is the Sun*. New York: Ballantine Books, 1991.

———. *The Front Runner*. Los Angeles: Wildcat Press, 1995, 20th anniversary edition.

Waters, Frank. *Book of the Hopi*. New York: Penguin Books, 1977.

———. *The Man Who Killed the Deer*. New York: Washington Square/Pocket Books, 1971.

Weatherford, Jack. *Native Roots: How the Indians Enriched America*. New York: Fawcett Columbine, 1991.

Wood, Nancy. *Taos Pueblo*. New York: Alfred Knopf, 1989.